D0319476

MUIRFIELD

HOME OF THE HONOURABLE COMPANY (1744-1994)

Beyond is the great estuary – a magic stretch of water whether dancing silver in sunshine and a brave wind, tranquil in the haze of summer or eerily haunted as ships, booming in the mist, steal upstream to Leith and Rosyth.

Pat Ward-Thomas on Muirfield

Duncan Forbes of Culloden

DUNCAN FORBES, Lord President of the Court of Session, was the moving spirit behind the formation of the Gentlemen Golfers, who were shortly renamed the Honourable Company of Edinburgh Golfers. His significance in Scottish history, however, stretches far beyond the Company of Golfers.

Forbes was strenuous in trying to prevent the 1745 Rising. Although a zealous Highlander, he espoused the Hanoverian cause and spent much of his personal fortune dissuading many Highland chieftains from joining Prince Charles Edward Stuart's army, whose right flank rested on Forbes' property before the battle was joined. Forbes himself took no part in the battle. Sickened by the brutality meted out by Cumberland to the Highland prisoners and wounded after the battle, Forbes used his position and influence to save many Highlanders from the gallows, including surgeon John Rattray, a staunch Jacobite and the first captain of the Honourable Company of Edinburgh Golfers.

MUIRFIELD

HOME OF THE HONOURABLE COMPANY (1744-1994)

NORMAN MAIR

A celebration of the two hundred and fiftieth anniversary of the Honourable Company of Edinburgh Golfers

EDINBURGH AND LONDON

Contents

First published in Great Britain in 1994 by
MAINSTREAM PUBLISHING COMPANY (EDINBURGH) LTD
7 Albany Street
Edinburgh EH1 3UG

ISBN 1 85158 617 2

A catalogue record for this book is available from the British Library

Book design by John Martin

Photographs: main photographs of the Muirfield course, clubhouse and staff © Glyn Satterley; additional photographs of paintings, plans, trophies, etc, in the clubhouse © John Sheerin of Forth Photography

For other photographic acknowledgments, see p.168

Typeset in Palatino by Saxon Graphics Ltd, Derby

Printed and bound in Great Britain by Butler and Tanner Ltd, Frome

Contents

Foreword *by Jack Nicklaus*

MUIRFIELD was not just the course where I made my Walker Cup début as an impressionable 19-year-old in 1959 but (which is the principal reason why it is so special to me) it is also the course where I finally proved to everybody, and not least to myself, that I had the game to win the British Open – or *the* Open as the Honourable Company would always call it. I had come close in both 1963 at Lytham when Bob Charles won and again at St Andrews in 1964 when Tony Lema took the title, but I was an undistinguished twelfth at Birkdale in 1965. There were murmurings that I hit the ball too high for the winds which are usually part and parcel of an Open over here, and that I would not have the variety around the green for all the shots you have to manufacture on a British links.

Muirfield in 1966 changed all that and it was particularly satisfying because, at first sight, many would have said it was not my kind of course – not the way it was set up with towering rough and narrow fairways. But I have always felt at home at Muirfield and I solved the problem of the rough by so often using my one-iron from the tee. Walter Hagen, Gene Sarazen and Tommy Armour had all said the same thing – that you couldn't call yourself a bona fide champion until you had won on both sides of the pond. Which, of course, was why Ben Hogan came to Carnoustie. Winning that Open in 1966 was a great feeling and I remember asking at the presentation if they would mind if I paused for a moment just to enjoy it.

I said things when I was young which make me wince now, because I did not fully understand then that the bad breaks, the bounces, the run of the ball, were all part of the challenge, the mystique of links golf. But, as I have said, I liked Muirfield from the first day I played it. It is essentially a fair course – as far as golf is meant to be fair – and, as everyone knows, it has more definition than most of the links on which the Open is played. What you see is what you get.

Jack Nicklaus studies the line of a putt with Prince Andrew during a recent Pro-Am match (photo: Scotsman Publications/Rutherford)

The turf is lovely, just made for hitting iron shots with the spin you want, the bunkers are so beautifully built as to be a work of art. As for the greens, I always thought that Logan, as the head greenkeeper, got it right in the way he knew when to leave it to nature or, as he would say, to God. No overwatering for him and he knew the value of sand.

I enjoy the element of run, which demands judgment and feel, but there is a point where bounce golf can become too much of a lottery. The balance between the two at Muirfield appeals greatly to me and so, too, does the part played by the wind. The way the course is laid out, with the front nine running clockwise as the outer ring and the back nine anti-clockwise inside it, means that the wind comes at you from all points of the compass and that adds to the shot-making.

I have always said that the Old Course at St Andrews is my favourite place in Britain to be playing golf because of its unique atmosphere, that feeling of history all about you. But Muirfield is my favourite course, to me the best on the Open championship rota. It would have been unforgivably presumptuous to call my course in Ohio Muirfield because there can be only one, but I much appreciated the response of the captain, the late Guy Robertson Durham, and of his committee, when I asked if it would be all right if I incorporated Muirfield into the name. It was a nice gesture, too, of the City of Edinburgh to acknowledge the link by presenting Muirfield Village at the Memorial tournament in 1980 with a Silver Club modelled on those they have presented to the Honourable Company.

A 250th anniversary adds up to an awful lot of golf shots. It is at once a pleasure and a privilege to have the opportunity, in contributing this Foreword, to congratulate the Honourable Company and, at the same time, wish them a year befitting so momentous a milestone.

Ted Ray making a speech after his Open victory at Muirfield in 1912

HCEG: THE MUIRFIELD YOUNG GOLFERS' TRUST

ON their 250th anniversary year, in 1994, the Honourable Company wish not only to celebrate the past but to look to the future. They propose to set up the Muirfield Young Golfers' Trust. This Trust is planned to benefit and coach selected promising young golfers – men or women – who live locally in the East Lothian or Edinburgh areas.

Steps are in hand to accumulate an adequate capital sum from which the club plans each year to help these potential local young champions of the future with their formal golfing educational training.

DOUGLAS FOULIS, *Captain*

Author's note

MUIRFIELD: *Home of the Honourable Company (1744–1994),* is a celebration of the 250 years' history of the Honourable Company and of the renowned links which has been their home since 1891. Of a club rich in character and golfing personality and of the great players, matches and championships which Muirfield has known. It is not a history as such because the club whose written records reach further into the past than those of any other has already been searchingly documented.

Edited by the eminent golf historian, Alastair Johnston, *The Clapcott Papers*, the painstaking researches of the erstwhile advocate and civil servant, Charles Clapcott OBE, run to over 500 pages. Stair Gillon's privately printed pamphlet covering the years 1891-1914 filled in much detail regarding the early years at Muirfield. Published by the Honourable Company in 1981, *The Original Rules of Golf*, by J. Stewart Lawson, was the definitive work on the Thirteen Articles.

Finally, George Pottinger's *Muirfield and the Honourable Company*, published by the Scottish Academic Press in 1972, was the history of the Honourable Company for which the club had been waiting. Readable and scholarly, it was a book whose guiding light had been that it should be a treatise which Henry Longhurst would enjoy – which he reportedly did.

The author would also like to acknowledge the permission given by the late Roger Newton of Programme Publications for permission to draw upon two of his previously published articles.

This book is dedicated to the memory of John Rattray and Guy Robertson Durham.

NORMAN MAIR

Edinburgh, January 1994

Acknowledgments

IN putting together this Celebration of the club's 250 years, many people have played an enthusiastic part – in particular the members and friends who have lent us valuable photographs for reproduction. But I think especially warm thanks are due not only, of course, to Norman Mair, but to Mainstream Publishing, always calm and professional, to David Ross Stewart, to Archie Baird, our archivist, with his astonishing knowledge of golf in the past, to John Martin, who designed the book and played a very distinguished part in putting it all together, and, finally, to Glyn Satterley who has produced recently so many marvellous photographs of the club and course we love.

DOUGLAS FOULIS, *Captain*

Edinburgh, February 1994

1 A course for champions

1 A course for champions

'WHILE maintaining to the full the traditions and rights of its members, and their privacy, the Honourable Company, as owner, also fully accepts that it is, as it were, trustee for Scotland – and for the world – of its great links. It is proud and privileged to accept the staging of the premier golfing tournaments – the Open and Amateur championships, the Ryder, Walker and Curtis Cups – from time to time.'

So spoke the Honourable Lord Robertson, Senator of the College of Justice and Captain of the Honourable Company, in 1972 in his admirable Foreword to George Pottinger's *Muirfield and The Honourable Company*.

All told, Muirfield has housed one Ryder Cup, two Walker Cups, two Curtis Cups, four Home International championships, one Scottish Ladies championship, seven Scottish Amateur championships, two Scottish Open Amateur Stroke-play championships, one St Andrews Trophy, two Vagliano Trophies, nine Amateur championships and 14 Opens.

Outside of the Open championship itself, the Amateur championships have provided the central thread, beginning with the sensational victory of Jack Allan in 1897. Allan, a medical student at Edinburgh University, was only 21 and, to render still more poignant the memory of his triumph, he did not live to defend his title. The field arrayed against him included two men who had already won the Open championship in Harold Hilton – at Muirfield at that – and John Ball; and amateurs of the calibre of Robert Maxwell, Johnny Low and J.E. Laidlay.

A Watsonian whose home course was the Braid Hills, Allan – the son of a surgeon-colonel who had once been the principal medical officer for Scotland – took the train each morning to Drem whence he cycled to Muirfield. He wore shoes with nary a tacket in them, arguing that such footwear forced him to stay in balance and swing within himself. He had broken the course record at the Braids with a 69 within two years of taking up the game. Endowed with an ideal temperament, he had a swing which had an ease about it which gave a misleading impression of looseness. In the quarter-finals, he beat Laurie Auchterlonie, in the semi-finals, Leslie Balfour-Melville, and in the final the renowned James Robb. Within a year he had contracted a lung disease and died in March 1898 when seemingly on the threshold of a great career both on and off the course. Those whom the Gods love . . .

Opposite: Cyril Tolley plays from a bunker during the 1920 Amateur championship

Where J.E. Laidlay's two Amateur championships in 1889 and 1891 had each been won at St Andrews at the expense of, respectively, Leslie Balfour-Melville and Harold Hilton, both of Maxwell's were captured on home soil. He beat Horace Hutchinson in the 1903 final by 7 and 5 and then, in 1909, he took the title at the expense of Cecil Hutchison in what was to pass into the annals of championship golf as one of the classic finals. Some conception of his reputation when he had the turf of his beloved Muirfield beneath his feet can be judged from the retort of Ben Sayers when the North Berwick sage was asked how he considered the final would go:

'It will be a good match – if Maxwell is off his game!'

In fact, Hutchison came tantalisingly close to winning. But let Bernard Darwin, whom Maxwell had beaten in the semi-final by 3 and 2 – at which juncture Maxwell was just one over fours – take up the tale: 'There never was a pleasanter final to follow, for the two, who had so often played together, played at the pace and in the manner of an ordinary friendly game. The golf was extremely good and accurate and Cecil was one up with two holes to play. At this point, Bobby produced a really great three at the seventeenth (the course was quite different from the present one), skirting the left-hand rough with obvious intention in order to get the easier approach, laying his pitch close to the pin and then holing his putt. He got his four at the home hole, where Cecil missed a shortish putt, and pulled the match out of the fire.'

Frank Moran, who covered golf for the *Scotsman* for 50 years, would tell of how one of the Fourth Estate's elder brethren complained bitterly that the play had been too good, practically every shot hit as it should have been hit with such a lack of deviation or incident that he had found precious little to report. Maxwell, who did not much care for the press, would have enjoyed that.

For the Honourable Company, in respect of the Amateur championship, it was something of a last hurrah. They had furnished not only the champion but four of the quarter-finalists, Maxwell, J.E. Laidlay, N.E. Hunter and Captain C.K. Hutchison. Other than administratively, they were never again to make such an impact on the premier amateur championship of the Old World.

It fell to Muirfield, though, to usher in the new era after the Kaiser's War and the championship of 1920 could hardly have had more dramatic undercurrents. There were 165 entrants and the 165th was to prove the victor. Cyril Tolley, then an Oxford University undergraduate, had had no intention of travelling to Scotland to play at Muirfield until a chance meeting in the street with his friend, Roger Wethered. Tolley was at that moment more intent on his cricket and it was ironical that it should have been Wethered, of all golfers, who changed his mind. After all, it was Wethered who, after tying with Jock Hutchison in the 1921 Open at St Andrews, had wanted to go south that night for a cricket match but was persuaded to stay for the play-off – which he lost.

Like many another, including the revered Freddie Tait, Tolley neither overlapped nor interlocked but the placement of his hands on the club was a thing of beauty. He was long and strong and, at his best, in the opinion of Darwin, there was no player in the world who could 'make the opponent feel how vain it is to struggle, and the spectator how futile it is ever to play again'.

But that week he was off his driving, using a spoon off the tee. His adversary in the final was America's Bob Gardner who was one of an American raiding party dubbed 'The Legislators' because the primary purpose of their transatlantic venture was to hold discussions with the R & A regarding the Rules of Golf. Having been three up with four holes to play on a man who had twice been the US Amateur champion, Tolley won with a two at the 37th, the old par 3 first hole. His putting had been wonderful-

Right: eight Amateur Champions pictured in 1920. Left to right - back row: Lassen, Maxwell, Barry, Gardner; front row: Jenkins, Balfour-Melville, Laidlay and Hilton

Left: Jesse Sweetser, 1926 Amateur Champion, with his boy caddie and the trophy

Below: R.T. Jones congratulates A. Jamieson who defeated him in the 1926 Amateur by 4 and 3

ly serene and it is said that, before he holed for that unanswered birdie two, he had already handed over to his caddie the five pound note he had promised to give him if he won. Walter Hagen, another who was to know what it was to win at Muirfield, would have approved.

In 1926, Bobby Jones was naturally the favourite – not so much hot as molten – but Andrew Jamieson, a 21-year-old Scot, earned himself Walker Cup honours, not to mention immortality in his own neck of the woods, the West of Scotland, by knocking him out in the quarter-finals. Jones, though he made nothing of it, was troubled by a stiff neck but the scalp above it was still the one to take. Jamieson, perhaps predictably, lost in the very next round.

His conqueror was A.V. Simpson, an Edinburgh golfer who, in the final, could not prevent the 1922 US Amateur champion, Jess Sweetser, a former Yale quarter-miler and a class golfer of much charm, from becoming the first American to take the trophy back with him since Walter Travis and his Schenectady putter in 1904. Not that it can have helped Simpson that his transport arrangements went so awry that he arrived on the first tee in the nick of time after a frantic taxi-journey with Keystone Cops connotations, right down to the flock of sheep, baa-ing and barring the way at Piershill.

In 1932, Scotland had four in the last eight – Eric McRuvie, S.L. McKinlay, W. Tulloch and J.N. Reynard – but only McRuvie in the last four. In the final, John de Forest beat Eric Fiddian but the champion was destined to be remembered less for this championship success than for the 1953 US Masters. By then Count de Bendern, with his ball lodged on the bank of Rae's Creek in front of Augusta's thirteenth green, he stripped off his left shoe and sock and rolled up the relevant trouser-leg. As the Masters booklet gleefully records, 'Johnny next, very carefully, planted the bare foot on the bank and stepped into the deep water with his well-shod right foot.

John de Forest receives the cup for the 1932 Amateur from John Cook, Captain of HCEG

The spectators who witnessed this incident will long recall the look of incredulity on the affable Count's face as he realised what he had done.'

That anecdote encapsulates one of the most idiosyncratic of all the assorted winners Muirfield has sired, not excluding the members. Even *en route* to the Amateur title at Muirfield, he would address the ball and apparently freeze until the more highly strung spectators wanted to cry out – but, eventually, as Moran wrote, 'Down in de Forest something stirred'. Forest and Fiddian had taken six and a half hours to play 35 holes: two and a half hours more than it had taken Maxwell and Hutchison, playing almost flawlessly, to go round twice in the final of 1909.

In the 1954 Amateur, the first at Muirfield after the Second World War, 'The Man from Rosebud', Doug Bachli, thwarted that fine golfer, Bill Campbell, triumphing in the final by 2 and 1 when not a few had thought that the Virginian would win in a canter. A quiet, stocky, 32-year-old Australian, Bachli, from the small seaside town outside Melbourne with a name which could have been culled from a romantic novelette, was a tough customer. He pitched and putted nervelessly on a day when the American Walker Cup luminary, as could happen with him, was finding a capricious right hand had him hitting if not from the top, then at any rate too early.

Alas, Bachli's title has always been unfairly dwarfed by the controversy surrounding the dashing Joe Carr's defeat of Bachli's compatriot, Peter Toogood, at the twentieth in the sixth round. At the second extra hole, Carr, to the surprise of most, was given a free lift and drop by officialdom from casual water and made the most of it. Moran did not bring himself to condemn the ruling in so many words but he did so by implication. He described it as 'one without parallel in golf law' and then, after Bachli's winning of the title, emphasised the satisfaction it had 'brought to Australian sentiment, following the unfortunate circumstances in which their brilliant youngster, Peter Toogood, had lost to Joe Carr'.

Out on the links, Moran had noticed that sightseers were over on the spot on the left of the second hole having a look at the locale that will be marked with a large X in championship memory. 'Ah well,' philosophised the humorists, 'you can't win 'em all.' A good crack, for the likeable Toogood and his family had made the trip – and acquired a spanking new car – on the back of the fortune produced by a winning ticket in their state lottery.

On to 1974 and a championship which will always owe its particular niche in the archives to the last hole of the last afternoon. Versus America's Jim Gabrielsen in a final of much sterling golf, England's Trevor Homer, who had won the Amateur at Royal St George's in 1972, was one up boarding the 36th tee but drove into a starboard bunker and took two to get out. Gabrielsen had hit a sumptuous drive but he pulled a six-iron into the farthest reach of the bunker lining the home green's left flank. Homer had taken four to reach the green and he was still wide of the flag.

Below: D.W. Bachli from Australia playing an iron shot during the 1954 Amateur

The gallery took it for granted that the match would go down the 37th but, among them, was Hugh Stuart, the Scottish Walker Cup player. Glancing from the flag to what he could see of Gabrielsen, he made a shrewd and prophetic remark: 'If he is anywhere near the back of that bunker he has got a very difficult shot.' Close enough to the rear wall of the bunker to give him all too little room in which to work, Gabrielsen came out too far, diagonally across the green. With all eyes glued upon it in petrified fascination, his ball slid on and on down into the island bunker.

Shaken, he was again much too strong with his recovery; back across the green, though short of the sand. His approach putt hurried several feet past. Homer himself putted down gingerly, by no means dead, but Gabrielsen by then was on skid row. Three putts left Homer's prospective six more than good enough. Dimly, one could remember when they had set sail from that last tee.

In 1990, the Amateur was won by Rolf Muntz from Holland and if it is correct that golf at Leith Links derived from the frozen lake pastime of *Het Kolven*, it was not inapposite that a Dutchman should take the title in the last Amateur before the Honourable Company's 250th anniversary. His achievement took even his own countrymen aback, Muntz confiding on the Saturday, after the final, that Dutch officials had made bookings for their two contenders to fly home on the Friday. 'The supposition was that neither of us would get through the qualifying rounds,' confessed the Leiden University student who had switched from law to psychology on the grounds that the latter would be more helpful to his golf. With golf in Holland having long been as flat as the land itself, the 21-year-old Muntz trusted that his win would fan the embers in a nation of but 45,000 participants. The powerful Muntz's victim in the final, by 7 and 6, was a Welshman, Michael Macara, who, in 1988, had required three operations on his back to stay in the game.

An international flavouring had long been a very welcome ingredient in the Amateur while, of course, the Honourable Company had, in their own distant ancestry, that match in which the Duke of York and the humble cobbler, John Paterson, defeated two English noblemen whose names have been expunged from history. Today, spanning the centuries, there is again a Duke of York who is addicted to the game and who brings to it, according to no less a personage than Jack Nicklaus, a heap of natural talent, a good swing and a deft touch.

Nor is that all, for he has already added to the store of golf's post-prandial oratory – the story of how, when the Duke of Edinburgh learned that Prince Andrew had taken up the game, he had exclaimed, 'Splendid. He can inherit some of his great-uncle's old clubs.' Into Prince Andrew's mind's eye, there had swum a pleasing picture of some beautifully preserved, perfectly crafted old hickories but the Duke, for his part, was thinking of Royal St George's, Royal St David's, Royal Ascot . . .

THE AMATEUR CHAMPIONSHIP

1897	A.J.T. Allan beat James Robb	4 and 2
1903	R. Maxwell beat H.G. Huchinson	7 and 5
1909	R. Maxwell beat Captain C.K. Hutchison	1 hole
1920	C.J.H. Tolley beat R.A. Gardner (USA)	at 37th
1926	Jesse Sweetser (USA) beat A.F. Simpson	6 and 5
1932	J. de Forest beat E.W. Fiddian	3 and 1
1954	D.W. Bachli (Australia) beat W.C. Campbell (USA)	2 holes
1974	T. Homer beat J. Gabrielsen (USA)	2 holes
1990	R. Muntz (Holland) beat M. Macara (Wales)	7 and 6

The eighteenth green and Clubhouse in 1920. Note the earlier bunker layout

William St Clair of Roslin, from the original portrait by Sir George Chalmers which hangs in the Archers' Hall in Edinburgh. It was commissioned by the Honourable Company in 1771 but was subsequently bought by the Royal Company of Archers in 1833. A copy of this painting hangs in the clubhouse at Muirfield

William St Clair of Roslin (1700–78)

THE last of a line said to have come to Britain with William the Conqueror, he was distinguished for his sporting prowess, particularly in golf and archery. He was captain of the Honourable Company in 1761, 1766, 1770 and 1771, having in those years won the Competition for the Silver Club. He was also 'Captain of the Golf' at St Andrews where he gained the Silver Club in 1764, 1766 and 1768. President of the Royal Company of Archers from 1768 to 1778, he won some 20 of their archery prizes. Having surrendered the hereditary office of Grand Master Mason of Scotland, 'Roslin' was appointed first Grand Master of the Grand Lodge of Scotland.

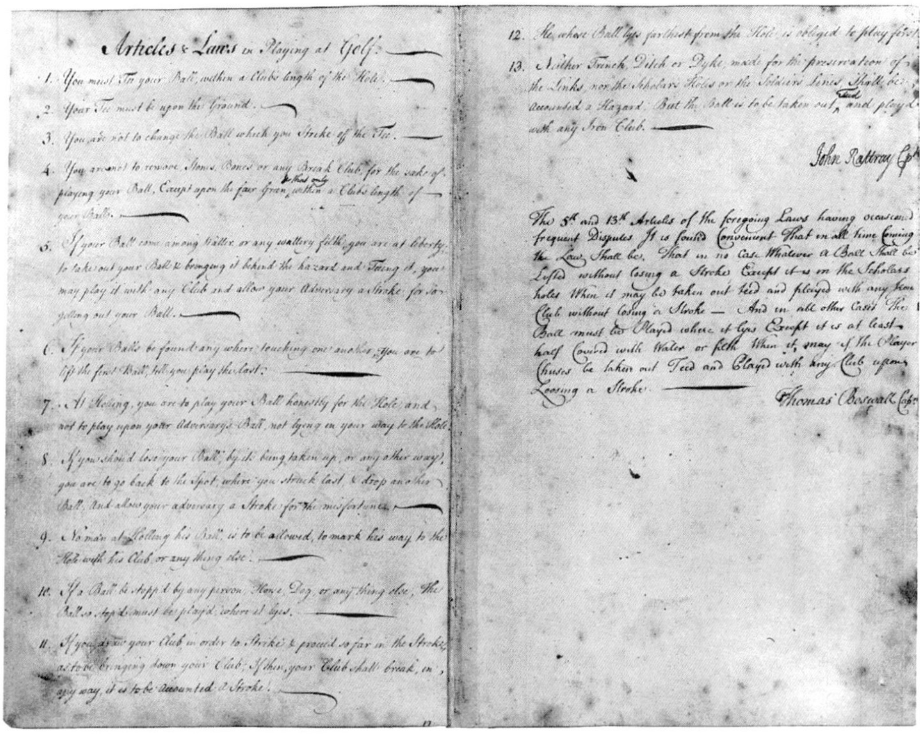

The two pages from the 1744 minute book of the 'Gentlemen Golfers' which record the world's first written rules of golf.
The text is given below

Articles & Laws in Playing at Golf

1. *You must Tee your Ball, within a Club's length of the Hole.*
2. *Your Tee must be upon the Ground.*
3. *You are not to change the Ball which you Strike off the Tee.*
4. *You are not to remove, Stones, Bones or any Break Club, for the sake of playing your Ball, Except upon the fair Green/& that only/within a Club's length of your Ball.*
5. *If your Ball comes among Watter or any wattery filth, you are at liberty to take out your Ball & bringing it behind the hazard and Teeing it, you may play it with any Club and allow your Adversary a Stroke for so getting out your Ball.*
6. *If your Balls be found any where touching one another, You are to lift the first Ball, till you play the last.*
7. *At Holling, you are to play your Ball honestly for the Hole, and, not to play upon your Adversary's Ball, not lying in your way to the Hole.*
8. *If you shou'd lose your Ball, by it's being taken up, or any other way, you are to go back to the Spot, where you struck last, & drop another Ball, And allow your adversary a Stroke for the misfortune.*
9. *No man at Holling his Ball, is to be allowed, to mark his way to the Hole with his Club, or any thing else.*
10. *If a Ball be stopp'd by any person, Horse, Dog, or any thing else, The Ball so stop'd must be play'd, where it lyes.*
11. *If you draw your Club, in order to Strike & proceed so far in the Stroke, as to be bringing down your Club; If then, your Club shall break, in any way, it is to be Accounted a Stroke.*
12. *He whose Ball lyes farthest from the Hole is obliged to play first.*
13. *Neither Trench, Ditch or Dyke, made for the preservation of the Links, nor the Scholar's Holes or the Soldiers' Lines, Shall be accounted a Hazard; But the Ball is to be taken out/Teed/and play'd with any Iron Club.*

John Rattray Cp^n

The 5th and 13th Articles of the foregoing Laws having occasioned frequent Disputes, it is found Convenient that in all time coming the Law shall be that in no case whatever a Ball shall be Lifted without losing a Stroke Except it is in the Scholars holes when it may be taken out teed and played with any Iron Club without losing a Stroke – And in all other cases the Ball must be Played where it lyes Except it is at least half Covered with Water or filth when it may if the Player Chuses be taken out Teed and Played with any Club upon losing a Stroke

Thomas Boswall Capn

2 The Thirteen Articles

IN all the kaleidoscope of sport, there can be few stranger coincidences than that the Company of Gentlemen Golfers (now the Honourable Company of Edinburgh Golfers) should have promulgated the first rules of golf in the very same year the laws of cricket were published for the first time. Namely, 1744.

No less notable is the extent to which, in each instance, the handiwork of the legal code's founding-fathers has stood the test of time. In a work published by the Honourable Company in 1981 entitled *The Original Rules of Golf*, J. Stewart Lawson, an acknowledged authority, observed that many of the fundamental rules of golf today derived from the 1744 code, the holy writ which has come down to us as the Thirteen Articles. 'It is a remarkable tribute,' he suggested, 'to the foresight and imagination of "The Gentlemen Golfers" that the general principles underlying seven of their thirteen articles (3, 5, 8, 9, 10, 11, 12) are incorporated with minor modifications in the current Rules of Golf and so far as Articles 4 and 6 are concerned, the only difference under the present rules is that the relief from interference by loose impediments or by another ball is available on a much wider scale.'

The cricket laws of 1744 numbered 21 and no fewer than seven of the nine ways in which a batsman could be out were the same then as today, though leg before wicket was still some 30 years away. Most strikingly, the length of the pitch was set at 22 yards and has never changed. The original laws of cricket could have been printed on a handkerchief but, like Topsy, they just growed. So with golf, for all Henry Longhurst's wistful but unproven submission that all the necessary rules of golf could be written on one side of a postcard.

As John Glover of the R & A is wont to point out, the principle that the ball had to be played where it lay was seemingly already so taken for granted that – shades of Longhurst – it was not deemed necessary to mention it specifically until Article 10 and then not again. But, in a foretaste of things to come, 'this facet of the common code', to borrow a phrase from the eminent golf historian, Alastair J. Johnston, was apparently so abused that the legislation had to be progressively more explicit and specific.

Article 2, 'Your Tee must be upon the Ground', puzzled many but, almost certainly, it was to prevent the kind of ploy favoured by as good a golfer as Sir Harold Gillies until the R & A made their displeasure known. Sir Harold – in the manner of a previous incarnation of Paul Hahn, of trick-shot legend – was in the habit of teeing his ball on the top of a piece of india-rubber tubing attached to the neck of a bottle. Johnston thinks that golfers at one time prepared their initial lie on each hole (and, in fact, wherever the rules permitted 'teeing' of the ball) by hacking the turf with a heel and perching the ball on the rampart thereby raised. If they did, it was to have echoes in the next two centuries in the launching pad many of rugby's goal-kickers dug with a heel but it was still not something too many would have fancied doing on the first tee at Muirfield with a Colonel Evans-

Letter from C.B. Clapcott printed in the Scotsman

London, April 30, 1938

Sir, – In your issue of April 28, under the heading of 'Oldest Clubs to Meet,' it is stated that 'Royal Blackheath was instituted in 1608, and Royal Burgess 127 years later. Next in order of seniority are Honourable Company of Edinburgh Golfers, Royal and Ancient,' &c.

Would it be out of place to point out that: –

(1) 'No written evidences of any society of Blackheath Golfers of earlier date than 1787 have come down to us,' (*Chronicles of Blackheath Golfers* by W.E. Hughes.)

(2) The earliest written evidence of the existence of the Royal Burgess is 8th April 1773.

(3) The earliest written evidence of the existence of the Honourable Company, under its then title of Gentlemen Golfers, is 7th March 1744.

(4) The earliest written evidence of the existence of the Royal and Ancient is 14th May 1754.

It is generally accepted that these four clubs are the four oldest golf clubs, but the order of their seniority would appear to require some rearrangement – I am&c.

C.B.C.

Lombe or a Paddy Hanmer in close proximity. There is no doubt, though, that caddies would often construct small castles of sand to give their employers a helpfully elevated missile site. Again, since, in the beginning, Article 1 decreed that 'You must Tee your Ball, within a Club's length of the Hole', one would not have wanted to be the first to interview a Nick Faldo after a bad putting round.

The rule forbidding the removal of a broken club, 'for the sake of playing your Ball' – Article 4 – conjures up a picture of a Leith Links infested by the forbears of such as John Daly whose prodigious power at one time had him breaking steel-shafted clubs as another man might break eggs, or Terrible Tommy Bolt whose clubs were said to have got in more flying time than a Pan-Am pilot. But even the hickory clubs of Henry Cotton's early years broke so readily that many kept a spare set for practice. Some of the distant prototypes were a deal more fragile.

Semantically, the centuries are further bridged by the use of the term 'fair Green' to indicate the putting surface and 'hazard' for what were then watery areas of varying mud and filth. Why, though, that stipulation in Article 13 that, from problem areas which were not hazards, 'the Ball is to be taken out, teed and played with any Iron Club'?

Judging by some of the early portraits, the favourite irons of many of the Gentlemen Golfers were their knife and fork. Nevertheless, one would have thought that even then there would have been among them one or two eighteenth-century John Pantons who would have been only too delighted to reach for an iron. But Johnston has surmised that being compelled to sacrifice distance, together with 'the danger to the delicate feathery ball from the clout of so ponderous an implement', was sufficient retribution for so straying.

On 2 July 1790, the Royal Burgess were still ruling that every person shall have it in his power 'to play his Ball in any direction he chuses, either upon his Adversary's Ball or otherwise'. Nonetheless, slow though it was to attain universal acceptance, Article 7, which forbade playing 'upon your Adversary's Ball, not lying in your way to the Hole', ensured that golf would never be glorified croquet however much it may sometimes feel like it. In that Article, too, as so many have noted, were sewn the seeds of the now abandoned stymie.

It was in 1937 that C.B. Clapcott, whose invaluable and painstaking perusal of the Minutes of the Honourable Company was to lead to his being made an honorary member of the Honourable Company, uncovered the code of 1744 as inscribed in the Minute Book of the Gentlemen Golfers. The Thirteen Articles or Leith Code had evaded the research of such chroniclers as Robert Clark and John Kerr, authors of, respectively, *Golf: A Royal and Ancient Game* and *Golf Book of East Lothian*. Both had accepted that the 'Articles and Laws in Playing the Golf', as recorded on 14 May 1754 in the first minute of the Royal and Ancient Golf Club of St Andrews, were the first rules of golf. (The one significant difference from the Thirteen Articles was that with the Gentlemen Golfers it was legitimate to lift and tee whereas at St Andrews the rule was to lift and drop.

Yet a Miss Marple, though precluded by her gender from membership of the Honourable Company, would have been on the trail of the

DINNERS AND THE BETT BOOK

The Bett Book is in direct line of descent from the dinners – first at Luckie Clephan's Tavern and later at the Golf House – which the Edinburgh Golfers were given to holding in the evenings of their Play Days at Leith Links. Since Play Days were usually on a Saturday, matches for the weekend ahead were recorded in the pages of the minute book until, in 1776, a separate Bett book came into being. By 1783, a 'Clerk to the Betts' had been appointed and, within two years, that title had been supplanted by that of the Recorder. In the ensuing 209 years, there have been only 33 Recorders. Among the most famous, if terse, entries in the Bett Book is

A preliminary study by David Allan for his portrait of William Inglis, Captain of the Honourable Company 1782-84, which is reproduced on our book jacket

that of 9 February 1880: 'C. v M. Not played. C. funked.' A message not lost on posterity. No strokes are involved in dinner matches, most of which are played at Muirfield. The captain will hammer a game which seems manifestly unfair. Matches, which must be played on a stipulated date, are for the Club Stake of two pounds plus whatever sum has been agreed among the prospective participants. There are seven dinners in a year, nowadays all in the clubhouse. Not just the captain but the ex-captains must wear their red coats of office. The match dinners and the dinner matches which they sire are at the very heart of the club, the stuff of banter and fellowship, of cut and thrust, of great shots held below the wind and short putts spilled.

Thirteen Articles from the moment she failed to identify on the Old Course at St Andrews the Scholar's holes and the Soldiers' lines. As late as 1907, H.S. Everard, in his *History of the Royal and Ancient*, was at a loss to explain the reference to the Soldiers' lines. Clapcott had still to discover the Thirteen Articles and there was no reference to either the Scholar's holes or the Soldiers' lines in the rules of the Honourable Company of 22 April 1775. Yet one would still have supposed that Everard would have thought to delve into the Leith Links and Honourable Company connections.

As a sleuth, Clapcott could have been an Agatha Christie creation, albeit for Inspector Slack read the disbelieving Jim Robertson-Durham.

'I recall,' wrote an elderly gentleman to Johnston, 'setting off in a foursome (not a bloody fourball) accompanied (as spectator) by Jim Robertson-Durham, then (1946–47) captain of the Honourable Company. As we moved down the first fairway after the drives, old Clapcott came puffing after us. "Mr Captain! Mr Captain! I must report to you that yesterday in a solicitor's office in Edinburgh I made a remarkable discovery affecting the early history of the Society of Gentlemen Golfers in a document contained in an eighteenth-century deed box. It throws much light . . ." But here he was violently and rudely interrupted by Jim R-D who had no interest whatever in antiquarian researches. "Tee Box! Tee Box! They didn't have tee boxes in the eighteenth century!" ("Silly old fool," aside to me!)'

Letter from *The Expedition of Humphry Clinker* by Tobias Smollett, 1771

I never saw such a concourse of genteel company at any races in England, as appeared on the course of Leith. Hard by, in the fields called the Links, the citizens of Edinburgh divert themselves at a game called golf, in which they use a curious kind of bats, tipt with horn, and small elastic balls of leather, stuffed with feathers, rather less than tennis balls, but of a much harder consistence. This they strike with such force and dexterity from one hole to another, that they will fly to an incredible distance. Of this diversion the Scots are so fond, that when the weather will permit, you may see a multitude of all ranks, from the senator of justice to the lowest tradesmen, mingled together in their shirts, and following the balls with the utmost eagerness. Among others, I was shewn one particular set of golfers, the youngest of whom was turned of fourscore. They were all gentlemen of independent fortunes, who had amused themselves with this pastime for the best part of a century, without having ever felt the least alarm from sickness or disgust; and they never went to bed, without having each the best part of a gallon of claret in his belly. Such uninterrupted exercise, co-operating with the keen air from the sea, must, without all doubt, keep the appetite always on edge, and steel the constitution against all the common attacks of distemper.

Shown here is the second Silver Club gifted by the City of Edinburgh when there was no more room on the first club for silver balls to be attached. The change from 'featheries' to 'gutties' is faithfully reproduced in the silver replicas

ACT of COUNCIL and REGULATIONS to be observed by those who yearly play for THE CITY of EDINBURGH'S SILVER CLUB. AT EDINBURGH the Seventh Day of March, One Thousand Seven Hundred and Forty Four Years, The Lord Provost, Magistrates and Council, with the Deacons of Crafts Ordinary and Extraordinary of the CITY OF EDINBURGH, being in Council assembled, AND it being Represented to them, THAT Several Gentlemen of Honour, Skilfull in the Ancient and Healthfull Exercise of the GOLF, had from time to time Applied to Several Members of Council for a SILVER CLUB to be annually plaid for on the Links of Leith, at Such time, and upon Such Conditions as the Magistrates & Council Should think proper: AND it being reported, THAT the Gentlemen Golfers had drawn up a Scroll, at the Desire of the Magistrates, of Such Articles and Conditions, as to them seem'd most Expedient, as proper Regulations to be Observed by the Gentlemen, who Should Yearly offer to play for the said SILVER CLUB, which were produced and read in Council, the Tenor Whereof follows.

I[st.] As many Noblemen or Gentlemen, or other Golfers, from any part of GREAT BRITAIN or IRELAND, as shall book themselves. Eight Days before, or upon any of the Lawfull Days of the Week immediately preceeding the Day appointed by the Magistrates & Council for the Annual Match shall have the priviledge of playing for the said Club, each Signer paying Five Shillings Sterling at Signing, in a Book to be provided for that purpose, which is to lye in Mrs. Clephen's House in Leith, or Such other House as afterwards the Subscribers Shall appoint from Year to Year; and the Regulations approved of by the magistrates & Council Shall be Recorded at the beginning of said Book.

II[d.] On the Morning before playing, Small bits of paper marked with the Figures 1, 2, 3, &c. according to the Number of players, Shall be put into a Bonnet, and drawn by the Signers, and every Couple shall be matched according to the Figures by them drawn beginning with Nos. 1, 2, and so on; but if there Shall be a greater Number of Subscribers, they Shall be match'd in Three's; and after the parties are thus matched, in case there be ane odd Number, the Gentleman who draws it Shall play along with the last Set.

III[d.] AFTER the Figures are drawn, the SET or MATCH beginning with No. 1, &c., shall goe out first, with a Clerk to mark down every Stroke each of them shall take to every hole; then, by the time they are at the Saw-Mill Hole, the Second Set, beginning with No. 3, or 4, according as the Match shall be made, Shall Strike off; and so all the rest in the Same Order, each Set having a Clerk: AND when the Match is ended, a Scrutiny of the Whole Clerk's Books or Jottings is to be made, and the player who Shall appear to have won the greatest Number of Holes shall be declared to be the Winner of the Match; And if there shall be two, three, or more, that are equal, then these two or Three &c. must play a Round themselves, in the Order of their Figures, before they goe off the Ground, to determine the Match.

Letter from Mr John Rattray (Captain, 1744–47 & 1751) to John Hamilton of Bargany.

Edinr 23 July 1752.

Dear Sir

The silver club is to be play'd for on Saturday, and it will be a particular pleasure to all the Gouffers here if you will favour us with your company. If you have any ambition for the prize you never can find a more favourable opportunity; Cross is at Glasgow, Davie Dalrymple is much out of play, the Commissary Leslie cannot attend, I am a criple, so that Alston thinks himself sure of being victor, pray do come and disappoint him. I intended you should have had more early intimation but M'Ewan neglected to write; how ever this may reach you in time enough I hope. I am dear Sir your most obedient humble servant

John Rattray

IVth. The Crowns given in at Signing are Solely to be at the Disposal of the Victor.

V^th. Every Victor is to spend a Gold or Silver piece, as he pleases to the CLUB, for the Year he wins.

VIth. That every Victor shall, at the receiving the CLUB, give Sufficient Caution to the Magistrates and Council of EDINBURGH for Fifty Pounds Sterling, for delivering back the CLUB to their hands One Moneth before it is to be play'd for again.

VIIth. THAT the CLUB is declared to be always the Property of the Good Town.

VIIIth. THAT if any Dispute shall happen betwixt any of the parties, the same shall be determined by the other Subscribers not Concerned in the Debate.

IXth. That the Victor shall be Called CAPTAIN OF THE GOLF, and all Disputes touching the Golf, amongst Golfers, shall be determined by the Captain, and any Two or Three of the Subscribers he shall Call to his Assistance; and that the Captain shall be entitled next year to the first Ticket without drawing.

The Procession of the Silver Club accompanied by 'Tuck of Drum' throughout the city of Edinburgh to announce the competition.
From the watercolour by David Allan dated 1787 (National Gallery of Scotland)

X^th. THAT no Coaches, Chaises, or other Wheel Machines, or people on Horseback, are to be allowed to goe through the Links, but by High roads, when the match for the SILVER CLUB is a-playing, or at any other time; and that the said Captain shall from Year to Year, have the Care and Inspection of the LINKS, and shall be at Liberty to Complain to the LORD PROVOST and MAGISTRATES of any Encroachments made upon them by Highroads or otherwise.

XIth. The Subscribers shall have power, if the Day appointed for the Match shall be improper for playing it, to adjourn to another Day, upon which, if it is fit for playing, the match shall proceed.

LASTLY, It is DECLARED, That, upon no pretence whatsoever, the CITY of EDINBURGH, shall be put to any sort of Expence upon Account of playing for the said CLUB annually, except to Intimate by Tuck of Drum, through the City, the Day upon which it shall be annually play'd for, Such time before the Match as the Magistrates and Council shall think proper, and to Send the SILVER CLUB to Leith upon the Morning appointed for the Match.

WHICH Regulations having been Considered by the Magistrates of Council, They with the Extraordinary Deacons, approved thereof, with and under this Express Condition, That nothing Contain'd in the above Regulations Shall in any Sort prejudge the Magistracy and Council to dispose, in Feu or otherwise, of all or any part of the Links of Leith, as they Shall think proper. AND they hereby Authorize the Treasurer to Cause make a SILVER CLUB not Exceeding the Value of Fifteen pounds Sterling, to be play'd for Annually, upon the above Conditions, with power to the CAPTAIN of the GOLF, and any Two of the Subscribers, to make Such Orders for Regulating the manner of playing from time to time, as they shall think proper; AND do hereby Appoint the first Monday of Aprile yearly as the Day for Playing the annual match for the SILVER CLUB.

EXTRACTED forth of the Council Records of the City of EDINBURGH, upon this & the three preceding pages By me.

Jos. Williamson.

The Masonic Influence

NOTHING could be more vividly indicative of the influence of the Freemasons on golf in the eighteenth century than the entry from the minutes of the Honourable Company, date-marked Leith, 2 July 1768. Elsewhere in *The Clapcott Papers*, it is revealed that when Alexander McDougall was elected secretary of the Gentlemen Golfers, he was already the Grand Secretary of the Grand Lodge of Scotland.

One of the game's foremost historians, David Stirk, goes so far as to say that, but for the Freemasons, golf might have died out. Those in the lower income brackets could scarce afford it while, in the century between 1750 and 1850, royalty whose patronage was so important had no interest in the game. Golf, if Stirk is right, was not initially much more to the masons than a way of working up an appetite and thirst, and another medium which lent itself to wagers. Wining, dining, ritual, speechmaking, good fellowship and wagering, he is convinced, had a higher profile within the brotherhood of masons but in time they succumbed to the lure of the game.

Their influence within the Honourable Company was not in any way exceptional. For example, the captain of the Royal Burgess was empowered to elect three new members a year 'on the shake of a hand'. Nor should those campaigning for the end to sex discrimination read anything into the fact that, all those years ago, the members of the Royal Burgess endorsed the purchase of three dozen aprons. They had nothing to do with what John Knox called 'the Monstrous Regiment of Women': they were merely part of the masons' uniform. Within the Blackheath Club was the Knuckle Club where, among the toasts they drank, was the 'three times three' which was, of course, characteristically masonic. These links are hardly surprising at a time when Andrew Duncan, a master mason, could be at different times captain of the Honourable Company, Blackheath and the R & A.

With the coming of the cheaper gutta-percha ball, and with railways accentuating the changing social conditions, golf experienced a resurgence which has continued to gather pace to this day. The hold of the masons waned and in some cases left little written trace. These were essentially secret societies and destroying records was an article of faith.

But the legacy lingered. The procedure whereby, until quite recently, Honourable Company members, voting on the suitability of a would-be new member, did so by inserting a hand into the opening in an otherwise closed box and dropping a wooden ball into the yes or no compartment, was vintage masonry. The rejected applicant was not entitled to an explanation. Nor did anyone know who had blackballed him.

The Bett Book, the hung portraits of the captains on the walls of the dining-room, the gold and silver medals for competition, all are part of the Honourable Company's masonic heritage. Nor is that all they left behind. As Stirk has observed, 'Leading masons encouraged clubs to honour the game of golf . . . and supported the playing of golf in a fair and sportsmanlike manner.'

THE SILVER CLUB

There are now four Silver Clubs, all presented by the City of Edinburgh. In the beginning, the winner of the annual competition for the Silver Club automatically became Captain of Golf but, on the move to Musselburgh in 1836, the practice ceased and the captain was elected.

The City Treasurer's accounts, dated 15 August 1744, read: 'That they having Examined ane Accompt due to Deacon Edward Lothian Goldsmith for Workmanship, in making, gilding and Engraving the City's Silver Club lately given as the Annual prize to be pla'd for by the Gentlemen Golfers, Fand the same right sum'd and sufficiently instructed – Amounting in whole to Seventeen pounds four shillings and Three pence Sterling.'

The Honourable Company's gold medals which are still competed for annually in the spring and autumn

Each captain attaches an inscribed silver ball to the club, each a faithful replica of the ball of his time. There is, however, a fifth Silver Club – the one presented to Jack Nicklaus at Muirfield Village in Ohio in May 1980. The Lord Provost, Tom Morgan and three other City of Edinburgh officials flew over for the ceremony. In his robes of office, amid the summer-clad crowd, the Lord Provost cut an unforgettably incongruous figure in the broiling heat. Nicklaus himself, though genuinely and graciously appreciative, appeared decidedly taken aback by this replica of a club of 1744. 'I didn't,' he gasped, 'realise my putting needed quite this much help!'

When the Royal and Ancient was established, a decade after the Company of Edinburgh Golfers had first competed for the Silver Club, many of the members were not just common to both clubs but fellow masons. But that was as nothing in the matter of the spread of the game by comparison with the role played by the masons in introducing the game to America. As long ago as 1743, David Deas, a native of Leith and the first Provincial Grand Master Mason in the United States, sent home from Charleston, in South Carolina, for 96 golf clubs and 432 balls. To Stirk's understandable gratification, the bill of lading is still extant as evidence of the order, the date of shipment, the destination and the identity of the consignee.

It proved to be the most momentous thing of its kind outside the pages of fiction and P.G. Wodehouse's classic, *The Coming of Gowf,* wherein the King of Oom was moved to ask his Grand Vizier who was the bearded little man with a face like a walnut making mysterious passes over a small round stone with what the King took to be a hoe.

'The Vizier', wrote Wodehouse, 'was a kind-hearted man, and he hesitated for a moment. "It seems a hard thing to say of anyone, your Majesty," he replied, "but he is a Scotsman . . ."'

THE UNIFORM OF THE GENTLEMEN GOLFERS

A Minute of 1771 reads: '*The Company of Gentlemen Golfers having resolved to have their present Captain's picture in full length in his golfing dress in their Large room, requested him to Sit for the same, which he having agreed to do Sir George Chalmers is appointed to paint the same.*' The captain was William St Clair and in the picture (see page 19) wears a round blue Kilmarnock bonnet and red coat cut after the fashion of that day, while it would appear that the waistcoat may have been red as well. The golfing dress as portrayed in the picture may be safely assumed to be the original uniform of the Gentlemen Golfers.

3 *The Links in the Chain*

Talking golf – Norman Mair in conversation with the Honourable Company's archivist, Archie Baird

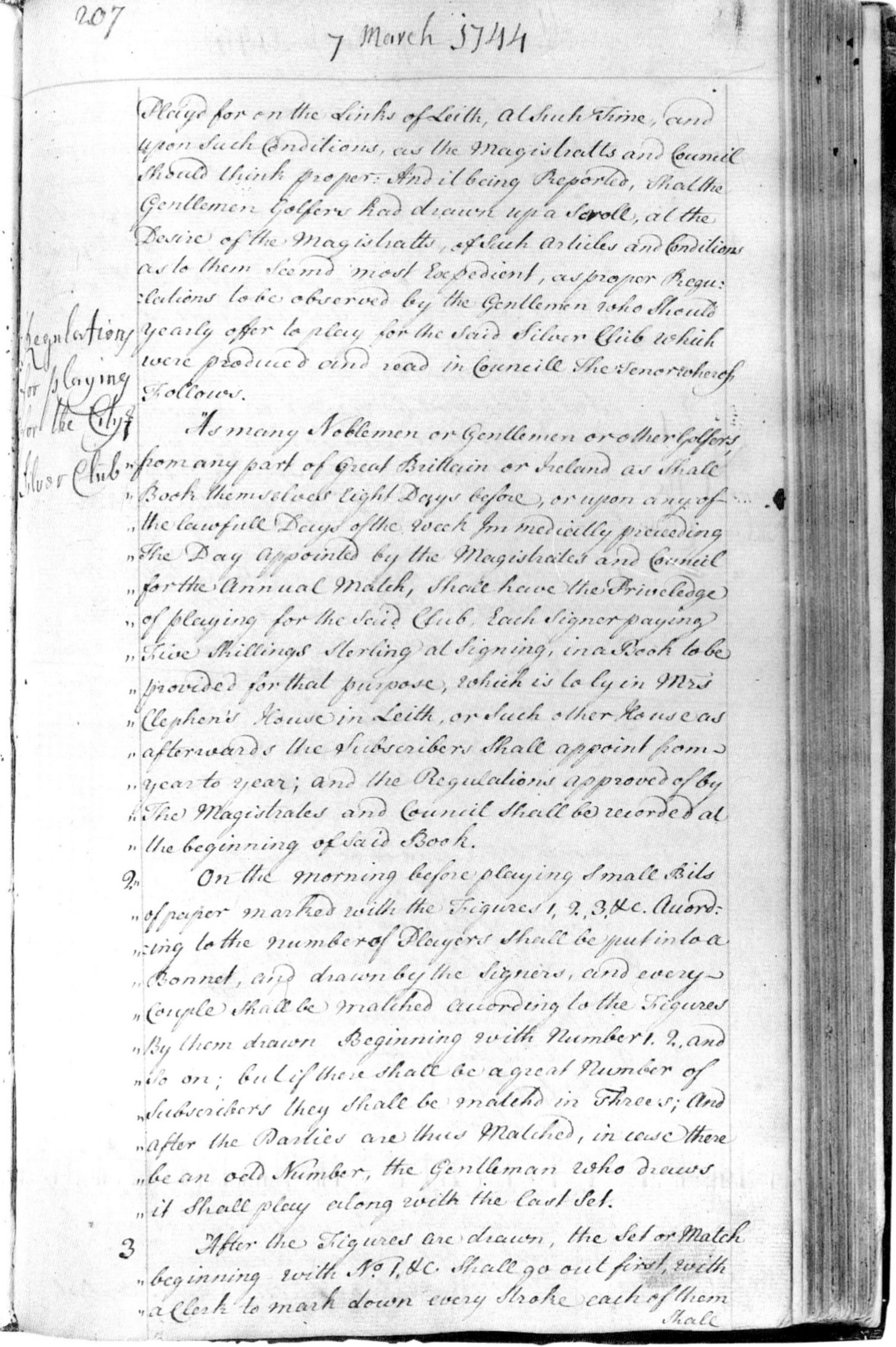
207

7 March 1744

Played for on the Links of Leith, at such time, and upon such Conditions, as the Magistratts and Councill Should think proper: And it being Reported, that the Gentlemen Golfers had drawn up a Scroll, at the Desire of the Magistratts, of such articles and Conditions as to them seemd most Expedient, as proper Regulations to be observed by the Gentlemen who Should yearly offer to play for the Said Silver Club which were produced and read in Councill The Tenor whereof follows.

Regulations for playing for the City's Silver Club

"As many Noblemen or Gentlemen or other Golfers, from any part of Great Brittain or Ireland as Shall Book themselves Eight Days before, or upon any of the lawfull Days of the week Immediatly preceeding The Day appointed by the Magistrates and Councill for the Annual Match, Shall have the Priviledge of playing for the Said Club, Each Signer paying Five Shillings Sterling at Signing, in a Book to be provided for that purpose, which is to ly in Mrs Clephen's House in Leith, or such other House as afterwards the Subscribers Shall appoint from year to year; and the Regulations approved of by The Magistrates and Councill Shall be recorded at the beginning of said Book.

2. On the morning before playing Small Bits of paper marked with the Figures 1, 2, 3, &c. According to the number of Players Shall be put into a Bonnet, and drawn by the Signers, and every Couple Shall be matched according to the Figures By them drawn Beginning with Number 1. 2, and So on; but if there shall be a great Number of Subscribers they Shall be matched in Threes; And after the Parties are thus Matched, in case there be an odd Number, the Gentleman who draws it Shall play along with the Last Set.

3 After the Figures are drawn, the Set or Match beginning with No 1, &c. Shall go out first, with a Clerk to mark down every Stroke each of them Shall

A page from the City of Edinburgh's minute book dated 7 March 1744, recording the 'Regulations for playing for the City's Silver Club'. (Reproduced by permission of the City Archivist.) The full text is printed on pages 24 and 25. The preceeding minute gives the full freedom of the City to a number of English gentlemen including Sir John Cope, 'Field-Marshal of His Majesty's forces in North Britain'. Cope's army was routed the following year at Prestonpans (a few miles from Muirfield) by Prince Charles Edward Stuart, whose entourage included (albeit unwillingly) John Rattray, first captain of the Gentlemen Golfers

MAIR: There is that tale, way back in 1571, about certain horsemen of Edinburgh happening upon nine prominent citizens of the city playing golf on Leith Links and slaying three of them by way of their own morning's sporting diversion. Though the better part of two centuries were to pass before the Company of Edinburgh Golfers came into being with that famous Act of the City of Edinburgh's Council, and their presentation of a silver club for competition, golf had obviously taken hold.

After all, as David Hamilton points out in his informative little treatise, *Early Golf at Edinburgh and Leith*, the contemporary records hardly suggest cries of 'Hold the front page!'. Both the fact that the nine burgesses were playing golf, and that three of them, however contradictory it may

Right: A Dutch winter scene by D. Teniers (circa 1650), showing at the extreme right of the picture two figures playing Kolven on the ice. The painting was donated to the club by Patrick Murray, Captain 1908-1909

Below: one of a set of four Dutch tiles circa 1650 depicting golfers, also donated to the club

sound, had pitched dead a long way from the hole, were treated as everyday occurrences.

BAIRD: There is no official mention of golf in Scotland before the middle of the fifteenth century but there is mention in Holland around 1300 of *Kolven* from which, I have no doubt, golf as we know it originated.

MAIR: How do you suppose it was brought to Scotland?

BAIRD: Partly, I think, through trade, particularly in wool. There were, too, something like 7,000 Scottish soldiers – mercenaries who had fought in the low countries – who married Dutch girls and they also, one would imagine, helped to bring golf, as well as other less welcome diseases, back to Scotland

MAIR: What exactly is the evidence substantiating that theory?

BAIRD: The Dutch, very fortunately for the golf historian, had a tradition of outdoor painting which had no counterpart in Scotland. There are sundry scenes of people playing *Kolven. Het Kolven* was the low countries' name for the sport and the most revealing painting was *The Frost Scene* by Van de Velde which dates from 1668. *Kolven*, as I suppose most golfers now know, was played on ice and, for obvious reasons, not to a hole but to a stake. The Van de Velde painting depicts two gentlemen in kilts but what, to my mind, really establishes the connection was that they were playing with Scottish clubs.

A 'featherie' from the collection at Muirfield

MAIR: How on earth can you tell that?

BAIRD: Because in Holland they don't have the wood that we have and their clubs comprised a shaft of hazel with a lump of lead for the clubhead.

MAIR: I take it, then, that you are very sceptical of the theory advanced toward the end of the last century by the Revd John Kerr in his *Golf Book of East Lothian* that golf derived from the Roman pastime of *Pila Paganica*?

BAIRD: I am no classical scholar but I don't buy that at all. It's much easier to believe that the wealthy merchants and mercenary soldiers picked it up in Holland and brought it back to the ports along the east coast where what we now call linksland – land left behind by the sea where the sand has acquired a covering of turf – lent itself so readily to the translation of the game from ice to land.

MAIR: From the records, particularly that famous match involving the Duke of York and the poor shoemaker, John Paterson, the traditional Scottish boast that golf north of the border is a game for all classes was taken for granted from the very first.

BAIRD: I've long belonged to the school which holds that it was the richer folk who could afford to travel from Edinburgh to Leith and the poorer who confined themselves to golf on Bruntsfield Links. But even if that is correct, there were both rich and poor at Leith and one obvious line of demarcation which soon materialised was that, for long, the wealthy could afford the feather ball while the more impoverished had to make do with wooden balls.

MAIR: What would a feather ball cost?

BAIRD: They could cost as much as a club. Sir John Foulis of Ravelston, who died in 1707, has recorded in his accounts the purchase of two clubs for ten shillings each, but Scots shillings were only one-twelfth of the value of English coinage. You have to remember that feather balls took a lot of making and even the most skilled practitioners could only make two a day.

MAIR: Who made them and how?

BAIRD: Originally, it was mostly the shoemakers because they were already skilled in stitching leather. The leather, which was thick, would be soaked in alum which dried it out. Then, when it had been partially stitched, it would be turned inside out so that the stitching did not show.

The next stage was to cram it full of feathers – goose or chicken but mainly the latter – and gradually to stitch up the aperture until, almost at the finish, it was so small that it took a finely pointed instrument to press in

An invoice from John Gourlay for supplying golf balls in 1850
Note the final item '1 percha'. This marks the demise of the feather ball as the gutta percha was much cheaper and more durable

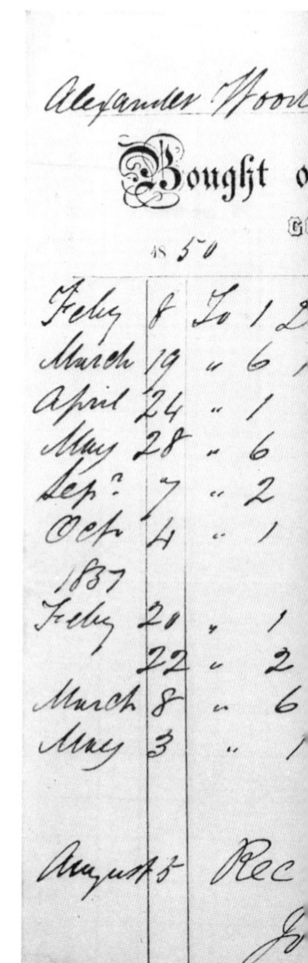
Alexander Wood
Bought o
1850
Feby 8 To 1
March 19 " 6
April 24 " 1
May 28 " 6
Sep. 7 " 2
Oct 4 " 1
1851
Feby 20 " 1
22 " 2
March 8 " 6
May 3 " 1
August 5 Rec

the last of the feathers. The best feather balls, relative to the materials involved, were of a very high compression.

MAIR: How far could one of those be hit with one of the clubs of the day?

A gutta percha 'bramble' circa 1860 from the club's collection

BAIRD: A good smack would travel 200 yards. The days of the 1.62 and the 1.68 might still be centuries away but even then some players played with the big ball and some the small. Some of them were numbered – 27, 28 or 29 – and I have a notion that those figures were to do with apothecaries' weights.

MAIR: Henry Cotton told me that Abe Mitchell, when there were not the regulations governing size and velocity there are now, used to play with balls which were unusually small and abnormally heavy. This ties in with the theory of Australia's Peter Thomson that, now that the distance the ball goes is in danger of rendering some of the great courses of the past obsolete – not to mention the amount of real estate required to build a modern championship course – a lighter ball would make more sense. It would not go as far and would additionally reward the better shot-makers in that it would be harder to control in any kind of wind.

BAIRD: Our forefathers worked out much of that kind of thing for themselves. The feather ball lasted until the mid-nineteenth century when, for 50 years, it gave way to the gutta-percha which, in the course of time, was itself replaced by the rubber-cored Haskell.

MAIR: What about the clubs?

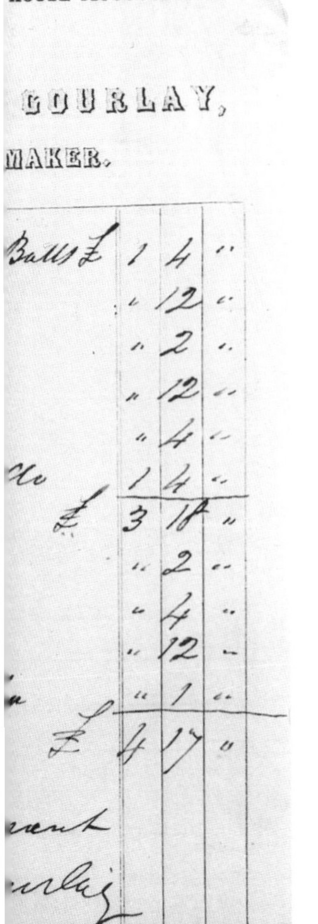

HOUSE MUSSELBURGH.

GOURLAY,

MAKER.

BAIRD: For the most part, they would be made by the bowmakers because they alone would have the skill. The early clubs may have been very brittle but some of the craftsmanship was very fine and the very hard wood which was used must have been difficult to work. Incidentally, there were left-handers even then but not as many as a novice golf collector might initially assume. It was simply that left-handed clubs were more likely to be put away in a cupboard than handed down from father to son and so, since they were much less likely to be broken, they have tended to survive.

MAIR: Foulis includes in his accounts the hire of a set of three clubs for a day at three shillings. Hamilton took those to be a driver (play club), an iron and a putter. But he also said that Old Tom Morris only carried one iron in his own set which I must admit surprised me.

BAIRD: It would vary from person to person.

MAIR: What would Leith Links have been like in the early years?

BAIRD: Pretty rough. Undulating rather than actually hilly in terms of slopes, and showing a great deal of wear and tear because it was used by the military, by archers, by folk hanging out their washing and, as is apparent from that Act of the Edinburgh Council in 1744, it was crossed by coaches and left rutted. There was a long building housing a ropeworks to the north and houses to the west but otherwise it would have been comparatively open. The Victorian houses you see today had still to come.

MAIR: It was interesting that recently when Alan Grossett (captain of

Duddingston Golf Club but a lawyer by profession) was contesting the rates assessment on the cricket club at Leith Links, he noticed the map which hangs in the locker-room at Muirfield of the long-defunct golf course. He was prepared to cite that map to prove that the cricket pavilion was within the boundaries of the original public park.

BAIRD: The area on which the Gentlemen Golfers, and no doubt many others with scant pretension to so grand a label, played their golf was expansive enough to allow five holes all of over 400 yards. However, what many have failed to realise was that most of the golf was played in the autumn or the spring. That was partly because high summer was not the time when most of the gentry were in residence in Edinburgh. Similarly, the staff and students of the university were on vacation. The principal reason, though, was that there was no greenkeeping as such. The grass would simply get too long. It was kept cropped, at least to a degree, by the horses and cows which grazed there but, when it had got out of hand, there was even less future in complaining to them than to the sourest of latter-day greenkeepers.

The five holes of Leith Links – 1744 to 1824 – drawn up over a 1953 Ordnance Survey map of Leith

MAIR: From Thomas Mathison's poem, *The Goff*, it would appear that the staple match at Leith Links consisted of four laps of the course (20 holes all told). Though, in the Thirteen Articles, the fact that a clerk went out with each match would suggest an element of stroke-play, the early golf was all match-play, wasn't it?

BAIRD: Certainly and, in fact, *The Goff* would suggest that much of it was not only match-play but foursomes. What has always intrigued me, since there is no clear-cut evidence, is how the early competitions for the silver club were conducted.

MAIR: I know there is no proof but I think that Alastair Johnston probably got it right when he opined that a hybrid format was in operation, the winner of the silver club being the golfer who had won most holes outright after comparison with the hole-by-hole scores of the other contenders. On the grounds that there is little new under the sun, I loved his surmise that it must all have been somewhat akin to the modern American concept of a Skins game without the accumulating wager which is carried forward to the next hole when there is no outright winner.

BAIRD: A Skins game as such would have appealed to them for they loved to wager. Either old Foulis did not bother to record his winnings or, judging by his accounts, he was the original losers' loser.

MAIR: What about the business of uniforms? Droves of red-coated golfers in the long ago was always a bit of a myth, one gathers.

BAIRD: That's right, but originally part of the reason for the uniform would be as a warning to others that golfers were letting fly. It is conceivable that, for that very purpose, the military may well have played in their tunics and perhaps later, the Loretto boys in their blazers.

Alexander Osborne, a secretary of the Honourable Company and a gigantic figure, portrayed by John Kay as a Royal Edinburgh Volunteer in 1794

MAIR: It does seem to have been dangerous judging by the memoirs of the Edinburgh physician, Sir Robert Sibbald. Mark you, he must have been

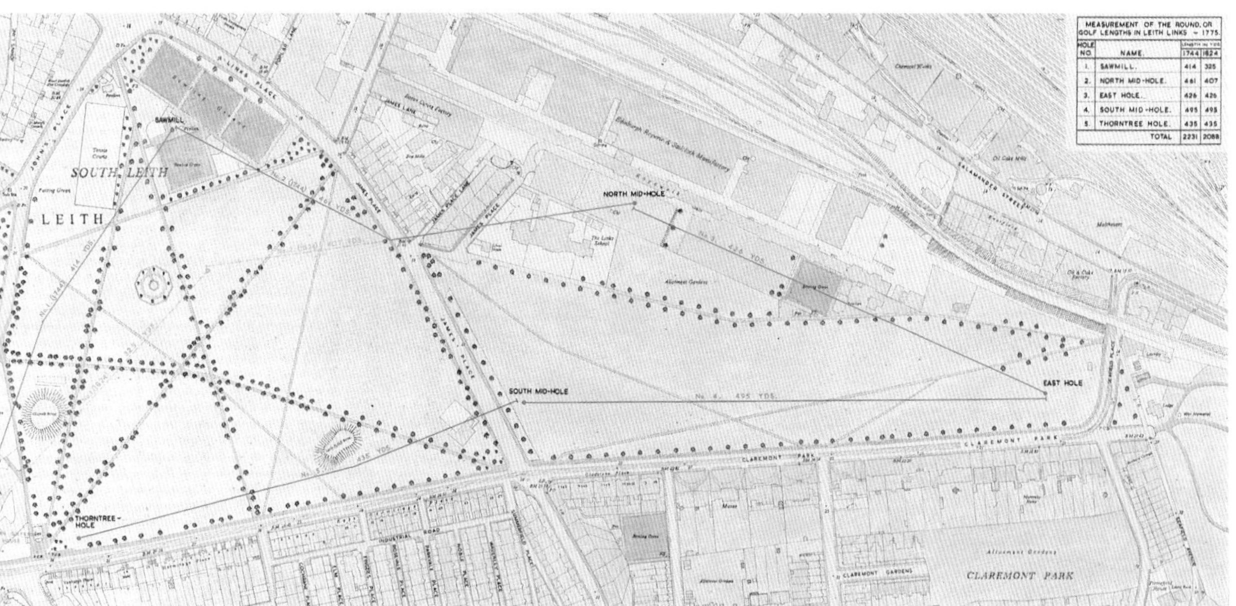

HOLE NO.	NAME.	LENGTH IN YDS 1744	LENGTH IN YDS 1824
1.	SAWMILL.	414	325
2.	NORTH MID-HOLE.	461	407
3.	EAST HOLE.	426	426
4.	SOUTH MID-HOLE.	495	495
5.	THORNTREE HOLE.	435	435
	TOTAL	2231	2088

partly to blame when that boy of 14 or 15 struck him 'with the back of the club with much force betwixt the eyes, at the root of the nose'. In fact, if it were an important shot, the youngster may have had the more legitimate grievance.

Sporting all-rounders have been such a feature of the Honourable Company that it greatly interested me to find that so many of those who had blazed the trail had themselves so many different outlets. Foulis is a case in point, what with his fishing, hawking, hare-hunting, curling and bowls. Since so many of the golfers of those bygone days were also archers, there can presumably be little argument that the gentlemen who petitioned the Edinburgh City Council for a silver club for competition got the idea from the Silver Arrow which the City of Edinburgh had presented to the Royal Company of Archers in 1709.

BAIRD: A club as such was a logical extension of the fact that so many of the golfers who frequented Leith Links gathered at the tavern, Luckie Clephan's – Luckie being the name of the widow who ran it. They ate and drank together though those tales of all the claret they drank have to be qualified by the fact that the claret they were imbibing in such quantity would be no stronger than the beer of today. They would leave their clubs there in boxes and eventually those coffins would be stood upright to become the forerunners of the modern locker.

MAIR: Do you think that the practice – after the inaugural year when, by definition, there wasn't one – of having the captain, as the previous year's winner, driving off first, was the origin of having the honour in today's golf. Or even, for that matter, of the ritual at various clubs, including the R & A, whereby the new captain has to drive himself in?

BAIRD: Maybe to both questions.

MAIR: Obviously, having an absconding embezzler such as Henry M. Low as secretary did not help. But surely, since there was no subscription from

1764 but only the five shillings which had to be paid annually to help pay for badly needed drainage, it is hardly surprising that the club got into such financial difficulties that they had first to sell the contents of the Golf House, which they had gone to so much trouble to have built, and then the Golf House itself.

BAIRD: My own conviction is that the financial troubles of the club had a great deal less to do with the move to Musselburgh in 1836 than the fact that Leith was becoming hopelessly crowded by people indulging a variety of pursuits. By the standards of the early nineteenth century, there was plenty of room for golf at Musselburgh. What is more, the course, as can still be detected, was much more like the golf courses of today and, particularly for those who were reasonably well off, it involved no great journey by horse or carriage.

MAIR: I was tickled by that story which J.E. Laidlay tells of studying the great golfers of the day in an Open at Musselburgh and of how impressed he had been by Young Tom Morris. Where everyone else was trying to stay off the road which runs through the links, he deliberately drove down it for the extra bounce and run it afforded.

BAIRD: Willie Park junior, my wife's great-grandfather, is said to have invented the brassie in order to sweep the ball off the road cleanly with a flat angle into impact rather than hit down on it with a more lofted club. True or false it's a good story but not as good as the one about how he came to invent the wry-necked putter. He had left his on the ground where it was run over by a cart and the moment he picked it up and saw the way it had been twisted so that the blade was offset, he knew that that was for him.

You never quite know which of such anecdotes is apocryphal but, on the other hand, somebody somewhere had to hit on such ideas and Young Willie was notoriously innovative.

MAIR: Young Willie, I noticed, held the record for the nine holes at Musselburgh with a 31, which was some score. The gutta-percha would by then have cornered the market.

BAIRD: The gutta-percha – *gueta*, a gum and *pertcha*, a cloth – was a big advance on the feather ball if scarcely so romantic. It was a tropical gum like rubber but, unlike rubber, it was 'thermal plastic'. When it was hot – say, after being placed in a bucket of piping hot water – you could mould it, but when it was cold, it went hard.

Inevitably, someone noticed that when it had been accidentally marked or scarred it flew better. At first, following that momentous discovery, the markings were hand-made, using the combination of a knife and a hammer but soon the ballmakers learned that it was much easier to put the dimples in the mould. Hence the Bramble with its bumps, and balls with a square-meshed surface.

MAIR: George Pottinger, in his history of the Honourable Company, spoke of how some players would have small pieces of lead incorporated in the centre of the ball to help them run true on the green. He hazarded that such balls must have made a splendidly resonant sound when struck. Cotton

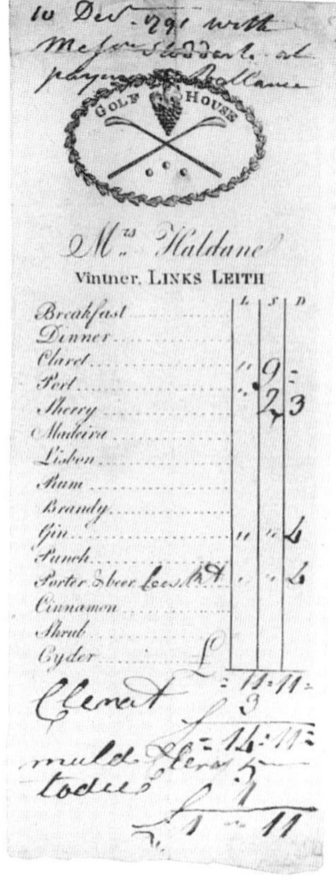
GOLF HOUSE

Mrs Haldane
Vintner, LINKS LEITH

	L	S	D
Breakfast			
Dinner			
Claret			
Port			
Sherry			
Madeira			
Lisbon			
Rum			
Brandy			
Gin			
Punch			
Porter & Beer			
Cinnamon			
Shrub			
Cyder			

A bill from the Golf House in Leith dated December 1791

always maintained that sound was an important element in putting and counselled anybody who did not believe him to try putting with cotton-wool in their ears. By the same token, when the other players complained at Wimbledon about the grunting of Monica Seles, they said that they could not hear the ball off her racquet strings and that the absence of that familiar noise threw their timing out. Clearly, though many may not have been aware of it, the sound the various golf balls have made over the years has been quite a pertinent point.

BAIRD: I should say that, as Cotton indicated, it would matter most on the green. But, of course, all the time the ball was evolving so, too, were golf clubs. The long-nosed clubs were giving way to shorter-nosed clubs which were also deeper and thicker.

MAIR: Musselburgh must have been a busy course once you had the three clubhouses of Bruntsfield, the Royal Burgess and the Honourable Company in a row and the members thereof sharing the links with the locals.

From the Statistical Account of Scotland

. . . the greatest and wisest of the land were to be seen on the Links of Leith, mingling freely with the humblest mechanics in pursuit of their common and beloved amusement. All distinctions of rank were levelled by the joyous spirit of the game. Lords of Session and cobblers, knights, baronets, and tailors might be seen earnestly contesting for the palms of superior dexterity, and vehemently but good-humouredly discussing moot points of the game, as they arose in the course of play

BAIRD: The congestion born of having four clubs sharing the same nine-hole course was the chief reason why the club began its search for pastures new. Eventually, they decided on what is now Muirfield, but not before they had considered, with varying degrees of seriousness, Hedderwick near Dunbar, Craigielaw to the west of Aberlady, and an overture involving, approximately, the land which is now Luffness Golf Club.

MAIR: Technique was plainly a talking point almost from the beginning, as witness the description of the action of Duncan Forbes in *Memoirs of Duncan Forbes of Culloden*: 'He struck the ball full, and having a nervous arm upon a well-pois'd body, he generally drove very far; when nigh the hole, he tipped with so much caution and circumspection that even a lesson might be learned from him at his innocent amusements.'

BAIRD: The subject of technique brings us neatly back to the origins of golf and the father figures of the Honourable Company. Most golfers are familiar with that portrait of William St Clair of Roslin who had a stance which would have made Bobby Locke blink. But why did he stand so absurdly closed? I think I know. He affected such a stance because it had come down to him from the exponents of *Kolven* who had found such a foot placement the best way of keeping their balance on the ice. Try it the next time your local loch freezes.

From the Edinburgh Evening Courant, *19 August 1833*

BY WARRANT OF THE SHERIFF

To be Sold by public roup on Thursday the 29th August current, within the Golf House, Leith Links

THE HOUSEHOLD FURNITURE, PAINTINGS, SILVER PLATE, etcet situated therein, among which are a Set of Mahogany Telescope Dining Tables, 18 feet long, 18 Chairs in Haircloth, Mahogany Side Tables, large carpet, three large Screens, a quantity of Silver Plate and Plated Goods, Cut Crystal Etcet Etcet; Full length Portrait of Sinclair of Roslin; D° of James Balfour, Esq., by Raeburn; D° of John Gray, Esq., by D°; D° of John Taylor, Esq., by Watson Gordon; and several other Portraits by eminent Masters.

Catalogues may be had on application to Dalgleish and Forrest, Auctioneers, Adam Square, Edinburgh.

The Sale to commence at 12 o'clock noon.

Ready Money

Sheriff Clerk's Office 17th August 1833

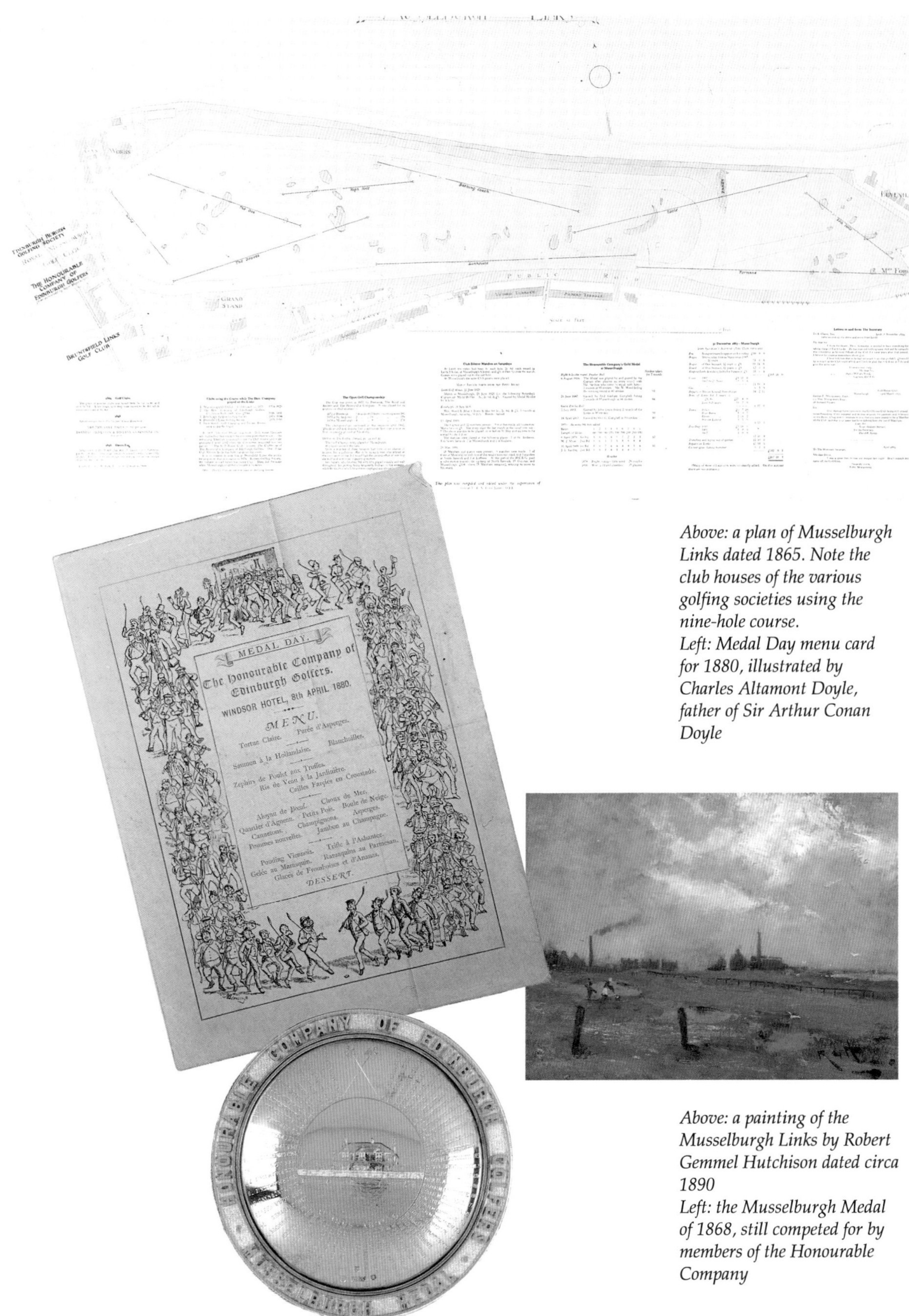

Above: a plan of Musselburgh Links dated 1865. Note the club houses of the various golfing societies using the nine-hole course.
Left: Medal Day menu card for 1880, illustrated by Charles Altamont Doyle, father of Sir Arthur Conan Doyle

Above: a painting of the Musselburgh Links by Robert Gemmel Hutchison dated circa 1890
Left: the Musselburgh Medal of 1868, still competed for by members of the Honourable Company

'A Summer Evening at Musselburgh' by Charles Lees, 1859

The Links at Musselburgh

George Pottinger on the Musselburgh course as the Honourable Company knew it:

George Pottinger on Mr Henry M. Low who, in the 1826 Club medal, when a round at Leith Links comprised two circuits of the five holes, had the best score ever recorded for the ten holes – 60 strokes.

Since 1764 there had been no annual subscriptions apart from the fifty shillings for maintenance of the links for the Silver Club competition, and entry money of half a guinea. Since this was not enough to meet expenses, the Golf House was mortgaged in 1824 to secure an advance of £500. In 1828 Mr Henry M. Low, lately captain and a Writer to the Signet in Edinburgh, arranged a second mortgage of £200. In 1829 Low was appointed secretary, and in February 1830 he fled the country, hopelessly indebted to his clients and others. (This makes it easier to understand why the last entry in the minute book of the period is merely a record of the 1830 Silver Club competition.)

ORIGINALLY the Musselburgh course had seven holes; another was added in 1838; and the full complement of nine was open for play in 1870 when the total length was about 2,800 yards. The first three holes went from the Racecourse Grandstand to Forman's Inn at the eastern end of the links. These holes measured 350, 430, and 450 yards and were named 'The Graves', 'Linkfield' and 'Forman's' respectively and were bogey fives. All three holes called for long, straight driving between the road on the right and, on the left, bunkers and gorse. On reaching Forman's, which still flourishes, the next hole went north towards the sea ('The Sea Hole') and was 180 yards in length. It was at this stage that the turf, which had been rather clay-like, changed to true seaside texture. The fifth and sixth holes went westward, adjacent to the sea – occasionally too close for comfort. The feature of the fifth (400 yards) was a cross-bunker aptly named 'Pandemonium' or 'Pandy' for short, which was faced with wooden sleepers that lasted until the 1920s. The hole was called 'The Table' after its plateau green. The sixth, of 346 yards, was called 'The Bathing Coach' after the old coach, or shelter, which was provided for bathers to change in. A splendid Victorian daguerreotype of bewhiskered bathers is evoked by the name of this hole. 'The High Hole', of 220 yards, looked innocent enough but it was difficult to get the ball to run true to the green. The eighth, the odoriferous 'Gas Hole' (270 yards), in the north-west corner of the course, was a bogey four, as were the sixth and seventh. 'The Home Hole' (ninth), which was a bogey three of some 150 yards, still exists as the first hole on the links today, and Loretto boys who still play there can testify that, even with all modern accessories and a reasonable putting surface, it is not an easy three.

4 *Men of Muirfield*

J.E. Laidlay

AT South Herts, they have a cast of Harry Vardon's hands moulded for eternity in the overlapping grip to which he gave his name. Alas, no such sculpture enshrines the hold on the club of J.E. Laidlay who is always held to have used such an overlapping grip some time before the paws of Jersey's most celebrated golfing son had been joined in holy wedlock.

Nor does legend lie. In 1884, Johnny Laidlay had been badly off his game – so badly, indeed, that he made various alterations to his game. Among them was that he 'took to the gripping of one finger of one hand over one finger of the other'.

The coupling Laidlay was to use for the remaining 45 years of his life had its first airing in open competition in 1885 when, in the space of a momentous fortnight, Laidlay won an event at Carnoustie which had the formidable figure of John Ball in the field, as well as the R & A's King William IV medal and a tournament at North Berwick in which he defeated in the final no less a personage than Horace Hutchinson. Mighty impressive, and all that eight years before the 23-year-old Vardon made his début in the Open championship and no fewer than 11 before he won the first of the six Opens on this side of the Atlantic which were eventually to have so many examining his style for clues to his pre-eminence.

In retracing how he came to overlap – though he did not himself initially use that term – Laidlay explained: 'The reason which started the idea in my mind was that, my hands being more opposite each other, were more likely to work together and swing the club like a pendulum, and less likely to operate against one another.' He noted that such a marriage of the hands particularly benefited his putting though, of course, like Bobby Locke in later years, he used the same overlap on the greens as he used for every other club, as distinct from the reverse overlap to which most modern golfers turn putter in hand.

Unquestionably, with such a persuasive track record wherein, among other feats, he had won two of no fewer than five finals in the Amateur championship and finished second to Willie Auchterlonie in the 1893 Open, Laidlay must have had his imitators even if there is no evidence to suggest that Vardon was among them.

Not that one should get carried away in relation to such suppositions. After all, in the eventual home of the Vardon overlap, Dai Rees, the club professional as Vardon had been before him, went his own heretical way, favouring neither overlap nor interlock but instead a highly personal, two-handed grip with the left hand showing just one knuckle.

Besides which, Laidlay had made more than one other alteration to his method at the same time as he had turned to overlapping. Above all, where he had always held the club at the very end of the shaft, he now went well down the grip for all his shots. The improvement was dramatic – 'It worked a miracle and I was back to my game in a day' – but, in retrospect, he supposed it had cost him length. Perhaps – but today Laura Davies does the same thing with every club in the bag, and it took a blow of 293 yards by Peter McEvoy, the Amateur champion of 1977–78, to beat her in a long-driving competition open to both sexes, her best effort of 284 yards being too much for the rest of a by no means undistinguished entry.

Finally, to complete the remodelling of his action, Laidlay had made a further modification which, a little mysteriously, he felt went with his down-the-shaft grip. Namely, the adoption of a stance known as 'playing off the left leg'. In other words, despite much criticism, and more references than ever to his unorthodox style, he played every stroke, including his putts, well forward in his address. But then so did Bobby Jones and many another luminary since, not excluding Ben Hogan and Jack Nicklaus.

He was a magnificent iron-player who was reckoned to be 'as good with his mashie as J.H. Taylor'. Which was rather like saying someone was as handy with a gun as Annie Oakley. But it was a different tale with his driver. As a boy in the park in which the family house was set, he had laid out one-shot holes with small greens, the length of each hole being decided according to whether he wished to get home with a wood, a cleek or an iron. Even when temporarily based in the south, some eight miles from Stonehenge; he would go for long walks, taking his driver with him and always teeing up for the next shot. The shades of the ancient druids must have been rudely disturbed, but his driving remained the weakest part of a game in which excellent putting was wont to complement his much acclaimed iron-play. Not that he putted simply by the light of nature. As a teenager, he had spent many an hour practising putting on the lawn of his home, using tins for the holes which were below regulation size so that the holes on the golf course would look encouragingly large.

Horace Hutchinson on J.E. Laidlay's ball position

And now let us turn our attention for a moment to the half shot as played off the left leg. We have said that the very large majority of players play the stroke off the right leg. Is the other method, then, worth consideration? We should have said 'No,' were it not that one of the very best approachers of the day, Mr J.E. Laidlay, habitually plays his approaches off his left leg; and this being so and golfing nature being what it is – highly imitative – he is sure to have many disciples, at least in style, if not in execution. The position for this stroke, then, is very similar to that for the drive.

No boy at Loretto School was allowed to use a cleek or an iron until he could go round the nine-hole Musselburgh course in 50 strokes or fewer, but the cleek Laidlay eventually obtained from old Willie Park was to stay with him all his days in its putting guise. It grew so worn and light that they said he could have shaved with it, but Laidlay continued to employ it to great effect in a stroke which reminded many of the forward defensive stroke in cricket.

Much the same, of course, could be said of, say, the left-elbow-up putting strokes of such as Jerry Barber and Lou Graham. In fact, coincidentally or otherwise, Laidlay had been a fine cricketer in his days at Loretto and had gone on to play for Scotland against Yorkshire.

As a fag at Loretto School, he had been compelled to heft the clubs of a prefect but, after that somewhat unwelcome introduction, he had taken to the game so quickly that in no time he had been invited to join the headmaster's Sunday morning foursomes. That headmaster was Dr H.H. Almond, the umpire who awarded Scotland the hotly disputed try from which the winning goal was kicked in the first-ever rugby international, between Scotland and England, on a Monday afternoon in March 1871.

Laidlay had quickly acquired sufficient power to attempt the coveted

J.E. Laidlay's Medals
Musselburgh:
Gold (spring) – 1883, 1887, 1888, 1890, 1891
Gold (winter) – 1885, 1886, 1887, 1888, 1890
Muirfield:
Gold (spring) – 1893, 1898, 1899, 1907, 1911
Silver (spring) – 1892, 1894, 1903, 1904, 1906
Gold (winter) – 1895, 1899, 1900, 1903, 1905
Silver (winter) – 1908, 1911, 1912, 1919

J.E. Laidlay in action

deed of driving a golf ball over the grandstand of the Musselburgh racecourse: 'It was not really much of a shot,' Laidlay was to concede long after his days at Loretto were over, 'but there was a spice of danger about it which added to the charm and made it a feat more or less necessary to perform before one could talk in comfort to the older boys in the school on the subject of golf. Of course, it was strictly against school rules, and there was a risk of breaking the stand windows; also, with a shade of very bad luck, it was conceivable one might hit the headmaster, who might be passing on the other side . . .'

At the age of 16, Laidlay went round Musselburgh 'on all fours' – nine on the trot – giving this precocious young talent a very remarkable round of 36. Statistically at least, it more than stood comparison with the 18-hole scores of 79 and 80 with which he won the Gold Medal of the Honourable Company in 1887, the best over the course in the annals of the club.

All told, he won ten medals when Musselburgh was the home of the Honourable Company, 19 at Muirfield, and played for Scotland against England in ten consecutive years. In such internationals, he proved the proverbial tower of strength even though the auld enemy had in their ranks a brace of Open champions in John Ball and Harold Hilton – the latter Laidlay's victim in the 1891 final of the Amateur championship. 'Strive as I will,' Bernard Darwin was to write many years later, 'I cannot wholly convice myself that young golfers of today stare with quite such reverential eyes at Mr Tolley and Mr Wethered as I did when, as a small boy, I first beheld Mr Mure Ferguson and Mr Horace Hutchinson or, at a later date, Mr John Ball and Mr Laidlay.'

Born at Seacliffe in 1860, Laidlay, as long ago as 1907, had written, with disarming diffidence, of the union of the hands he had helped to pioneer: 'I believe it is quite a common grip nowadays.' By the time he died, in 1940, he could, to borrow an Americanism, sure say that again.

Leslie Balfour-Melville

Scotland's greatest all-rounder

THESE islands have harboured some astonishing all-round sportsmen over the years . . . Men such as Dr Kevin O'Flanagan of Old Belvedere and Arsenal who, in addition to being a crack track sprinter and playing rugby and soccer for Ireland on successive Saturdays, played single-figure golf both left and right-handed. Or C.B. Fry who, besides being a brilliant classical scholar, held the world long-jump record for 21 years, captained England at cricket, played for Southampton in an FA Cup final and turned out as a wing three-quarter for the Barbarians.

Yet, even those two immortals would have to give best in terms of sheer versatility to the Honourable Company's L.M. Balfour-Melville. A triple international who played rugby, cricket and golf for Scotland, Leslie Balfour-Melville won the Amateur championship and was also the Scottish long-jump champion, the Scottish lawn tennis champion and the Scottish billiards champion. As if all that were not enough, he was also an uncommonly skilful skater and curler. He was, too, in his time, captain of the Honourable Company and captain of the R & A; president of the Grange Cricket Club and captain of the Scottish Universities Golfing Society; president of the Scottish Rugby Union and president of the Scottish Cricket Union.

And all that though he was, by profession, a lawyer; a member of the Society of Writers to His Majesty's Signet, his own firm being Messrs Balfour and Scott. He also had an appointment in the Inland Revenue where he was Clerk to the Property and Income-Tax Commissioners for General Purposes in the County of Edinburgh.

A sketch of Leslie Balfour-Melville

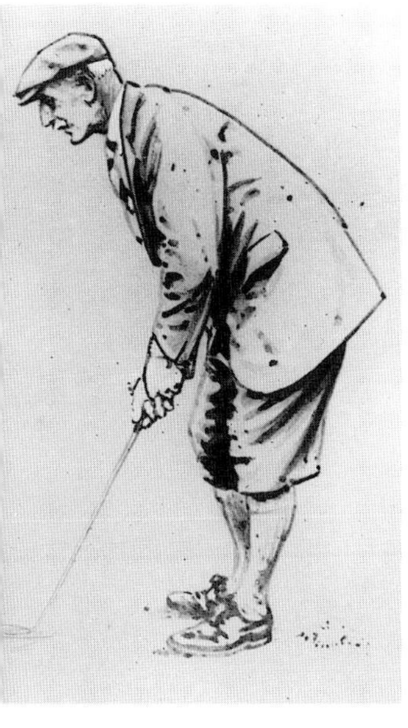

His father, James Balfour, was a member of the legal profession in Edinburgh and a familiar figure in St Andrews. A keen golfer, he had won three R & A medals and was the author of a little book of reminiscences of the St Andrews links and the personalities they begat.

Leslie Balfour, as he originally was, had taken the name of Melville when his father succeeded to the estate of Mount Melville near St Andrews. A brother, Elliott, was himself a good enough golfer to win the Silver Cross of St Andrews. One of the two sons by L.M.'s first marriage, J.E. Balfour-Melville, was also a superb cricketer and an Oxford soccer Blue but he was killed in the Kaiser's War. As for his grandson, Ronnie Balfour-Melville, he was destined to become secretary of Gullane Golf Club and one to rank, in the very pertinent opinion of Guy Robertson-Durham who knew both so well, with Muirfield's Colonel Brian Evans-Lombe.

Endowed not only with exceptional hand, eye and foot co-ordination but also the turn of pace befitting a boy who was one day to win, in the Academy games, both the 100 yards and the hurdles, Leslie Balfour-Melville was in the Edinburgh Academy Football XI at the tender age of 13. Four years in the side and captain in his last season, he was still a schoolboy when, in 1871, he was selected at full-back to play against England at Raeburn Place in rugby's inaugural international.

A bite from a dog robbed him of the distinction of going down in the archives alongside the 21 players who have played for one of the four Home Unions while still at school. (That canine bite has also left Merchiston's T. Anderson alone in his glory as the only man to have played for Scotland at both rugby and cricket before his schooldays were ended.)

Even so, Balfour-Melville had still not turned 18 when he won his rugby cap against England. The match was at the Oval – a not inappropriate venue for one who was four years in the Academy XI and captain in 1871 when he played for the XXII of Scotland against George Parr's All England XI. The 17 he made in his maiden knock for his country may not sound much, but it was the highest score in Scotland's first innings. For more than three decades, he was an automatic choice for the Scotland XI, his late cutting and on-side play being described by no less a personage than W.G. Grace as 'quite first-class'.

At Raeburn Place in 1882, he was captain of the Scotland XI which lost in two days by an innings and 18 runs to the Australians but which gained a measure of revenge in a hastily arranged, but still serious, one-day match. A brilliant and chanceless 75 by Balfour-Melville, which included a six from the Grange ground into the Academy field, laid the foundations for the Scots' total of 167 for seven – the Australians, amid great excitement, being dismissed for 122.

A decade previously, in 1872, he had played in just one cricket match because of injury but the game in question was the first Inter-City with Glasgow and he made 150. He was a member, too, of the Edinburgh side which made a little matter of 672 in the 1878 match with Glasgow, his own contribution being a typically attacking 70. Even the most dauntless statisticians lost count of his centuries though no one who saw it ever forgot his scintillating 207 not out versus Drumpellier.

A most effective batsman, he seems to have been less concerned with technique and theory as a cricketer than he was as a golfer where, according to Bernard Darwin, he never ceased experimenting. One attempt, in a bid to offset a certain loss of length in later life, entailed the purchase of a peculiarly heavy driver such as Abe Mitchell (he whose statuette stands atop the Ryder Cup) was using.

The powerful Balfour-Melville got his runs quickly as might be inferred from his feat of hitting the very first ball he received from F.R. Spofforth – the dreaded 'Demon' – into the pavilion at Scarborough. Playing for Grange, he was given to landing Bothamesque sixes in the Water of Leith. A singularly adhesive slip-fielder when he surrendered the gloves, he was a highly accomplished wicket-keeper and never better than when whipping off the bails from the squirming underhand lobs of H.J. Stevenson. It is a matter of record that when he made his last appearance on a cricket field in 1924, at the age of 70, in a centenary match for a team of old Academy captains against the Academy XI of the day, he kept quite beautifully, stumping two batsmen and catching a third.

Over the border, other than when playing for Scotland, he contented himself with frequent appearances for I Zingari, the Free Foresters and the MCC. But it was often said that he would have played Test cricket for England had he joined one of the English counties.

Bernard Darwin on Leslie Balfour-Melville

One of the most amusing things I ever saw, though I do not hope to convey the fun of it, was in an Ayrshire garden where, Mr Balfour-Melville being present, Mr Laidlay gave an imitation of him playing in a big match. He fidgeted about on the tee; he shouted several loud and ferocious 'Fores' to the spectators; he turned with a sweet smile and an exaggerated gallantry to ask two imaginary ladies to stand away from behind; he returned more stormily than ever to shouting to the offenders in front; finally, he topped the ball hard along the ground.

It was an admirably mischievous impersonation at which Mr Balfour-Melville looked on, not severely, but with a slightly puzzled air, as if wondering at such frivolity.

As it was, the most lasting claim to fame of 'Essie', as he was known, was to lie in his deeds on the golf course. In both 1902 and 1903, he played for Scotland against England and, over his career, he won 15 medals of the Honourable Company and no fewer than 31 of the Royal and Ancient.

Where Bobby Jones and Joyce Wethered had to be content with just two holes-in-one apiece, Balfour-Melville had none at all in man's allotted span of three-score years and ten. However, having at last broken his duck as a septuagenarian, he had four more before he died at the age of 83 – having, just the day before, presented, with an almost boyish enthusiasm, the medals at a putting competition in North Berwick. 'His naturally happy, genial and witty disposition', to draw from the pages of the Edinburgh Academy *Chronicle*, 'made him deservedly popular with all who had the good fortune to meet him.'

'Mr Laidlay,' Bernard Darwin opined, 'was a golfer of genius. Mr Balfour-Melville was rather one of great talent, talent for playing any kind of game, carefully cultivated. His swing was as good a model as anyone could want, upstanding, firm, strong and steady with a certain air of rigidity which was compensated for by a big, free follow-through. Mr Everard prophesied that, of all the leading amateurs of the '80s, Mr Balfour-Melville's style was that which promised to serve him best and longest in later life and this forecast was on the whole well borne out. He went on playing and playing well for a long time. His iron-play was sound and good, his putting less so; he could indeed miss very short ones but, though he never looked very comfortable on the green, he could often putt well, as it seemed by sheer, resolute determination.'

Horace Hutchinson on Leslie Balfour-Melville

On both sides of the house, the subject of our sketch inherits very great strength of grasp and wrist power, which cannot fail to be of service to him in his cricket and golf. He is a very strong driver, and a particularly good scorer in rough weather; indeed, many of his medals have been won on very bad days, in scores which would defy criticism under the most favourable meteorological conditions.

Engrossed heart and soul in the game, he is not one who lets a chance slip if any care on his part can avoid it and besides being – apart from his skill – a right good partner, he has the enviable gift of being able to play up 'all he knows' whether fortune smiles or frowns. Nor, when matters wear their rosiest aspect, does he ever allow himself to drop his

In all, he reached the semi-final of the Amateur championship six times and was the beaten finalist when J.E. Laidlay won in 1889. In 1895, when he took the title, the man he defeated was none other than John Ball, the 1890 Open champion. Ball had leapt away, winning the first three holes, but Balfour-Melville was two up on the penultimate tee only to lose the seventeenth to a five and the eighteenth to a four. For the third match in tingling succession, Balfour-Melville – who, through the wind, had had to lay dead a wood to the last to survive against Laurence Auchterlonie in the semi-final – was taken to the nineteenth.

Willie Greig and Auchterlonie had both obligingly scuttled their chance by putting their shots to the green in the Swilcan, but it seemed too much to hope that the great John Ball would follow suit. Against the stiff wind, Balfour-Melville had taken three to reach the green and Ball was similarly short in two.

A master of the straighter-faced irons when it came to manufacturing the shorter approaches, Ball was compelled by the Swilcan to resort to his less familiar pitching mashie. Again the waters opened, thereby preserving, to quote Darwin, 'a curious symmetry of ending that must have made the winner believe in some higher power.'

Rather touchingly, when Balfour-Melville was captain of the R & A in 1906, the Amateur returned to St Andrews and it fell to him to present the trophy to the man he had defeated in that final 11 years earlier. The crowd on that afternoon in 1895 had been unashamedly partisan, rallying behind Balfour-Melville after their idol, Freddie Tait, had gone down to

Ball in the semi-finals. The *Scotsman* newspaper took it upon itself to apologise: 'The glorious reception he [John Ball] received on presentation of his prize more than testified any display of feeling during the game was very far indeed from being directed against him personally.

'I'm afraid the truth may be that we Scots are an excitable lot. Personally, I blame the porridge and oatcakes, not the whisky!'

Horace Hutchinson, who had described Balfour-Melville's semi-final with Auchterlonie as 'the strangest medley of good and bad strokes as was ever seen in an important contest', wrote of the Balfour-Melville–Ball final, 'Then, even as Scamander arose "that he might stay noble Achilles from slaughter, and ward destruction from the men of Troy", so did the Swilcan once more intervene in favour of the man of St Andrews, and Hector this time triumphed over his Grecian, or Hoylake, foe.

'Thus did Xanthus, the river god, win for Mr Leslie Balfour-Melville his Amateur championship, to the exceeding contentment of St Andrews and his many friends.'

The *Sun* could not have put it better.

game and run the common risk of being unable to take it up again, thus imperilling, or even losing after all, a match to all intents and purposes practically won.

The conditions under which alone prophesy may be safely indulged in are well known but, looking at all the leading amateurs, Mr Balfour-Melville strikes one as being one of the most likely to carry his fine play late into life – to be, in fact, a counterpart in the amateur section to the veteran Tom Morris among professionals.

Robert Maxwell

JOHN BALL who, in 1928, was made an honorary member of the Honourable Company, won the Open championship at Prestwick in 1890 and the Amateur championship a record eight times. In measuring the greatness of Muirfield's Robert Maxwell, suffice it to say that he led Hoylake's favourite son by five matches to two in the context of their Scotland–England jousts, trouncing him by 7 and 6 in 1903 and by the still more brutal margin of 12 and 10 in the international at Muirfield which preceded the 1909 Amateur championship.

Maxwell was born in Edinburgh and educated at Eton, where Bernard Darwin remembered him not as a golfer but as 'a good oarsman and a large and formidable figure in the football field'. He had had no idea that the young Scot was a golfer, he was to recall in later years, 'until, in 1897, three years after we had both left school, I heard from some North Berwick golfers that a certain young Maxwell was becoming alarmingly good and might astonish people in the Amateur championship which, that year, was at Muirfield.'

Astonish some people? Entered from Tantallon, Maxwell, materialising for the first time as Ball's *bête noire*, beat him at the twenty-first and then, by a resounding 6 and 4, claimed the scalp of a second Open champion, Harold Hilton, on the very links where, in the Open of 1892, Hilton had ended the monopoly of the Scottish professionals. Maxwell lost to a fellow countryman, James Robb, in the quarter-finals but, within three more summers, on the tragic death of Freddie Tait in the Boer War, he had, in Darwin's words, 'largely succeeded to his position as the acknowledged champion of Scottish amateur golf'.

The two Amateur championships which Maxwell won were both on his beloved Muirfield where, head to head, he was for long reckoned to be close to unbeatable. They still tell at Muirfield of how, having won the last

The portrait of Maxwell by Stanley Cursiter, a copy of which hangs in the smoking-room at Muirfield – the original is on loan to the Scottish National Portrait Gallery

medal before the First World War, he won the first post-war medal from his renowned rival, Johnny Laidlay. In between those two medals was another – an MC won in 1916 while on active service in France with the 1/8 Battalion, The Royal Scots. His war ended when he was invalided home with trench feet.

When he was made a Trustee of the Honourable Company in 1928, Maxwell, the most unostentatious of men and one who notoriously abhorred a fanfare, was moved to present the club with his medals, a hoard which twinkled as might the once buried treasure of some bygone pirate. There were 84 all told with 20 from the Honourable Company and nine from the Royal and Ancient.

'As to his technique,' wrote Darwin on Maxwell's death in 1949 at the age of 73, 'I have a clear vision of him in my mind's eye – his broad, massive and powerful figure addressing the ball with a particular and threatening waggle all his own. His method was certainly neither orthodox nor elegant but he had obviously worked it out for himself and found that it was good.'

Bobby Jones, for much of his enfabled career, used a very narrow stance, primarily on the grounds that it facilitated the very full body turn which he had come to regard as the most important factor in his method. In contrast, a golfer like Major Charles Hezlet, a Great Britain and Ireland Walker Cup player, who looked at the address as if he were about to do the splits, had so jammed his turn that his swing was, perforce, relatively restricted in length. There was, in the width of his stance, more Hezlet than Jones about Maxwell, as Darwin has recorded: 'He stood decidedly open with a wide straddle, the right shoulder noticeably down, the left hand well over the club, the right hand under with the thumb down the shaft. His swing was what would then have been called a three-quarter swing, rather stiff than otherwise.'

The face of his club at the top of the backswing – as might have been suspected from the nature of his grip – was almost completely shut. Not that being shut-faced had then acquired the pejorative connotations which attended it in these islands for much of the Henry Cotton era or, in fact, that it was even a phrase in use in Maxwell's earlier years. 'Big and strong,' enthused Darwin of his old friend, 'Bobby Maxwell could hit very hard but his swing always suggested power under control and he was as straight and accurate as he was long.'

Jack Nicklaus – who, in 1959, won the St George's Challenge Cup as Maxwell himself had done at the turn of the century – has sought all his golfing days to keep the shape, rhythm and pace of his swing the same right through the bag. All those years ago, Darwin noted in Maxwell's game 'a noteworthy similarity in his swing for all his strokes. In that respect, he seemed to make a very simple game of it.'

Darwin liked to apply a sentence which Alfred Lyttleton had once penned of W.G. Grace's batting methods to Maxwell's golf: 'Though sound, serviceable, powerful and not without the dignity attaching to all high efficiency, they were not ornamental.' The dignity and high efficiency were unquestionably there, explained Darwin, 'but there was perhaps a certain superficial heaviness about it all.'

Maxwell, by common consent, was another of those golfers who, down the ages, have been able to administer massive blows to the wee cowering beastie that is the ball but who yet have had a singularly delicate touch in the realm of miscellaneous short pitches, pitch-and-runs and outright chips. Maxwell's putting was deemed by Darwin to have been less than graceful but that, to the eyes of 'Bernardo', might have been because he had already discovered the virtues of a locked left wrist. (Three-quarters of a century later, Lee Trevino, another with good reason to have fond memories of Muirfield, was advocating a plaster cast for practice to promote the requisite feel.)

'Day in, day out,' conceded Darwin, 'Bobby was, I should say, a very good putter.' He also saluted his ability to putt more than soundly on the Muirfield greens which, he added, having clearly suffered himself, 'is more than many people can do'.

Robert Maxwell as seen by 'Spy'

BENCH AND BAR
by Wig and Pen
The Bench and Bar have always been part of life at Muirfield. Internal competition regularly takes place but the most prestigious event is the annual match against the English for the Scott Baker trophy. The fixture began between the wars as a private match and has gone from strength to strength. Played every other year at Woking, the weekend consists of two rounds of matches and two opportunities for private games. A dinner is taken in the Garrick or Inns of Court and when in Scotland the New Club or Advocates Library.
Over the years many distinguished lawyers and golfers have played. Both the successful prosecutors in the notorious 'Manuel' trial graced the team, Gordon Gillies in the 1950s and more recently Ranald Sutherland. Bill Hook has been selected over five decades and Robin McEwan has played continu-

ously over four. In the last 25 years the English have produced some very strong golfers. Charles Russell, Victor Lemieux, Trevor Reeve, Richard Rougier, and the best of all, Hugh Griffiths. The Scots matched these with Ian Robertson, Robert Johnston, Bertie Grieve and the now distinguished financier, Angus Grossart. The fun of the occasion conceals the serious competition and often liquid sabotage attacks have to be mounted on the side ahead at half-time during the Saturday dinner. After one such Percy Harris left his trousers at Muirfield. The elegant Savile Row garment was still there two years later and the Englishman had to pay the rent of the coat hanger to Neil Gow with a round of drinks. Fathers and sons have been a regular feature. George and Derek Emslie, Alasdair and Alan Johnston, Bob and Christopher Purchas and the most famous duo, Bill and Jim Milligan. Bill Milligan produced more legends than anyone. A fine and natural athlete he was a better golfer than ever given credit for (he once defeated the mighty Griffiths). He lent his name to Milligan's Hill – the small bump in front of the tenth tee, and latterly his favourite shots were the practice swing and the conceded putt.

In recent years England has again produced some very fine players, with Nigel Wilkinson and Richard Hayward being almost unbeatable. Hayward, in particular, may qualify as the best player ever selected, having been chosen when only a 'pupil'. Only Robert Henderson, Jim McGhie and Sandy Philip ('the Duke') have been able to match and resist these latter day Sassenachs.

Yet, reading between the lines, the most revered of golfing essayists – at a time when there were many more wristy putters about than there are now – seems to have felt that Maxwell's success was despite his style rather than because of it. 'There was,' he observed, somewhat reprovingly, 'something rigid about his grip and stiff left arm.'

'There is a general impression,' asserted Horace Hutchinson, 'that, of resident Scottish players, Mr Robert Maxwell is individually the strongest. Of extremely powerful physique, no conceivable bad lie holds any terrors for him.' Mr Maxwell, concluded Hutchinson, who had lost to him by 7 and 6 in the final of the 1903 Amateur championship, 'can make a match' for any professional.

Indeed, in 1902, at Hoylake, he had finished fourth in the Open championship which was won by a stroke from Harry Vardon and James Braid. Herd was the first to capture the Open with the rubber-cored Haskell ball and Maxwell, using it himself in the closing round, had a 74 to pull up just two strokes behind the new champion.

Maxwell, who was again the leading amateur in the Open of 1903, may well have missed his best chance when he had to withdraw from the 1901 Open at Muirfield because of a family bereavement. That season, at a time when many an amateur in Scotland and England would, in Hutchinson's phrase, have 'scorned to take odds' from any professional, he had numbered among his achievements not only the spring and autumn medals of both the Honourable Company and the Royal and Ancient but also, in November, a new course record for a competitive round at Muirfield of 77.

Where Laidlay – 'wiry, active and well-knit', as Hutchinson described him – was the only boy at Loretto who could draw himself up on the horizontal bar by the use of one hand alone, Maxwell was still more physically imposing. 'No more formidable figure ever stepped on the tee in relation to height, bulk and muscularity,' declared Frank Moran of the *Scotsman*. 'Quite literally, Maxwell was one of the giants of the game.' Many an opponent, averred Moran, must have been in awe of him – 'but he was a gentle giant with a pleasant smile, a soft voice and quite a shy manner.'

Darwin said of Abe Mitchell, Henry Cotton's idol but a professional whom the Open always eluded, 'Abe is very fond of golf but not *big* golf. By nature a gentle and peaceful creature, he never really enjoyed, as some more fortunate people do, the trampling and the hum of the crowd and the clash of battle. He has fought hard and well but he did not like the fight for its own sake. In that respect, he reminds me of another great player who was always happier in playing with his friends and disliked the fuss of playing in championships, Mr Robert Maxwell.'

The natural choice to lead Scotland in the inaugural international with England at Hoylake in 1902, Maxwell defeated Ball and then met him again in 1903 at the head of the English order on the day after he, Maxwell, had won the Amateur for the first time. Darwin missed many of their international tussles for the very good reason that he was otherwise engaged, battling for England 'in a humbler position toward the end of the team'. He did, though, witness the 1903 encounter and could scarce believe what he was seeing. 'It had seemed likely,' he was to write, 'that Maxwell would be suffering from reaction. On the contrary, all his cares had dropped from him and he was at his triumphant best. He was always apt to be at his very best at Muirfield but I never saw him so overpowering there as he was that day. John Ball had something of an off-day and was completely crushed. I imagine he had never before had such a beating.'

Maxwell – whose portrait by Stanley Cursiter hangs in the smoking-room at Muirfield, entitled simply but pleasingly *Portrait of a Golfer* – played for his country for eight years but, by the time war broke out in 1914, he was, as Moran put it, 'already, in effect, a golf recluse at his beloved Muirfield and North Berwick links'.

Captain of the Honourable Company in 1912 and 1913, he urged the club 'to consider acquiring more land to the north and building a course more worthy of its prestige'. When, after the 1914–18 war, that came to pass, he brought the golfing savvy of a great player and an unsurpassed local knowledge to bear in co-operating with the architects, Harry Colt and Tom Simpson.

No lover of the limelight or of the attentions of the press, he had departed the tournament scene while still in his prime, leading Scotland for the last time in 1910, just a year after his second victory in the Amateur championship. But he was still a tremendous golfer. Even in his heyday as one of the country's foremost amateurs, those who knew him best, as Darwin has related, always maintained that the time to see him at his most overwhelming was when he was playing the best ball of the other three in a friendly four-ball.

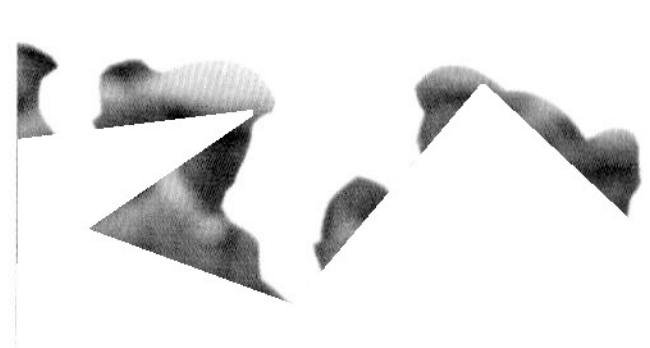

'If there was one shot of his to be envied more than another,' mused Darwin, 'it was his long-iron shot in a wind. He used to say that to judge of a golfer's quality he would choose to see him holding up long irons into a right-hand wind and he certainly possessed this art himself to great perfection.' Shades of Jack Nicklaus and the three-iron to the home green he banked against the wind in winning the 1966 Open.

His fellow golfers gave what Darwin called 'onomatopœic' names to two of his favourite strokes. His long half or three-quarter shot with an iron was dubbed a 'dunch' though the word would conjure up a very different shot today, while he had a species of bunker shot, taken almost clean and not so much hit as sensually caressed, which passed into Lothians' folklore as 'Bobby's pussy-cat shot'.

As John Ball might have exclaimed, ruefully, 'Some pussy-cat!'

David Blair

THOUGH he won a singles point in the first of his two Walker Cups in 1955, Major David Blair always said of his Walker Cup career that he should have been picked a little earlier and omitted at the time he was chosen. Cheerfully wry assertion though that was, he would back it up with a story of how, on the first tee of an earlier Walker Cup trial, the first thing his caddie had somewhat inopportunely produced from the Blair golf bag was a fishing rod!

But if the selectors saw this as evidence that he could not be serious about his golf, the same did not apply to his peers. Laddie Lucas, in summing up the virtues of those who returned to the golfing fray after the Second World War, referred to Blair as 'a fine, composite golfer; the best out-of-practice player I ever saw. When he turned up at a tournament not having played for a month, with a pair of guns and fishing rods in his luggage, that was the moment to watch him.'

Blair, whose second Walker Cup appearance was in 1961, began golf as a five-year-old in the productive golfing nursery that is the children's course at North Berwick. He also played at Nairn, where Willie Whitelaw, who would become the Deputy Prime Minister under Margaret Thatcher, was a frequent golfing companion. The two followed each other in winning the Nairn Under-16 Cup and Lord Whitelaw can well remember the effect a win in that company had on his mother, a lady who could not bear to see her son lose. 'She would come and watch, which I found ghastly,' said the Viscount, who felt that her ambitions for him in golf had been a foretaste of the 'burning zest' she was to develop to see her son become Prime Minister.

Back in North Berwick, Blair won what was the first of the Scottish Boys' championships in 1935. In 1985, as the Scottish Golf Union were preparing to celebrate the fiftieth anniversary of that championship at Dunbar, the venue that year, word came that Blair was dead. The next morning the Union's flag flew at half-mast.

A full-back in the Harrow rugby XV, he went from Harrow to Sandhurst and was with the Seaforth Highlanders when, in 1938, he won the Army championship. Serving with the Cameron Highlanders in the Middle East, Blair came to grief in the desert war, being captured in 1942 in the fall of Tobruk – a misfortune which Leonard Crawley was later to insist on seeing as preordained in that he had always been uneasy whenever he sighted his old Halford Hewitt comrade-in-arms in sand . . .

Whatever problems Blair may have had in escaping from bunkers, he had none in escaping from the Italians as early as 1943. He was soon back on active service, serving with the Seaforths in the 51st Division in the invasion of France in 1944 and adding an MC to the MBE he had been awarded in 1944.

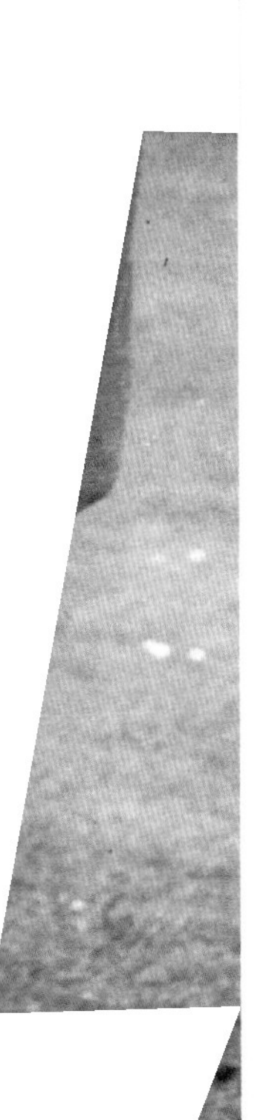

On the strength mainly of his past winning of the army golf title, he was singled out in India one week to play with Field Marshal Lord Wavell. If it appeared that India and its problems had to take a back seat as the Viceroy played his daily game of golf, that was misleading. He saw the golf course as a place not only to relax but to think. Indeed, he preferred not to talk at all. Blair discovered that the best way of handling these somewhat eerie games of golf was to ensure that Wavell always had the honour. On those occasions Wavell hit right, he would hit left – and vice versa. Only on the greens did their paths cross.

At the end of the week, Blair was puzzled to receive his instructions for the following day. There was an important four-ball to be played at eight o'clock the next morning and Blair was expected to be there on the dot and on his best form. He was to refuse any invitations to parties the previous evening. The ADC who picked him up divulged the nature of the match. Apparently, Wavell and the American General with responsibility for US Forces in the Indian Ocean had a difference of opinion about who had the last word on the use of the available 'strategic airlift'. Rather than refer the matter to London and Washington, they had decided to resolve the problem with a game of golf – which must have had the local KGB agents wondering how on earth to phrase their next dispatch home. They would each choose a golfing partner from their own men and play a four-ball, with the Viceroy and the General to be in receipt of strokes but their partners, whomsoever they might be, playing off scratch.

Previous page: David Blair in a typical, beautifully balanced finish to his swing. Photograph kindly loaned by his brother, Lt-Gen Sir Chandos Blair

It is not too difficult to imagine Blair's reaction when his opposite number turned out to be no less a player than the 1939 US Open champion, Byron Nelson, who had won 11 tournaments in a row in 1945 on the US tour, ending the year with a stroke average of 68.33. Blair, in an early demonstration of the sang-froid which was to permeate the great golfing years which lay ahead, scored well enough to have his team level leaving the penultimate green.

At the last hole, both senior officers had a stroke but the pressure was beginning to tell on the US General who put a shot out of bounds. The Field Marshal, always the tactician and mindful of the stroke he had in hand, played short of the green in two. Blair and Nelson were both on the putting surface but far from the flag.

Thus the match could scarcely have been more excitingly poised when there came a distraction in the shape of a 'near-naked native' who appeared through the undergrowth and picked up the two balls on the green prior to wrapping himself round the flag 'like a snake'.

Though today the automatic assumption would be that some tabloid journalist was behind the arrival of the native or was even the native himself, it transpired that the man was, in fact, the bearer of a lengthy missive for the Viceroy. It was never deciphered for public consumption, so posterity may never know whether it had to do with a sudden threat of World War III or was merely the result of the 3.30 in Calcutta, together with a long list of the next day's runners.

East Lothian County Cup winners in 1967. Left to right: J.G. Salvesen, R.S. Waddell, Col T.R. Broughton (captain, HCEG), C.D. Lawrie and C.N. Hastings

Once normal service had been resumed, Wavell, whose ability to concentrate on a given matter on a golf course has already been recorded, pitched dead and, by dint of that masterly stroke, won the match. Winners are winners.

On retiring from the army in 1949, Blair joined The Distillers Company as an export representative, eventually becoming a director. Holidays and weekends were devoted to shooting, fishing, stalking and skiing as well as golf, while he further negotiated ditches and other hazards on horseback, being a regular winner at point-to-point meetings.

The low amateur in the Open of 1950, where he finished thirtieth equal, Blair was the beaten finalist in the Scottish Amateur championship at Prestwick that same summer. In 1953, though, he took the title at Western Gailes, becoming the first player to complete the double of Scottish Boys' championship and Scottish Amateur.

In the Centenary Open of 1960 at St Andrews, Blair – who was captain of the R & A in 1978–79 – tied for eighth place but was beaten to the amateur medal by Joe Carr. In the course of the championship, Blair had partnered Sam Snead who, making something of a late entrance, elicited from the major a remark of which there is now more than one version. The

Bernard Darwin on Muirfield

The stone wall round the course has nearly vanished and some of the wilder sandhill country has been taken in but there is still to me something park-like about those lines of fairway. But I like to be there and I love the view of the sea and Archerfield Wood – the Garden sea wood of the 'Pavilion on the Links', with its trees bent and writhing under the wind.
And it is good golf too, almost too long and too good for some of us; and there are one or two great holes, such as the ninth, with the blackboarded bunker and that narrow terrifying second, where it is so hideously easy to hook on the wall. I admire it very much but I cannot find in it the supreme charm and the supreme thrill that belongs to some courses.

preferred rendering? 'Now Mr Snead' – with the unmistakable inflection of an army officer in the habit of being obeyed – 'you aren't going to keep me waiting all the way round, are you?' Perhaps not since the Duke of York, the future James VII of Scotland and James II of England, partnered the 'poor shoemaker', John Paterson, to victory over two English noblemen at Leith Links in the first of all golfing internationals had there been so diverse a pairing in terms of backgrounds as the Harrovian army major and the erstwhile hillbilly from Hot Springs, Virginia. But class on a golf course has its own connotations and two such lordly swingers of a golf club will be twin souls in the Elysian Fields.

Where James Braid's length came to him in the night, transforming him from a short hitter into a long one, Blair came by an additional 20 yards by less mystical means. A driver purchased from a sports store in Chicago at once made him not just that much longer but more accurate. As to his relatively erratic bunker-play, Crawley always ascribed it to the major's assumption that it ought to come to him as easily as did the rest of the game. To Crawley, it was one aspect of golf which even the David Blairs of this world could not perfect without a goodly measure of practice.

His brother, Chan, also a member of the Honourable Company, was a 3-handicap and a Halford Hewitt golfer himself. He had need of his sense of humour since he was constantly introduced – which was a little hard when he was a lieutenant-general and the said sibling a mere major – as 'David Blair's brother'.

A member of the Scottish side in 26 internationals between 1948 and 1962, Blair played for Harrow in the Halford Hewitt from 1949 to 1984, figuring in five winning teams. It was always said of David Blair that he had 'a swing which was built to last' and, at the age of 67, he was selected yet again for the 1985 side. Alas, he was found dead in his car in Deal on the eve of the event, the victim of a heart attack.

Simply having him in their thoughts was enough for the Old Harrovians. In what was a fitting tribute to the man and the golfer, they won that year's Halford Hewitt.

Charles Lawrie

CHARLES LAWRIE was originally more of a cricketer than he was a golfer, with a batting average in a golden summer at Fettes College of 87.33. Cricket, too, was, one of the five sports in which he represented Oxford against Cambridge during the Second World War, the others being hockey, tennis, squash and, of course, golf. Since he was also the full-back in the Fettes First XV, he may fairly be classed as an outstanding all-rounder even by the standards of the Honourable Company – a club where a species, now endangered by the specialisation deemed necessary by the demands of modern sport, once abounded.

He and another outstanding Fettesian cricketer, Donald Steel, hold the record in the Halford Hewitt with 30 consecutive foursomes wins – a tremendous run which included the foundation they gave the side as an opening partnership when Fettes won in 1964. A Scottish Amateur international, Lawrie, who could hold on to his game with a minimum of practice, reached the semi-final of the 1955 Scottish Amateur and six times figured in the last eight.

His own experience partly explained why, for all the abundant innate talent with which he had been blessed, he believed so devoutly in the coaching drive which, by the early '70s, had enveloped even his native land. In Scotland, more perhaps than in any other country, he had been constantly irritated by that – to him – idiotic boast: 'Never had a lesson in my life!'. He could recite the litany of the great self-taught champions as readily as the next man, but if Jack Nicklaus was not ashamed to acknowledge his debt to Jack Grout, why on earth should so many lesser mortals consider it an admission of inadequacy to repair to a good professional for tuition. 'I think,' he would say, 'that a winner in golf depends on his heart, head and technique. I am never quite sure of the proper order but, if you press me, I think I would put heart first. However, way back, when I was just beginning to take golf seriously, Leonard Crawley wrote some nice things about me but told me bluntly that I would always have unnecessary limitations, unless I changed my hooker's grip.

'Like a fool, I ignored him – and, though I played for Scotland in 1949–50, I then had three years in the wilderness belatedly putting Leonard's advice into practice. Thus, I am all for the kind of coaching which makes sure youngsters are sound in the basic fundamentals of such things as grip and set-up even if – as I consider I can justifiably claim I was myself – they are born with a natural swing.'

Captain of Scotland in 1960, he was captain again the next year when, at Portmarnock, Scotland performed the phenomenal feat of winning all ten singles against England *en route* to taking the Triple Crown – an additional touch of romance being furnished by the fact that Lawrie's father, A.A. Lawrie, had been president of the Scottish Rugby Union when, at Twickenham in 1938, 'Wilson Shaw's match', the rugby version was secured. Non-playing captain of the Walker Cup team in 1961 and 1963, and chairman of the R & A selectors from 1963 to 1967, he was chairman of the R & A championship committee when Lee Trevino won the Open at Muirfield. In contrast to 1966, the rough cultivated for Trevino's Open was graded but, if not as spectacularly fierce as it had been six years earlier, it was still better avoided. Lawrie brought to bear the eye not just of an international golfer but of the golf course architect which he was by profession, one of his best-known creations being the Duke's course at Woburn where there is a commemorative Lawrie room in the clubhouse.

At Muirfield, he was, of course, very much aware that at every hole save the third, fifth, ninth and seventeenth – and from one flank of both the sixth and the fourteenth – a player going for the flag from the rough had to carry a bunker on the overfly with all the attendant problems of getting the ball to stop from such a lie. The greens at Muirfield are traditionally swift and, as Lawrie always bore in mind, depending on the weather, they were always liable to quicken still further toward the end of a championship as they had done in 1966. The weight of traffic of a field of Open championship numbers, apart from anything else, tended to harden them.

As for those who wanted the greens to attain a pace more akin to

MATCH IN PROGRESS
Glyn Satterley followed the fortunes of a recent dinner match (36-hole foursome) played on a sunny but cold winter's day

those of Pebble Beach in the US Open earlier that summer – greens which, according to Lawrie, had been triple-cut and rolled – he would remind them that the putting surfaces on the last nine holes at Muirfield embraced one particular factor which had to be included in their calculations. With the exception of the tenth and seventeenth, all the putting surfaces were on a gradient. That could in itself add considerably to the test of nerve and touch, especially with a wind blowing.

Lawrie, who sadly died young, being only 53, recognised the threat to some of the older courses posed by the distance the ball could now be propelled by the longer hitters, armed with the marvels of modern technology in respect of clubs and balls. Even so, he was convinced that Muirfield, as an Open championship test, would remain long enough for the foreseeable future without anything too radical in the way of lengthening. Nor, he would underline, for he felt too many made the mistake of doing so, was it to be compared in that dimension with St Andrews. The Old Course was a case apart and anyway its comparative lack of any very demanding length was partially offset by the fact that it had only two par threes. As an R & A official, he abhorred the notion of the Open championship one day becoming all-ticket: 'It must never become absurdly pricey, beyond the pocket of the rank and file of the golf fraternity. Nor is there any reason why it should. What is often lost sight of is the fact that the R & A is a non-profit-making organisation. They have no shareholders to satisfy or dividends to declare. All the money from an Open is channelled back into the game.

'Some of it, of course, goes into the reserve fund and some immediately towards the installation of further facilities at the relevant courses – telephones, toilets and so on – and the purchase of new machinery, including such relatively sophisticated equipment as that for aerating courses. And aeration, in my time, is something which has often been very badly needed – though not, I may say, at Muirfield.'

As long ago as 1972, Lawrie was already worrying that the Open championship was in imminent danger of growing too big for its own good. 'Certainly,' he averred, 'we wouldn't want the tented village to get much larger. The Open must never be swallowed up in the general circus. In the last resort, it must always be the golf, the play, the actual Open, which remains paramount.'

Lord Robertson, captain of the Honourable Company in 1970 and 1971, on the 'Scotch foursome'.

The Honourable Company is the Home of the Foursome – sometimes called the 'Scotch' Foursome – and regards it as the true game, the epitome of all that is best in golf. A prominent Notice hangs beside the entrance to the clubhouse at Muirfield, saying: 'Fourball games are forbidden at weekends and on public holidays.' Any member (or visitor) who attempted to break this rule would get short shrift. And, if it be retorted that a player plays twice as many shots in a fourball game as in a Foursome, the Muirfield man would reply – 'Play 36 holes in 4½ hours (as we do) and you will get the same number of shots, twice the exercise, far more fun, and you won't have to wait between shots. Furthermore, you will learn to play golf better.'

5 Notable Secretaries

Singing Jamie Balfour

OVER the centuries, secretaries to the Honourable Company have provided some diverting character studies but none in the long litany has been more colourful than 'Singing Jamie' Balfour. Nor many, if any, more popular. Balfour was an accountant, as is Stuart Wyllie, assistant to the present secretary, Group Captain John Prideaux. A sportsman of what may euphemistically be termed comfortable contours, Balfour, 'an amiable, upright and able man', was so shrewd in business affairs that it was said that he could do as much in one hour as many another man in three. He had, too, the handy knack of being able to generate business whenever he so chose, which was only when he considered himself in somewhat urgent need of funds.

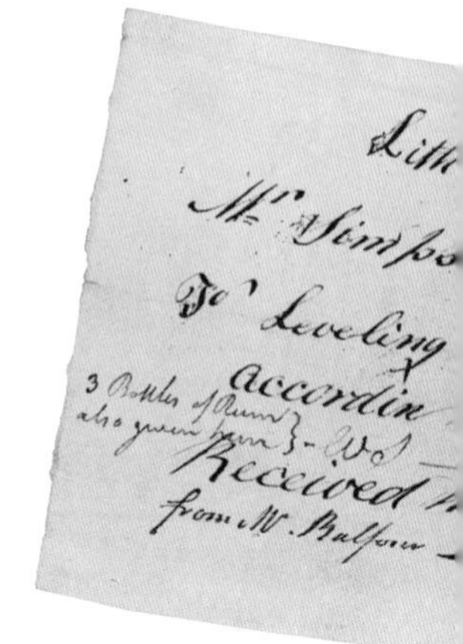
Leith
Mr Simpso
To Leveling
accordin
Received
from Mr Balfour

Right: a membership certificate of May 1784 signed by James Balfour as secretary of the Honourable Company, and, below, a receipted bill for work on the Links at Leith – and for three bottles of rum! – dated March 1791

One of the Honourable Company's newer members in the late twentieth century, Ronnie Corbett, would have recognised a frustrated Thespian. Chambers' *Traditions of Edinburgh* explained that Balfour was 'usually called "Singing Jamie" on account of his fascinating qualities as a vocalist'. His forte was Scottish songs of all kinds. Indeed, there is some sheet music in the famous portrait of this convivial, larger-than-life personality, and legend has it that Balfour is on the verge of his party piece – the song 'When I ha'e a saxpence under my thoomb'. The painting, which was by Sir Henry Raeburn, who was himself a member, was among those sold when the club was in dire financial straits in the 1830s but the print, which hangs at Muirfield, has an attachment in Raeburn's own hand: Edinburgh, 6 May 1793: 'Received from James Balfour, Esq., the sum of thirty Guineas for his own portrait done for the Society of Golfers, Henry Raeburn.'

Jenny Ha's Tavern, opposite Queensberry House, in the Canongate in Edinburgh, was a regular haunt where Singing Jamie quaffed cappie ale (ale laced with brandy and drunk from a wooden bowl). Tales of his carousing and powers of endurance were rife and it was always said of him that he could see off three sets of boon companions in a night, a fresh platoon stepping into the breach as the others fell.

There was one anecdote to which Sir Walter Scott was given to alluding: 'Jamie, in going home late from a debauch, happened to tumble into the pit formed for the foundation of a house in James's Square. A gentleman passing heard his complaint, and going up to the spot, was entreated by our hero to help him out. "What would be the use of helping you out," said the by-passer, "when you could not stand though you *were* out?" "Very true, perhaps, yet if you help me up I'll *run* to the Tron Kirk for a bottle of claret." Pleased with his humour, the gentleman placed him upon his feet, when instantly he set off for the Tron Church at a pace distancing all ordinary competition, and accordingly he won the race, though at the conclusion he had to sit down on the steps of the church, being quite

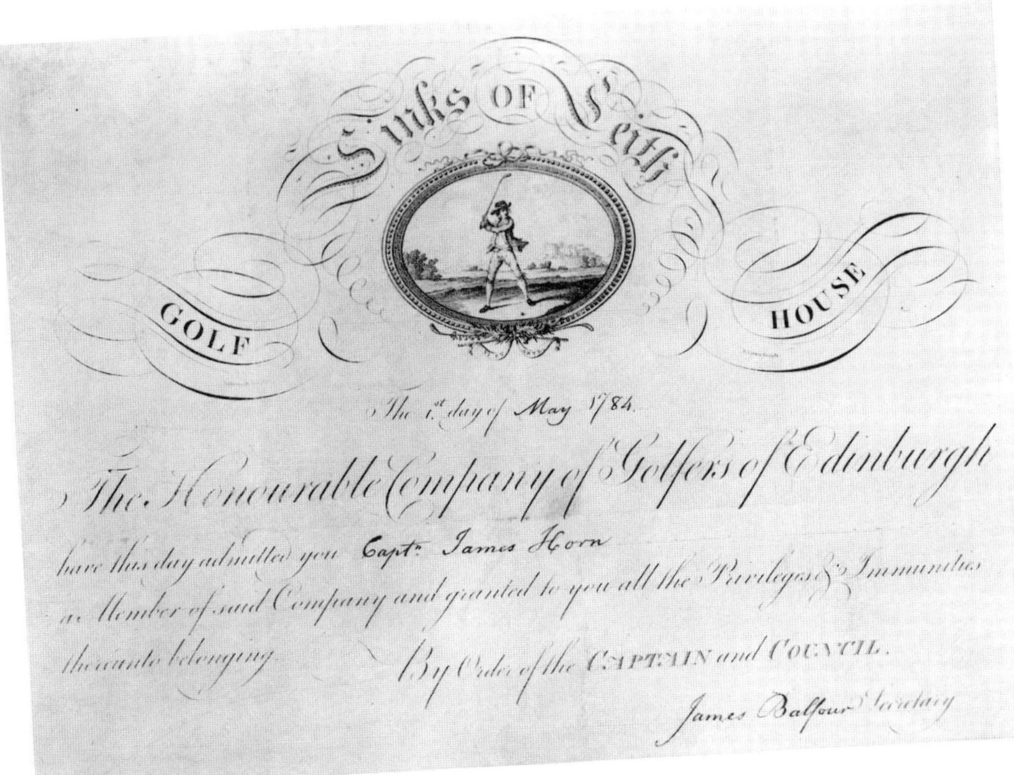

Links of Leith

GOLF HOUSE

The 1st day of May 1784.

The Honourable Company of Golfers of Edinburgh

have this day admitted you Capt. James Horn
a Member of said Company and granted to you all the Privileges & Immunities
thereunto belonging.

By Order of the CAPTAIN and COUNCIL.

James Balfour Secretary

unable to stand. After taking a minute or two to recover his breath – "Well, another race to Fortunes for another bottle of claret!" Off he went to the tavern in question, in the Stamp-office Close, and this bet he gained also. The claret, probably with continuations, was discussed in Fortunes and the end of the story is that Balfour sent his new friend home in a chair, utterly done up, at an early hour in the morning.'

Jamie was of Jacobite leanings and in *Traditions of Edinburgh* there is the story of how a lady, who dwelled in Parliament Close, was wakened from her sleep one summer morning: 'Going to the window to learn what was the matter, guess her surprise at seeing Jamie Balfour and some of his boon companions (evidently fresh from their wonted orgies) singing "The King shall enjoy his own again" on their knees, round King Charles's statue.' His custom, when anxious to repair the effects of intemperance, was to bathe his head and hands in icy water: this, it was said, made him quite cool and collected almost immediately.'

'Pleasure being so predominant an object in his life', the fact that he failed to make it to his sixtieth birthday occasioned much less surprise than that he died in possession of a tidy sum of money. After his death, the Honourable Company held a general meeting on 24 November 1795 'in memory of their worthy secretary'. Twenty-seven members in mourning clothes attended with, at their head, the Lord Provost of Edinburgh. Among the toasts they drank was one 'to the Memory of our worthy and late departed friend, Mr James Balfour, whose benevolent and cheerful disposition, and happy social powers, while they captivated all, particularly endeared him to his numerous friends.'

The portrait of Balfour commissioned by the Honourable Company from Henry Raeburn (who was a member) and, below, the receipt for payment for it in Raeburn's own hand

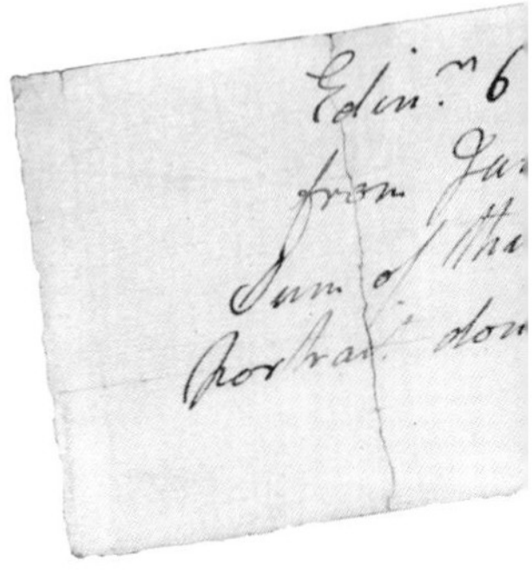

Then came the plea to posterity and Prideaux: 'May the offices in this society held by Mr Balfour be agreeably supplied and attended to with that accuracy and precision for which he was generally distinguished.'

Brian Evans-Lombe

IF you ask Colonel Brian Evans-Lombe, OBE, who last year celebrated his own centenary, how he came to be secretary of the Honourable Company, he will tell you, with a twinkle, that it owed most to the fact that the difference between high and low tide at Muirfield is a matter of 35 feet. It mirrored exactly the tides on the beaches of Normandy, which is how Evans-Lombe and sundry pillars of the Pioneer Corps came in 1944 to be checking, in the immediate vicinity of Muirfield, the loading and draught of the vessels which would land the lorries and other vehicles on the shores of France on the opening of the Second Front. Evans-Lombe himself crossed on D Plus Two and was affectionately assisted from the water by men he had helped to train. It was his second world war but again he survived.

Having politely declined postings to Cairo and Berlin, the former of which had been to 'an area which would have been fine if I had been a ravenous mosquito', he had retired from the army in 1947. Friends at Muirfield such as James Dallmeyer and Colonel Jock Mitchell, the latter of whom had been secretary of the Army Golfing Society, had tipped him off that the Honourable Company were in need of a secretary. Though there was a short leet of three, he, in the best traditions of the military, used the contacts he had made in 1944 to get in behind the lines and secure a tactical advantage. Having obtained an interview 24 hours ahead of his rivals, he was off to a flyer, winning in a canter – though a stewards' inquiry would surely have upheld an objection. The real point, though, was that the Honourable Company had indisputably got the right man.

A mere year later, he was, to all intents and purposes, in charge of the 1948 Open championship at Muirfield for, in those days, much of what is now the preserve of the R & A championship committee was down to the club secretary. However, he had from the first treated with scorn the notion that he, a former staff officer, would find the organisation of such an event beyond him. He had been to the Open at Hoylake the previous summer to study such a championship for himself. So thorough was his preparation, so shrewd his delegation, by the time the first shot was struck at Muirfield, he himself was mainly holding no more than a watching brief. Nor was he remotely fazed by the visit of King George VI on the day the eventual winner, Henry Cotton, handed in a never-to-be-forgotten 66.

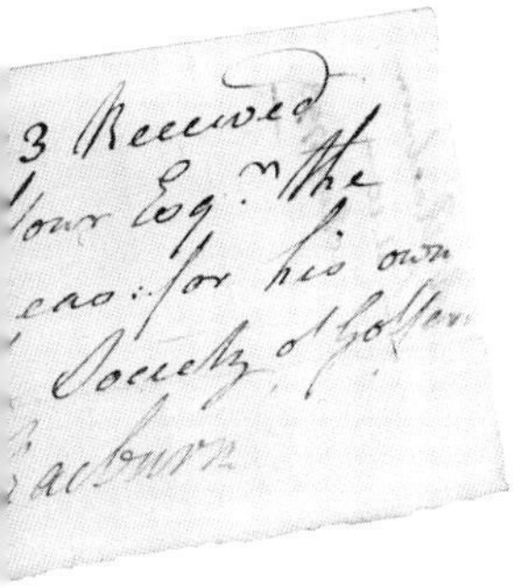

It was all a far cry from the Muirfield which had awaited him when he took over as secretary from Major Kerr who had gone south to become the secretary at Royal St George's. The links had been overgrown and covered in ragwort and thistles. He used German prisoners, 90 all told, whom he divided into three platoons of 30, operating a morning, afternoon and evening shift. He paid them but, in his second week at Muirfield, they went on strike in protest at their meagre wage. There was very little money in the bank, even allowing for the compensation the club had received for the damage done by the army. Eventually, despite much incredulous opposition, the subscription was raised from – wait for it – six guineas to nine guineas. When, after a month, the Germans were repatriated, he had members adopt specific holes and continue clearing the weeds. Even when he had built up a pool of six greenkeepers, the same principle applied with each personally responsible for three holes. Nor was there much scope for slacking, the Lone Ranger on his bicycle being Evans-Lombe himself.

He was given a lady secretary but he steadfastly refused to have anything to do with the accounts, a former bank manager being enlisted at his instigation. 'There was no club-tie,' he explains, 'and no one had a handicap. When they needed one for a medal, I gave them it, though the captain sometimes also wanted a say.'

Farming in New Zealand when the Kaiser's War broke out, he was persuaded home by his father, a regular soldier who promised confidently that the Secretary of War, a relative of theirs, would give him an immediate commission. In fact, the Secretary of War had enough of the Evan-Lombes in him to do no such thing, and the returning son of the soil had to go through Sandhurst like any other aspiring officer.

Commissioned in the cavalry, the King's Royal Irish Hussars, Evans-Lombe fought on the Somme, being greatly tickled by the fact that the German response to the raids they made was invariably to shell the French on the British flank. By 1939, he had transferred to the Pioneer Corps because his beloved horses had given way to tanks in which 'abominations' he had no desire to be entombed.

His eyes trouble him, a legacy of service in the Far East and an occasion when the supplies of quinine, which would have made the difference, had expired. Indeed, the mepacrine they used instead, he remembers indignantly, poisoned him. Otherwise the centenarian – a non-smoker and not far off a teetotaller – enjoys wonderful health, which he attributes in part to his years in the saddle: 'No one who rides has any back trouble unless he has had an accident.'

He played golf until he was 90. He had been scratch, in the less exacting golfing realm of Egypt, in pre-war days, but he was off seven both when he won the handicap division of the 1924 Army championship at Hoylake and throughout his reign as the secretary of the Honourable Company. As a polo player, his other principal sporting outlet in his years in the cavalry, he had a handicap of five; and, when he was a schoolboy at Cheltenham, his play behind the scrum had him marked as a promising disciple of the famed Harlequin, Adrian Stoop.

Latterly resident in Hove, Evans-Lombe – incidentally, the oldest surviving Boy Scout – looks back on his 17 years at Muirfield as being among the happiest of what, he cheerfully owns, has been a wonderful life. But only once, when he had to come north to St Andrews anyway in his capacity as captain of the Society of Senior Golfers, has he been back.

He cannot recall a row in all his days at Muirfield. 'We were a team – the members, the clubhouse staff, the greenkeepers, the caddies.' As for Logan, the legendary head greenkeeper, here was an adversary worthy of his steel. 'He fought me,' recalls Evans-Lombe, with reminiscent relish, 'but I had the last word. And besides, in order the better to take him on, I had travelled to Yorkshire to take a fortnight's course in greenkeeping!'

The years in the army, especially the war service in the Far East, had left their mark and it is a fact that, in his time at Muirfield, not one Japanese visitor played a round over the historic links. 'We are full up,' he would say, politely, looking out over the largely deserted course. He could, too, be autocratic and imperious and, in truth, there were those who swore that in him a great Pope had gone to waste for the mantle of papal infallibility would have rested easily on his shoulders. Yet humour was never far away and he will admit, chuckling, that, yes, the best of all the many anecdotes he inspired was perfectly true. He really had insisted that the members of a visiting society mend their ways and replace their divots with the nap facing the right way though it was not, alas, as legend has it, a dental society whose inability to fill their cavities correctly who had incurred his wrath.

Nothing encapsulates his days as the most revered of all

Below: Colonel Evans-Lombe aged about 81, from a photograph kindly loaned by his daughter

the Honourable Company's long litany of secretaries more felicitously than the lines he penned as a guest of those impish versifiers, the Monks of St Giles, among whom he was known as Father Superfluous:

Club members to me, I think you'll agree,
Are as to a shepherd, his sheep;
I chase them off here and pen them in there,
And I count them as I go to sleep.

I have to listen as their eyes glisten
And they tell me of marvellous putts;
All I've seen them sink, is a great deal of drink;
It's gradually driving me nuts.

They tell me with force what to do with the course
And how drinks are cheaper in pubs.
I'd like to suggest, if I ever was pressed,
What they could do with their clubs.

And when at last the ultimate blast
Of the dear old trumpet calls,
They'll all expect me on the first fiery tee
With a box of asbestos balls.

Paddy Hanmer

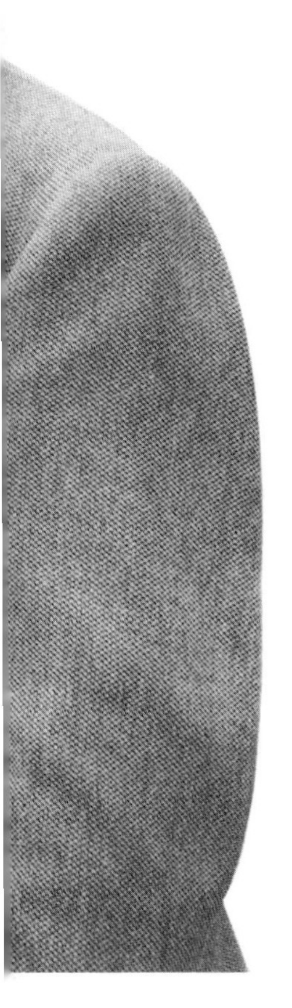

THE conversation concerned Captain Paddy Hanmer, former secretary of the Honourable Company, as it so often does in the vicinity of Muirfield.

First party: 'Have you met Sadie?'

Second party: 'No, I haven't. In fact, I had no idea Paddy had got another labrador. How nice for the old boy.'

First party: 'It's not another labrador – it's a wife!'

It was the biggest sensation in those parts since America's Johnny Miller sank his second for a two at the long fifth. The most confirmed of bachelors, Hanmer had been faced with drawing up his will and – which conjures up a rather more romantic image than many have had of him over the years – had wanted to leave something to a petty officer in the Wrens whom he had once known in Rosyth but had not seen for 38 years. A letter sent to her last known address reached its target thanks to a thousand-to-one chance chat between the current occupant and a neighbour. In no time at all Captain Hanmer and the lady were wed.

Rosyth was also responsible for introducing him to the Honourable Company who, for almost two and a half centuries, had been even warier of the female of the species than Hanmer himself. It had taken more than that, of course, to convince two eminent members, Bill Napier and Teddy Gordon, that he was the man for them when, by chance, it fell to Hanmer, as captain of HMS *Cochrane* and president of the navy's golfing community north of the border, to play host to the seniors from Muirfield. In the course of the match, the then 52-year-old Hanmer had mentioned casually that he had a mind to stay in Scotland when he left the navy which, with the service contracting and fewer and fewer opportunities for further promotion, was becoming increasingly imminent. Alerted by an obviously impressed Teddy Gordon to the vacancy at Muirfield occasioned by the retirement of Colonel George Elsmie from the post of secretary, Hanmer applied. In 1968, he began his eventful tenure of office. It lasted 15 years and embraced not only two Open championships, a Ryder Cup, Walker Cup and Curtis Cup, but also many equally spirited contests off the course.

He loved and lived his role 365 days a year to a degree which might not have been possible for a man with with a wife and family. He may not always have been on speaking terms with every member but he was fiercely loyal to the Honourable Company. 'A great lot,' he recalls, a little wistfully. You have the impression that even though, like Colonel Evans-Lombe before him, he was made an honorary member in recognition of his outstanding service, he will always regard the years in office as the great years. His previous career as a supply officer in the Royal Navy had been, he rapidly came to believe, an ideal preparation.

'Dealing with cooks, stores, clothing and all the rest had been an everyday way of life and wonderful conditioning for the demands made upon a golf club secretary!'

Above: Paddy Hanmer
Below: the secretary's office, with, from right to left: John Prideaux, Carol Robertson, Stuart Wyllie and Elspeth Mustard
Below right: the dining-room staff and caddie master

In other ways, however, it was a whole new world. If it had been highly advisable in the war years to ascertain what flag a passing ship was flying, the consequences now of failing to identify one old school tie from another were liable to be scarcely less explosive. 'I had heard of Loretto because my mother had once had a fleeting fancy to send me there, but most of the other great Scottish schools were new to me.' Still, this erstwhile pupil of the Nautical College of Pangbourne had not been 35 years in the navy without recognising a minefield when he saw one. At one committee meeting, the captain, Rob Macgregor, wished to know if the proposed dates for the biennial match with the R & A and the annual encounter with Prestwick clashed with the Halford Hewitt. 'I'll check,' promised Hanmer, as if the same thought had been troubling him. In truth, the Halford Hewitt could have been a rugby match for all he knew.

He was surprised that there was so little forward planning, especially in terms of the club's finances. The yearly figures were in the red, the new secretary's solution being to get more visitors playing what was, after all, one of the world's great courses. Only, he was told, if it could be done without upsetting the members. 'Damn it,' protested Hanmer, 'we employ seven greenkeepers and they are lucky if they meet up with one member a week!' Facility fees from the Open were another source of income but soon there was an assumption that, basically, members' subcriptions paid for the clubhouse, visitors' fees for the course. Not that too many of those same visitors could have been readily persuaded that this testy old sea dog had ever been their patron saint. There are many stories surrounding the Hanmer legend, but as he himself says, 'No one ever gets these things right. Take the last night of the 1980 Open when Tom Watson and Ben Crenshaw played a match after dinner with ancient hickories up the tenth and down the eighteenth. I was in the Bissets Hotel relaxing when word came that

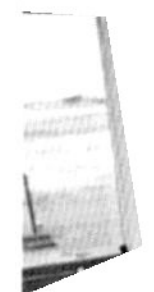

there were folk dancing on the last green to the skirl of bagpipes. When I got to the course, the giant stands stood out black against the last light of day and the whole scene looked less like Muirfield than Coney Island. "What the hell are you doing?" I roared before I realised that the golfers and the crowd with them were mostly players and wives from the Open who had been staying at Greywalls. Had they sought permission, I would probably have given it though the watchers would have had to keep off the greens. In fairness, I think most of the women had taken off their shoes.'

Just once he hit back, because the offending passages were enshrined in what he deemed 'an otherwise beautiful book, *The Spirit of Golf*' and would therefore be perpetuated ad infinitum. He sued and won his case.

Jerry Pate, telling humorously at the 1980 Open of the day he played Muirfield as a student, painted a picture of 'this man and his black dog' which made Muirfield's old mariner sound about twice as sinister as Long John Silver and his parrot. By a cruel irony, three hip operations have left him hardly more fleet of foot than Long John. As for his eyesight, which had threatened to put paid to his boyhood ambition to join the navy, it has hardly been improved by his having been shot in the eye, not by an irate member or a visitor who would not take no for an answer but by a stray pellet when out with the guns.

Where the Honourable Company had given him a dinner and the Edinburgh Provost put on a lunch, ten Americans, three of whom were not even members, had marked his retirement with the gift of a motorised golf cart. The use of a golf cart at Muirfield is subject to strict conditions but, in any case, Hanmer's golfing days are done. Instead, he sits in the clubhouse, revolving, like Sir Belvidere, many memories.

John Prideaux

AS they broke cloud, Acting Pilot Officer John Prideaux, now Group Captain Prideaux, secretary of the Honourable Company, looked down anxiously. He did so at the casually blasé behest of his flying instructor, who was not about to admit to his young pupil that he had not, in an all too apposite phrase, the foggiest idea where they were. The landmarks for which Prideaux was searching were roads, buildings, rivers. Instead he saw individual blades of grass which he could distinguish with alarming clarity. Moments later, in a species of pitch-and-run which will go with him to man's last bunker, the grave, they had hit and were tearing through a bush. Immediately ahead were power lines and Prideaux had a sudden conviction to which he had sometimes fallen prey in his horse-riding days. A conviction that this was one hurdle he was not about to clear.

The next thing he knew they were enveloped in a thick white mist. For the merest fraction of a second, he says, laughing at himself, he thought he was in heaven but unless they were beating retreat on some runway in the sky, the pounding he could hear was presumably his own heart.

The wings on a Vampire jet are set behind the pilot and, glancing out on his side, Prideaux was left in no doubt that they had caught the power lines. Speechless, he tapped the shoulder of his instructor who, getting the message, checked on his flank where what he espied was no more comforting. A golf ball as 'visibly cut, cracked and out of shape' – Rule 5 (3) – would have been taken out of play. They, though, had somehow to get down. Though unable to slow to the speed which was mandatory for such a landing, they got enough check, in golfing parlance, to hold the runway. A veritable Frank Spencer, of *Some Mothers Do Have 'Em*, hopped up the ladder and opened the canopy. 'You've had an accident,' he revealed.

To this day, Prideaux has a comemmorative drink every year on 2 February. The plane never flew again but the flying instructor was exonerated on the score of a faulty altimeter. Which was as well, because Prideaux's response to his superior's suggestion that they could attribute the mangled plane to a bird strike had been more realistic than respectful: 'Not unless they were pterodactyls!'

When he enlisted to train as an RAF pilot, he had never flown before and, initially, was quite horribly airsick, but he won his wings. He flew Shackletons for Coastal Command from Northern Ireland before being invited to join the V Force and fly the delta-winged Vulcan bombers which, in the days before Polaris and Trident, were Britain's ultimate deterrent with regard to nuclear defence.

His RAF service included a spell as an instructor at Staff College and a period at the Ministry of Defence. In the latter case, he acted as an adviser on nuclear policy to the Secretary of State (Michael Heseltine followed by George Younger) and to the Prime Minister, Margaret Thatcher: 'She would take her time absorbing the information you gave her, almost to the point of seeming hesitant – but, once she had made up her mind, she was

ELSPETH MUSTARD

'I am sorry,' said the secretary's secretary, Mrs Elspeth Mustard, to the very large daughter of Uncle Sam who had loomed through the portals of the Honourable Company, 'but we don't allow ladies in the clubhouse.'

The American ran her eyes disdainfully up and down this latter-day Horatius. 'Then what,' she asked, interestedly, 'are you?'

PASS MUSTARD was one American headline she inspired atop an article on the alleged – and she would say greatly exaggerated – problems of obtaining permission to play Muirfield. But, unfailingly courteous and helpful, and armed with a sense of humour, she takes it all in her stride.

Even when one singularly vulgar transatlantic worthy, sensing that his energetic chewing of gum was not taking too many tricks with Major Vanreenan, the then secretary, plucked it from his mouth and handed it to her. Mrs Mustard reached for a piece of paper and, fastidiously wrapping the remains in it, dropped it into a wastepaper basket. Jeeves could not have done it better, nor Lady Bracknell.

Another American applicant who, revealing that he had only six months to live and dearly wanted to play Muirfield before shuffling off this mortal coil, turned up in the rudest of health. 'You are looking very

well,' said Mrs Mustard, and the timbre of her voice should have alerted him. But no. 'Never felt better in my life,' he agreed, cordially.
'You must have made a marvellous recovery,' said Mrs Mustard, icily.
'Eh?' said the other, puzzled.
'You were telling me when you made your booking how very ill you were,' explained Mrs Mustard, her voice now far below freezing point – and at last he remembered.
'That's right, I was. The doctors,' he ended, lamely, 'say that I've made medical history.'
After all of which, it was by no means certain that he enjoyed his round quite as much as he had thought he would.
On the other hand, there are innumerable guests whose obvious pleasure in playing Muirfield she finds infectious and sometimes they are more appreciative than might be supposed. And, of all the presents she has received, there is one which will always stand apart. Namely, the medal which the late Tommy Dempster gave her to remember him by – a medal he had won long, long ago at Longniddry but always treasured. 'When he could no longer play golf,' she recalls, 'he would come in every Monday just for a chat – but wasn't that a lovely gesture. I was really very touched.'

wonderfully decisive. In that respect, a service man's dream.'

He did not, however, like Whitehall as a place to work and, after commanding a flying station responsible for training over half the pilots for the RAF, all the pilots for the navy and many from foreign lands, the prospect of flying a desk in Whitehall held scant appeal. At which juncture in his life, he noticed that the Honourable Company were advertising for a secretary. He had by then turned 50 and a change of direction seemed very inviting. The interview, though, twice had him puzzled. Would he, if he were appointed, mind playing quite a lot of golf with the members? Mind? He would be delighted.

The second requirement went against all his service training. They would not want him to use his initiative. 'They were right, of course,' he says now. 'They do not like change for change's sake and, even when the time has come for it, they prefer to take their time as befits a club of so much cherished tradition. But, within my own domain, I have a free hand.' Nor is he expected to be involved in the everyday minutiae of the finances as are many club secretaries. 'Again,' stresses Prideaux, 'I think that they have got it right – at least for a club such as the Honourable Company.'

As to finance, he was hardly in danger of being overawed, his command of a flying training station in North Yorkshire having entailed handling a budget running to £24 million. But, other than on the broader scale, that realm of the club's affairs is left to a retired chartered accountant, Stuart Wyllie, an enthusiastic 24-handicap golfer whose other sporting interest is rugby union, wherein his son, Douglas, is a Scottish international.

Turning to the administrative framework, Prideaux would warmly recommend it to golf clubs everywhere, though he concedes that, in its entirety, it might not suit other clubs as well as it does the Honourable Company. 'The club,' he explains, 'is run on the lines of a good business. The captain is the Chairman of the Board and is normally in office for two years. The committee, who meet only five or six times a year, could be said to be the Board of Directors – six-strong with each of them serving for no more than three years in any one spell and with two demitting office each year. There are no subcommittees as such save for something exceptional like the club's 250th anniversary. No handicap committee, no green committee and no house committee. Concluding the parallel, my own role is that of the Chief Executive, putting policy into action.'

The Honourable Company have no professional as such, but Prideaux has a staff of 28; two-pronged in that eight of them are greenkeepers working under Chris Whittle, the course manager, with the remainder under the club steward. He deems Whittle the complete professional in a calling which is very different from the days of Shay Logan, the head greenkeeper whose name was for so long synonymous with Muirfield. Very much his own man with his own way, Prideaux knows that what was right for yesterday is not necessarily right for today. And he is practical: 'Take the visitors away and the annual subscription would have to double.'

THE UNITED STATES

Back row – from left to right: T.D. Aaron, J.W. Nicklaus, H. Ward Wettlaufer, W. Hyndman III
Front row – from left to right: E. Harvie Ward jnr, Deane R. Beman, C.R. Coe (Capt), W.J. Patton, F.M. Taylor jnr

IN 1938 at St Andrews, when Great Britain and Ireland won the Walker Cup for the first time, Henry Cotton practised with the home team. His accounts of the prodigious hitting and spectacular scoring of Jimmy Bruen, the idiosyncratic Irishman with a loop in his swing which his wife always said had its origins in the sport of hurley, had made great propaganda, capturing the headlines from the Americans.

It was perhaps not entirely a coincidence that, on the eve of the 1959 Walker Cup at Muirfield, Cotton was again in evidence. He was, in any case, on his way north to give a clinic at Nairn but, as a graduate of Muirfield in that he had won his third Open championship there in 1948, he obviously had a lot to offer. Dai Rees, with the aura of a man who had captained the home side to victory in the 1957 Ryder Cup at Lindrick, was also present since he was to be involved in the film of the Walker Cup match.

They were still competitive, Rees having just won the PGA championship and Cotton having come second to Peter Alliss in the Dunlop. It was too good an opportunity to miss. Cotton and Rees took on Joe Carr and Guy Wolstenholme in a match followed by a gallery which swelled rapidly. Carr, even in such illustrious company, held centre stage, being round in 70 as the amateurs beat the professionals at the last. 'On a fast-paced course,' wrote Frank Moran in the *Scotsman*, 'he hit the ball terrific distances and, at several holes, with the breeze behind him, drove well over 300 yards.' Rees was much impressed: 'I can't see any Americans beating Carr and Wolstenholme.'

Both Cotton and Rees had offered Gerald Micklem, the Great Britain and Ireland captain, any help he wanted with his team and many saw their defeat as the stuff of 1938 and Bruen at St Andrews. Which was not to say that they had connived at it: they were not perhaps quite as selflessly patriotic as that.

On the debit side, though, there had been something of a setback for

GREAT BRITAIN AND IRELAND

Back row – from left to right: D.N. Sewell, A.E. Shepperson, M.F. Bonallack, M.S.R. Lunt, D.M. Marsh, W.D. Smith
Front row – from left to right: A.H. Perowne, J.B. Carr, G. Micklem (Capt), R.R. Jack, G.B. Wolstenholme

the Great Britain and Ireland side with the neck injury sustained earlier in the week by Dick Smith, the Scottish champion. Having begun in practice on the Tuesday 4, 3, 3, he had had to drop out at the fourth having mysteriously damaged his neck. He slept that night, after prolonged massage, with a felt bandage round his neck. It was all the more of a blow in that Micklem had already lost Scotland's Jimmy Walker, who had been injured in a car accident, Smith, ironically, being the replacement. Smith was fit in time to be fielded in the singles but fate followed its original rabbit punch with a real haymaker, bequeathing him Nicklaus.

The Americans, too, had a problem. Harvie Ward's golf had been on the decline for two years and the descent had not been arrested with his arrival at Muirfield. Charlie Coe, America's playing captain, was detected on the practice ground helping him with his driving, while at dinner in Greywalls, Ward was to be seen rising from his table to mime his swing in order to obtain not just a second opinion but a third and a fourth. The 19-year-old Nicklaus was in no doubt: he was picking the club up too abruptly on the backswing.

The view among the Americans was that there was a close match in store; one in which everything might hinge on the final match on the Saturday night. The aforementioned Moran, writing in the midst of an epidemic of 'guessin' and calculatin'' suggested that Great Britain and Ireland would win the first two foursomes, lose the third 'and at least halve the touch-and-go third'.

The great day began, as Moran would relate, 'with a song in our hearts'. Muirfield was at its picturesque best, with the sun spotlighting the sandhills and 'a thin veil of haze' over the sea. By evening, it was not just the sun which had retreated behind a cloud. The grim scoreline read: United States 4, British Isles 0.

Six thousand spectators had followed play which, for all the final outcome, could scarcely have been more compelling. Two matches had gone to the home green and another to the 35th, with the only rout occurring in the third match in which Michael Bonallack and Arthur Perowne – 'innocents to the slaughter', as was said at the time – lost to the tune of 9 and 8. Bonallack, at least, was to have his revenge, captaining Great Britain and Ireland to victory at St Andrews in 1971.

In the top match in which Reid Jack and Doug Sewell met Ward and Dr Frank Taylor, Ward holed from seven yards for a birdie on the home green to close the door on the luckless British pair. Ward, by Coe's calculations, had rolled in '150 yards of putts!'.

As for Wolstenholme and Carr, they lost on the last green as Carr, from 12 yards, failed by the proverbial whisker to avert a one-hole win for Bill Hyndman and Tommy Aaron.

In the fourth and final game, Michael Lunt and Alec Shepperson had been four up after four holes in the morning in losing by 2 and 1 to Ward Wettlaufer and a certain Jack Nicklaus. 'Snow White and Baby Fat', Harvie Ward, in handing out the nicknames, had dubbed them – but no, you are wrong, it was the 220lb Wettlaufer who was Baby Fat.

Having said, ruefully, that he would like to have broken the rusty old putter which Harvie Ward had used to such telling effect, Micklem was the umpteenth Great Britain and Ireland captain to note that his players had 'missed too many six-footers'.

Coe, in his end-of-day comment, was the reverse of complacent: 'I said last night that it would be close and I don't think you could cut it any finer. You could turn round and do the same to us tomorrow. The ball does not bounce the same way every day.'

What had to be done if Great Britain and Ireland were to climb back from the abyss? It needed six wins and a half from the second day's singles.

Carr had drawn Charlie Coe who, as always, looked as if he had stepped straight out of a Hollywood Western on to the course. But the Irish sharp-shooter gunned down the man Harvie Ward had christened Wyatt Earp. In this duel of national champions, Carr was five up at the turn on a morning when the American took time to find his putting touch. Only one to the good at lunch but back to three ahead after the 27th, Carr made light of an extraordinary piece of bad luck at the 29th. As he trailed his putter behind him, someone in the crowd inadvertently stood on it, snapping the shaft. Two seasons before, Carr had regularly putted with a three-iron and it was not without some confidence that he turned to that club again in the crisis. Having sunk six-footers at both the 29th and 31st, he holed a seven-footer for the winning half at the 35th. 'In the fighting mood he was in against Coe,' judged Moran, 'he could have putted with a shillelah.'

Reid Jack, playing third, was four under fours in defeating Billy Patton by 5 and 3. Patton, who failed by just one stroke to join Sam Snead and Ben Hogan in the play-off for the 1954 US Masters, was nothing if not entertaining to watch if the word 'watch' is permissible since, as Nicklaus had it, his backswing was so fast you could not actually see it!

Après Reid Jack, *le deluge*. With the exception of Shepperson – who, out in 43 and four down against a future US Masters champion in Tommy Aaron, annexed six of the next eight holes to win by 2 and 1 – Micklem's

At Muirfi

Great Britain
Matc
R.R. Jack/D.N. Sewell
J.B. Carr/G.B. Wolstenholme
M.F. Bonallack/A.H. Perowne
M.S.R. Lunt/H.E. Shepperson
Matc
J.B. Carr (2&1)
G.B. Wolstenholme
R.R. Jack (5&3)
D.N. Sewell
A.E. Shepperson (2&1)
M.F. Bonallack
M.S.R. Lunt
W.D. Smith
Grand Aggrega

At Sea

USA
Matc
J. Nicklaus and D.R. Beman (6&5)
C.R. Coe and D. Cherry (1 hole)
W. Hyndman/R. Gardner (4&3)
R. Cochran/E. Andrews (4&3)

USA
Matc
D.R. Beman (3&2)
C.R. Coe (5&4)
F. Taylor (3&2)
W. Hyndman (7&6)
J. Nicklaus (6&4)
C. Smith
R. Gardner (1 hole)
D. Cherry (5&4)
Grand Aggreg

men foundered all down the line.

Wolstenholme succumbed to Ward by 9 and 8: so much for form in the phoney war. Bonallack, Lunt and Smith lost the last three singles, with Smith losing at the fourteenth to Nicklaus. 'From the beginning,' Nicklaus was to write ten years later, 'I liked Muirfield very much. I think we all did. While it has the intrinsic qualities of a British seaside links – fairways that tumble every which way, magnificent low-cropped turf, deep bunkers, and hard, unwatered greens – it is a frank and open course.'

The result was 9–3, the post-mortem underscoring again and again the superiority of the American work on the greens. Much of putting, though, is about expectation of success and, despite the heady morale of the practice days, the habit of defeat was soon taking its familiar toll.

The 1959 instalment of the biennial contest ended with both sides affirming that the Walker Cup must continue, the American captain, Charles Coe, assuring his hosts afresh that 'it would cause the greatest disappointment in the United States if it were discontinued. In the amateur game, it is reckoned the highlight of our year.'

However, as Frank Hannigan of the USGA said in the programme for the 1979 match, the American press were not greatly interested. 'Its attention,' wrote Hannigan, 'is now centred on athletic events in which one of two factors must be present: the best players must be so rich that they can barely tolerate the bother of playing; or there must be a considerable potential for the manifestation of hatred – preferably among players on the same side.' Sex, he added, was also a favourite subject of the sporting press and there had been a bitter suggestion that, for future Walker Cups on American soil, the USGA should 'confect a major sex scandal'. He did not say whether the idea was to have a member of the USGA directly involved or whether, if one were to be, the chap who drew the shortest straw was to be considered the winner or the loser. But his point, though lightly made, was taken.

However, it was not just America's Fourth Estate whose attitude had been called into question. The Muirfield Walker Cup coincided with the NCAA, the major collegiate event in the United States. The US Amateur champion, John Cook, who was to come so close to winning the 1992 Open at Muirfield, Gary Hallberg and the much publicised Bobby Clampett were among those who were, consequently, unavailable. The fact that they were on college golf scholarships had left them in an invidious position. Declared Hallberg: 'I picked the NCAA because of my school, my scholarship, the golf and the academics.'

One other part of the build-up was of especial interest to the Honourable Company members to whom foursomes golf is a way of life. Rodney Foster, the Great Britain and Ireland captain and a veteran of five Walker Cups himself, had practised no foursomes as such, in line with his belief that the thing that mattered was to pair players 'who enjoy each other'. But he did concede that he would not want to yoke a player with a long and slow swing to one whose swing was short and quick lest each disurb the other's rhythm. One had a notion that Honourable Company members were going to be studying their partners in their next Dinner Match in a new light, worried lest their own syrupy rhythm be imperilled.

d 16 May 1959

RSOMES

USA	Matches
Ward/F.M. Taylor (1 hole)	1
yndman/T.D. Aaron (1 hole)	1
Coe/W.J. Patton (9&8)	1
Nicklaus/H.W. Wettlaufer	1
)	4

LES

	Matches
Coe	0
arvie Ward (9&8)	1
Patton	0
yndman (4&3)	1
Aaron	0
Beman (2 holes)	1
. Wettlaufer (6&5)	1
Nicklaus (5&4)	1
	5

, 9; Great Britain, 3

2 September, 1961

RSOMES

Great Britain	Matches
lker/B.H.G. Chapman	0
Blair/M.J. Christmas	0
arr/G. Huddy	0
Bonallack/R.D.B.M. Shade	0
	0

LES

Great Britain	Matches
Bonallack	0
R. Lunt	0
lker	0
. Frame	0
arr	0
Christmas (3&2)	1
B. M. Shade	0
Blair	0
	1

, 11; Great Britain, 1

The US captain, Dick Siderowf, had been warning his men how a real wind could so change the course, 'about the only thing you'd still recognise would be the clubhouse.' On the last day of reconnaissance, to his undisguised satisfaction, there was enough venom in the elements to give the nine members of his ten-strong team, who were new to golf in Britain, some practical experience. The average age of his side was just 24. Yet Siderowf was sure that his players were already so steeped in golf they could mostly sort out any last-minute technical problems for themselves.

Foster, in contrast, emphasised the value to the British of having so respected a teacher as John Jacobs on hand in an advisory capacity. England's John Davies, who had been plagued for some time by a pesky hook, was the grateful recipient 'of one of the most fantastic lessons of my life'. Jacobs altered his left-hand grip to show a less bristling array of knuckle and persuaded him to extend his left thumb and push his hands forward a little. After which, with his stance which had got a little shut also corrected, he was invited to hit as hard as he could. But it was late to be making four changes.

The home anchor-man was to be Jimmy Buckley of Wales even though, because of a troublesome sciatic nerve, he had played no tournament golf all season other than one monthly medal. 'Clear and clip' was the slogan under which Jacobs had the Welshman working, by which he meant the co-ordination of the clearing of the left hip with a very definite hit. Jacobs, who had undoubtedly played no small part in the famous win at St Andrews eight years earlier, had wrought a transformation in both players but how deep did it go?

On the morning of the match, the *Scotsman* ran an article suggesting that the Americans might well be looking askance at so much last-minute tinkering with swings in the British camp: 'It is one thing to hit the ball on the flat of a practice ground, another to do so out on the course, under fire with possibly an uneven stance and bunkers snapping like crocodiles at any stray shot which escapes the jungle.' Suffice to say that Davies, out in 46, lost to Clarke by 8 and 7; Buckley to Scott Hoch – Nick Faldo's play-off victim in the 1989 US Masters – by 9 and 7. Those who, the day before, had been quoting the old professional adage, 'If you havn't brought it with you, you won't find it here', merely nodded.

Even though they had lost the afternoon singles 4½-3½, the home team finished the opening day only a point behind because they had shared the foursomes, Foster's tail-gunners having repaid his hunch. He had bracketed Allan Brodie with Iain Carslaw to give Britain, in the language admittedly more of a Blackpool postcard than of Agincourt, 'a better back end'.

The eventual margin – US 15½ points, Great Britain and Ireland 8½ – was a painful reminder that it is not just cricket teams which collapse. Still only a point to the bad after the morning foursomes, Foster's men, at four o'clock, were up in five of the eight singles, square in two and down in only one. A short and grisly hour later, the foe, having already taken the British flagship in the shape of Peter McEvoy, led in six of the other seven matches. This was always going to be a bad match to lose because the Americans were without at least four first-choice players but the manner of the capitulation made it that much more unpalatable. As both captains agreed,

At Mui

FIRST

Great Britain

M

P. McEvoy/B. Marchbank
G. Godwin/I.C. Hutcheon (2 hole
G. Brand/M.J. Kelley
Allan Brodie/I. Carslaw (2&1)

P. McEvoy (halved)
J.C. Davies
I.C. Hutcheon
J. Buckley
B. Marchbank (1 hole)
G. Godwin (3&2)
M.J. Kelley (3&2)
Allan Brodie

First day's aggr

SECOND

Great Britain

Ma

G. Godwin/G. Brand
P. McEvoy/B. Marchbank (2&1)
M.J. Kelley/I.C. Hutcheon (halve
I. Carslaw/Allan Brodie (halved)

P. McEvoy
G. Brand
G. Godwin
C. Hutcheon
Allan Brodie (3&2)
M.J. Kelley
B. Marchbank
I. Carslaw
—

Second day's aggr

Grand Match aggr

and 31 May 1979

)URSOMES

USA	Matches
Ioch/J. Sigel (1 hole)	1
West/H. Sutton	0
Fischesser/J. Holtgrieve (1 hole)	1
Moody/M. Gove	0
	—
	2

NGLES

igel (halved)	½
Clarke (8&7)	1
Ioltgrieve (6&4)	1
Ioch (9&7)	1
Peck	0
Moody	0
Fischesser	0
Gove (3&2)	1
	—
	4½

eat Britain 5½; USA 6½

)URSOMES

USA	Matches
Ioch/J. Sigel (4&3)	1
Fischesser/J. Holtgrieve	0
West/H. Sutton (halved)	½
Clarke/M. Peck (halved)	½
	—
	2

NGLES

Ioch (3&1)	1
Clarke (2&1)	1
Gove (3&2)	1
Peck (2&1)	1
West	0
Moody (3&2)	1
Sutton (3&1)	1
igel (2&1)	1
	7

eat Britain 3; USA 9

eat Britain 8½; USA 15½

Hoch's defeat of McEvoy 'had provided a momentum which had spread down the order'. Alone of either side, Hoch had taken four points out of four and that Scottish grandmother of his who had left Galashiels as a lass of 15 had a lot to answer for.

Afterwards, Siderowf told of how comments on BBC television by Alex Hay, to the effect that the college boys obviously lacked the experience to cope with the pressure, had incensed his team, 'really fired them up!'. No, he had never seen Hay play, but 'any of our team, including me, would be only too happy to give him three up and take him on.' The hazards of commentating – because Hay was adamant that he had said no such thing.

Not that commentating does not have its more rewarding moments. Clarke – one up partnering Michael Peck on the second morning versus Brodie and Carslaw – crossed himself before descending into the abyss of the cross-bunkers at the seventeenth. But thrice they left their ball in the sand.

'You can't,' said Peter Alliss, sadly, 'trust anyone these days . . .'

Curtis Cups

MARGARET and Harriot Curtis, who would meet in the final of the 1907 US Women's Amateur championship, had been so captivated by the impromptu and informal match which preceded the British Women's championship of 1905, that they nurtured dreams of an official fixture.

It began in 1932, with the legendary Joyce Wethered as official captain, but it was not until 20 years later that the British side would win. This milestone in the history of the women's game occurred at Muirfield, where, in a scenario to suggest that the women must have had a somewhat uncomfortable week, the members of the Honourable Company allowed them into the clubhouse on the eve of the match but not thereafter.

The elements were no less rudely masculine, with the wind cold and blustery. The links, too, seemed hostile to the Americans. Hostile and totally alien . . . Like so many lunar explorers, the visitors were stunned at the sight of Muirfield's lone tree, photographing its gnarled branches from all angles. They were foxed, too, by the putting surfaces. 'The fast subtle greens,' wrote Pat Ward Thomas, 'did not suit the Americans and only Miss Kirby was able to save herself by putting.'

On a day when the Americans donned balaclavas and ear-muffs against the midsummer cold, Great Britain and Ireland captured the foursomes by the odd match. Jean Donald and Elizabeth Price won the top game; Jessie Valentine and Frances Stephens lost the second; and Philomena Garvey and Moira Paterson beat Pat O'Sullivan and Polly Riley in the decider to have the home team bedding down at Greywalls leading 2–1. The next morning – a day of 12 singles played over 36 holes – began in glorious vein for Britain. By midday, four players were ahead, while Frances Stephens had recovered from three down to square. But let Bernard Darwin paint the ugly scene which developed over tea: 'I cannot hope to convey to those who were not there how great were the agonies to be suffered. The thought of writing that stuff yet again with insincere congratulations to the conquerors was really unbearable, just as was the strain of watching, the apparent tragedy developing with appalling slowness.' Hardest to bear was the demise of the local player, Jean Anderson. Five up with 11 to play, Gullane's favourite daughter lost at the 36th hole to Dorothy Kirby.

But even as Anderson succumbed, so Elizabeth Price was getting the better of her nerve-wracked clash with Grace de Moss. One up coming to the thirteenth and still one up with five to play, Price pulled her drive at the fourteenth into a bunker while de Moss hit her ball straight down the fairway. Price came out well, only for her ball to flop into sand for a second time. 'Only a socket can save us now,' said a well-known amateur who was standing beside the green as de Moss stood to her third, a seemingly straightforward pitch.

'No sooner were the words out of his mouth,' wrote Tom Scott, a renowned editor of the old *Golf Illustrated*, 'than Miss de Moss executed a socket which will be for all time immortal. The ball flew off the club at right angles into long rough. She had one hurried and ineffectual stab at the ball in the deep grass before perpetrating the father and mother of all sockets, one which flew off at an even greater angle than the first one. The crowd looked on in silent sympathy. Miss de Moss had now played five against our girl's four and had still to reach the green. This she did with her next shot, but Miss Price was calm and won the hole with ease. So ended one of the most dramatic holes ever played in international golf.'

Two up with four to play instead of all square, Price, a diabetic whose caddie would recognise before she did herself that she was in need of a quick fix of glucose, won the fifteenth to draw three ahead, thereby ensuring that Britain could not lose the match.

At the sixteenth, a downwind par 3, Price, to use the words of Jeanne Bisgood, a team-mate, 'swung her iron as smoothly as if playing a friendly game at Hankley Common.' Her ball finished above the hole and she duly laid her long, downhill putt stone dead to complete the long-awaited British win.

If the British had had their turn of glory in the 1950s, the '60s and '70s belonged to the Americans – exclusively as it turned out. Nor did things improve until, in 1984, the match returned to Muirfield.

The vibes were not good on the eve of the match, for the LGU's selectors had arrived at Muirfield with a British team which included not a single Scot – and that though the credentials of Jane Connachan and Gillian Stewart outstripped those of at least half the players who were in the side. In his time the Minister for Sport, Sir Hector Munro, who follows women's golf with much interest and who knows a thing or two about picking teams, having served on the Scottish Rugby Union's selection committee, was moved to describe the decision as disgraceful.

As for Laura Davies, who was destined to win the British and US Opens, and earn the tag of the longest hitter the distaff side of the game had known, she did not hesitate to say that she had been one of the beneficaries of the somewhat erratic selection process: 'I'm lucky,' said she, 'but I'm going to make the most of my good luck.'

At Muirfi

Great Britain & Irel
J Donald & E Price (3 & 2)
F Stephens & Mrs G Valentine
M Paterson & P Garvey (2 & 1)
Jean Donald
Frances Stephens (2 & 1)
Moira Paterson
Jeanne Bisgood (6 & 5)
Philomena Garvey
Elizabeth Price (3 & 2)

Aggregate: Great Britai

At Muirfi

FIRST D

Great Britain & Irel
C Waite and B New (2 holes)
J Thornhill and P Grice
M McKenna and L Davies

Great Britain & Irel
J Thornhill
C Watte
C Hourhane
V Thomas (2 holes)
P Grice (2 holes)
B New

SECOND D

Great Britain & Irel
C Waite and B New
J Thornhill and P Grice (2 and 1)
V Thomas and C Hourihane

Great Britain & Irel
J Thornhill
L Davies (1 hole)
C Waite (5 and 4)
P Grice
B New
C Hounhane (2 and 1)

Aggregate: Great Britain

2

JRSOMES	
ted States	
irby & G DeMoss	0
oran & M Lindsay (6 & 4)	1
ley & P O'Sullivan	0

GLES	
othy Kirby (1 up)	1
jorie Lindsay	0
y Riley (6 & 4)	1
Murray	0
re Doran (3 & 2)	1
ce DeMoss	0

nd 5; United States 4

and 9th June, 1984

JRSOMES	
ted States	
cillo and A Sander	0
nith and J Rosenthal	½
Vidman and H Farr (1 hole)	1
	1½

GLES	
ted States	
cillo	½
ammel (4 and 2)	1
senthal (3 and 1)	1
Iowe	0
ander	0
Vidman (4 and 3)	1
	3½

JRSOMES	
ted States	
nith and J Rosenthal (3 and 1)	1
Vidman and H Farr	0
Iowe and P Hammel	½
	1½

GLES	
ted States	
cillo (3 and 2)	1
ander	0
nith	0
Iowe (2 holes)	1
arr (6 and 5)	1
ammel	0
	3

and 8½; United States 9½

Diane Bailey, who would go on to captain the winning sides of 1986 and 1988, had been indoctrinating her players for months with the notion that they were undoubtedly good enough to beat America's latest offering – a team which took in six newcomers and a couple of players very much in the evening of their careers.

Four thousand turned out to watch a first day's play which saw the Americans, after the three morning foursomes and six singles which make up the modern format, leading by the odd point in nine. Just like that American side of 1952, the visitors were in awe of Muirfield, the course. They had by the mid-1980s become well used to greens at least as fast as those the Honourable Company had to offer but, by nightfall on the first day, Tish Preuss, the American non-playing captain, was expressing pained surprise that her players had not holed out better.

The second morning's foursomes were shared which meant that the contest was still very much alive going into the last afternoon's singles. The crowd was double the first day's figure and the excitement reached fever pitch.

In the end, the home side were just one putt away – a Penny Grice four-footer – from halving the contest. Not, mind you, that anyone would attach any blame to the Yorkshire player, for her two and a half points out of four represented the top tally in the British camp. Claire Waite, Claire Hourihane and Laura Davies were the British winners on the last afternoon, with Davies describing her win over Anne Sander as the highlight of her amateur career. What finished Sander was the way in which she had to take a wood for her second to the last green where the long-hitting Davies needed but a trifling eight-iron.

Although at Muirfield, the LGU were never allowed to forget the error of their ways in having none of the natives in the side, the comments were mostly more mischievous than malicious. There was, for example, that choice moment detonated by an LGU announcement about there being evening entertainment in the shape of Scottish country dancing. Tongue-in-cheek, a lady of the Fourth Estate inquired innocently of the LGU chairman if perchance any Scots had made the Scottish dancing team . . .

Ryder Cup 1973

WHEN it comes to the Ryder Cup, few, if any, have had a greater stomach for the fight than Bernard Gallacher, non-playing captain in 1991 and 1993. But not at Muirfield on the second day of a 1973 instalment which remains to this day historic as the only occasion on which the foremost international contest in the professional firmament has been staged in Scotland.

The previous evening, Gallacher had bedded down having collected, in tandem with his compatriot, Brian Barnes, two points out of two with Great Britain and Ireland – as, for the first time, the team were officially labelled – on fire and ahead 5½–2½. In the small hours of the night he awoke, sick and dizzy, cold yet sweating. Around 4.30 a.m., his wife, Lesley, summoned medical help. Food poisoning was confirmed. These things can happen but usually in foreign fields, many a sportsman having been reared on the story of Alf Gover running in to bowl in India – only, with a look of gathering concentration and consternation, to continue on past umpire and batsman and up the pavilion steps. But as a native of Scotland, the embattled Gallacher was among familiar dishes – not like America's Julius Boros who, coming face to face with a haggis for the first time in the 1966 Open at Muirfield, waved it away in some alarm, protesting that, on 144 at the halfway stage, 'I'm not out of it yet!'

Folklore would have you believe that Hobbs had lost his Sutcliffe and one of the great opening partnerships had been untimely rent asunder. In fact, before Hunt named them to open the batting at Muirfield, Gallacher and Barnes had never previously partnered each other. None the less, it would have been difficult to exaggerate the severity of the blow to home hopes. As the only players from either side to emerge from that unforgettable first day with two full points, the Scots had got Great Britain and Ireland off to a resounding start by triumphing on the home green in their morning foursomes versus Lee Trevino and Billy Casper who, between them, had won six Opens and a US Masters. Then, in the afternoon four-balls, they had blithely added two more Masters champions to their bag in Gay Brewer and Tommy Aaron. What was more, they had done so by the record margin, for a British coupling in the four-balls, of 5 and 4.

Barnes had not figured in the foursomes in either of his previous Ryder Cups – choosing, in his own incorrigible way, that format's spiritual home among the Honourable Company of Edinburgh Golfers to denounce it as 'the lousiest form of golf imaginable!'. Nevertheless, if he had to play what he considered a mongrel version of the game, let it be with 'wee Bernard'. They knew each other well while Gallacher's adhesive temperament and lethal short game duly proved complementary to Barnes's very different approach and, in those days, booming length.

When Gallacher and Barnes shook hands with Brewer and Aaron on the fourteenth green, at which point they were seven under par, Gallacher's record in the Ryder Cup read: played 11, won seven, lost three and halved one. Tremendous going viewed against the results of yesteryear. It did not need too much imagination to picture how Hunt had felt when, at 6 a.m., Gallacher, who had been up since 2 a.m. intermittently vomiting, phoned him with the news that he had been laid low by, as it were, the enemy within. The first Peter Butler knew of his call to arms was a knock on his bedroom door shortly before 7 a.m. After a hasty rather than hearty breakfast, he was on the tee at 8.30 a.m. He and Barnes were round in the foursomes in a one-under-par 70, succumbing to Jack Nicklaus and the reigning Open champion, Tom Weiskopf. At the 180-yard sixteenth, Butler inserted his three-iron for a hole-in-one – the one shot which the Scots in the gallery had reluctantly to concede Gallacher might have been pushed to play all that much better.

Despite that defeat at the head of the column, Hunt's troops still led after the morning foursomes by three clear points as they had overnight. Now, at an emergency team conference, the Americans decided to throw in all their heaviest armour. The intention had been to rest Arnold Palmer, in order that he would be fit to play twice in the singles of the last day. How-

At Muir

FIRST I

Great Britain and Ir

B.W. Barnes/B.J. Gallacher (1 hole
C. O'Connor/N.C. Coles (3&2)
A. Jacklin/P.A. Oosterhuis (halved
M.E. Bembridge/E. Polland

B.W. Barnes/B.J. Gallacher (5&4)
M.E. Bembridge/B.G.C. Huggett (3&I)
A. Jacklin/P.A. Oosterhuis (3&1)
C. O'Connor/N.C. Coles

First-Day Totals – Great B

SECOND I

B.W. Barnes/P.J. Butler
P.A. Oosterhuis/A. Jacklin (2 hole
M.E. Bembridge/B.G.C. Huggett (5&4)
N.C. Coles/C. O'Connor

B.W. Barnes/P.J. Butler
A. Jacklin/P. Oosterhuis
C. Clark/E. Polland
M.E. Bembridge/B.G.C. Huggett (halved)

Second-Day Totals – Great Br

THIRD I

B.W. Barnes
B.J. Gallacher
P.J. Butler
A. Jacklin (3&1)
N.C. Coles (halved)
C. O'Connor
M.E. Bembridge (halved)
P.A. Oosterhuis (halved)

B.G.C. Huggett (4&2)
B.W. Barnes
B.J. Gallacher
A. Jacklin
N.C. Coles
C. O'Connor (halved)
M.E. Bembridge
P.A. Oosterhuis (4&2)

Singles Totals – Great B
Grand Aggregates – Great Br
Non-playing Captains – B.J. H

, 21 and 22 September 1973

)URSOMES

ɜA

Trevino/W.J. Casper	0
Weiskopf/J.C. Snead	0
Rodriguez/L. Graham (halved)	0
V. Nicklaus/A. Palmer (6&5)	1

)UR-BALLS

Aaron/G. Brewer	0
Palmer/J.W. Nicklaus	0
W/eiskopf/W.J. Casper	0
Trevino/H. Blancas (2&1)	1

d Ireland, 5; USA, 2 (1 halved)

)URSOMES

V. Nicklaus/T. Weiskopf (1 hole)	1
Palmer/D. Hill	0
Rodriguez/L. Graham	0
Trevino/W.J. Casper (2&1)	1

)UR-BALLS

:. Snead/A. Palmer (2 holes)	1
Brewer/W.J. Casper (3&2)	1
V. Nicklaus/T. Weiskopf (3&2)	1
Trevino/H. Blancas (halved)	0

d Ireland, 2; USA, 5 (1 halved)

NGLES

ɔrning

J. Casper (2&1)	1
Weiskopf (3&1)	1
Blancas (5&4)	1
Aaron	0
Brewer (halved)	0
:. Snead (1 hole)	1
V. Nicklaus (halved)	0
Trevino (halved)	0

ternoon

Blancas	0
:. Snead (3&1)	1
Brewer (6&5)	1
J. Casper (2&1)	1
Trevino (6&5)	1
Weiskopf (halved)	0
V. Nicklaus (2 holes)	1
Palmer	0

d Ireland, 3; USA, 9 (4 halved)
d Ireland, 10; USA, 16 (6 halved)
reat Britain and Ireland; J. Burke, USA

ever, Burke and his men agreed that they were already so far behind that nothing less than their optimum octet would do: that it had become a case of now or never.

'Lee told me he took one look, picked his spot on the green – and didn't dare look again until the ball was in the hole.' Thus spoke Jackie Burke, the American captain, of the three-foot putt which Trevino had holed on the last green of the last game. It halved the hole and his match and thereby completed the American counter-attack, sending the twentieth Ryder Cup into the last day with the score agonisingly poised at eight points apiece.

Hunt predictably fielded Peter Oosterhuis as his anchor man but controversially 'hid' Tony Jacklin at No. 4. Jacklin responded by beating Aaron but, by then, the first three singles had been lost and thereafter it was always America's Cup. In picking the team, the three selectors – Hunt as captain, Oosterhuis as leader in the Order of Merit, and Dai Rees, captain of the winning team in 1957 – had simply continued down the order in respect of the four places they had at their discretion. Thus, their nominations were John Garner, Eddie Polland, Clive Clark and Brian Huggett who had lain, respectively, ninth, tenth, eleventh and twelfth in the Ryder Cup table.

Much was made of the length of the tail. Maybe too much. Hunt had got nary a point from the cumulative six appearances of Butler, Polland, Clark and Garner but, on the other hand, Burke, from the collective seven of Aaron, Dave Hill, Chi Chi Rodriguez and Lou Graham, garnered just the halved match Graham and Rodriguez had wrested from Jacklin and Oosterhuis in the opening series of foursomes.

A doggedly calm and unobtrusively conscientious captain in the wake of the abrasive but dynamic Eric Brown, Hunt wound up with one thing in common with that highly combustible Ryder Cup hero – to wit, that one of the sticks with which some critics sought to beat him was the pencil-slim Garner. Both at St Louis and at Muirfield, Garner was widely regarded as the captain's choice but, where Brown had at least given him one four-ball, Hunt never took him out of the wrapper.

Nothing could be more indicative of the vastly different circumstances of a Ryder Cup of today than that Jackie Burke, the American captain, had gone into the match having never seen nine of the home team play. No, not even on television! Burke, intelligent, humorous and articulate, admitted freely that, having been the American captain when the cup was lost at Lindrick in 1957, the strain had been made all the worse for him by the fact that, by the close of play on the first day, he had been face to face with a ghoulish double which would have gone with him all his days: 'But, even aside from that, American golfers never take representing their country lightly even if politicians do!'

The cold, as much as a links which was relatively hard and fast, had troubled the visitors. In truth, on the practice days, it had been so chilly that when Palmer drove into the tented village and set off in pursuit of his ball, Jack Nicklaus had beseeched him to pick up a couple of thick woollen sweaters while he was about it!

The Ryder Cup was, of course, played with the 1.68 ball – the concensus of opinion among the Americans being that its adoption on this side of the Atlantic had already brought a discernible improvement, especially in the realms of pitching and chipping. But Burke had marvelled all through at the length some of his men hit the ball and, in victory, he reiterated his conviction that, all other things being equal, 'distance will eventually get you!'.

As a spectator much more than as a player, Hunt had been struck by the size, strength and stamina of golfers hardened by the remorseless grind of the American tour by comparison with what was then available to the Great Britain and Ireland players. He cited a remark Jack Nicklaus had made to him: namely, that while Oosterhuis and Barnes were the only two really strapping fellows in the home side, professional golf in America in the late 1960s and early '70s had been attracting sundry large and husky young men from other sports. One obvious example was, of course, Jesse Snead who, for all his lineage, was once addicted to baseball.

There had, though, never been enough rain to leave the shorter hitters at an overwhelming disadvantage. Indeed, two of the British team's smallest men, Brian Huggett and Maurice Bembridge, had taken a large share of the battle honours, Huggett demolishing Homero Blancas with six successive threes from the eleventh. As for the cheerful and cherubic Bembridge, he spent most of the Ryder Cup in the eye of the storm in that he drew Nicklaus in four out of his six matches. Which made all the more acceptable his tally of two wins and two halved matches. 'Maurice played very well this afternoon,' a Scottish scribe observed to Nicklaus, on the evening of the third day. 'I played very well today,' retorted Nicklaus, with mock indignation, his way of generously stressing how pressed he had been to get the better of the little Englishman.

Top: scars left by the spectator stands after their removal and, above, one of the many stands spread around the course for an Open championship

It was to such as Bembridge and Oosterhuis that Hunt pointed in support of his rueful post-match conclusion that only those who toured the world for much of the year, competing week after week, had the toughness and stamina to stand up to the Americans through possibly six gruelling matches in the space of only three days. It was a judgment which was to look all the better once the Great Britain and Ireland team had been translated into Europe and the Americans found themselves tangling with players who were every bit as tournament-hardened as they were.

Bernard Gallacher had learned to pace himself but he, too, had done his share of travelling. In the morning singles, he had hung on tenaciously to Weiskopf before losing by 3 and 1 but had little left to offer when confronted by Brewer in the afternoon. Small wonder perhaps, since not only had he spent the whole of the previous day sick in bed but he had had nothing more than a plate of soup since falling ill.

Oosterhuis and Jacklin had gone into the match as Britain's so-called 'Big Two' and, on the afternoon of the first day, had lived up to that billing with a vengeance. They were out in 28 in a stunning four-ball of 17 birdies to close out Weiskopf and Casper on the penultimate green, a rather bashful par creeping in at the eighth in a front nine otherwise comprising four birdies from Oosterhuis and four from Jacklin.

The news that his father had been in a car crash was kept from Jacklin but he heard about it through a chance comment in the clubhouse before he teed off against Casper on the last afternoon. In fact, he played by no means badly against Casper, but that bland killer just kept rolling putt after putt right through his heart.

A putter like Nicklaus, whose stroke has something of a shove in it, will tell you that he greatly prefers fast greens. Yet, intriguingly, Burke owned to a theory that, on greens as quick and dangerous as were those of Muirfield, what was needed, ideally, was a player whose putting stroke put some check on the ball: 'Both Billy Casper and Gay Brewer have putted beautifully in this Ryder Cup and they both squeeze the ball a little.'

Two years before at St Louis, Oosterhuis had wanted, got and beaten Palmer, and at Muirfield he had again defeated that living legend. Having halved with Trevino in the concluding singles, he sped south on the first stage of the journey to America to pre-qualify for the school which would decide whether he were good enough for the US circuit!

Trevino had promised – or should it be threatened – 'to kiss the asses of the American team' if he failed to defeat Oosterhuis. Understandably perhaps, they waived their claim but it is said that there is in existence a photograph of the US side with their trousers down to their knees waiting for a not so Merry Mex to pay his dues. A unique picture in its way, for one doubts if you could find one of, say, the Great Triumvirate in similar *déshabillé*.

THE PROBLEMS OF HOSTING AN OPEN

After the 1972 Open championship, the Honourable Company held a referendum among the members. The point at issue was whether they wished to continue to have the Open championship at Muirfield with all the upheaval which that nowadays entails. Predictably, the answer was in the affirmative and not by any means only because the facility fee given by the R & A to a club staging the Open is now very substantial.

Of course, the referendum did not alter the fact that not all the members view forthcoming Opens with unabridged enthusiasm. The skeletal stands are in place weeks before, causing one purplingly apoplectic colonel to complain that it was 'like playing golf in and out a damned shipyard!'

Colonel T.R. Broughton, Captain 1965-67 (left), speaking to members of the Honourable Company

The question now arises whether we still want to be considered for future Opens. The committee are firmly of the opinion that any inconvenience caused to members and the hard work which it entails is more than compensated by the financial gains and the prestige it brings to the club. If Muirfield ceased to be a championship course, the number of visitors, especially from overseas, would drop; Gullane would suffer financially as well; members would lose the opportunity of seeing the world stars play on their own course at little cost and under reasonable conditions for spectating; and the green staff would lose a great deal of incentive in keeping the course in first-class condition.

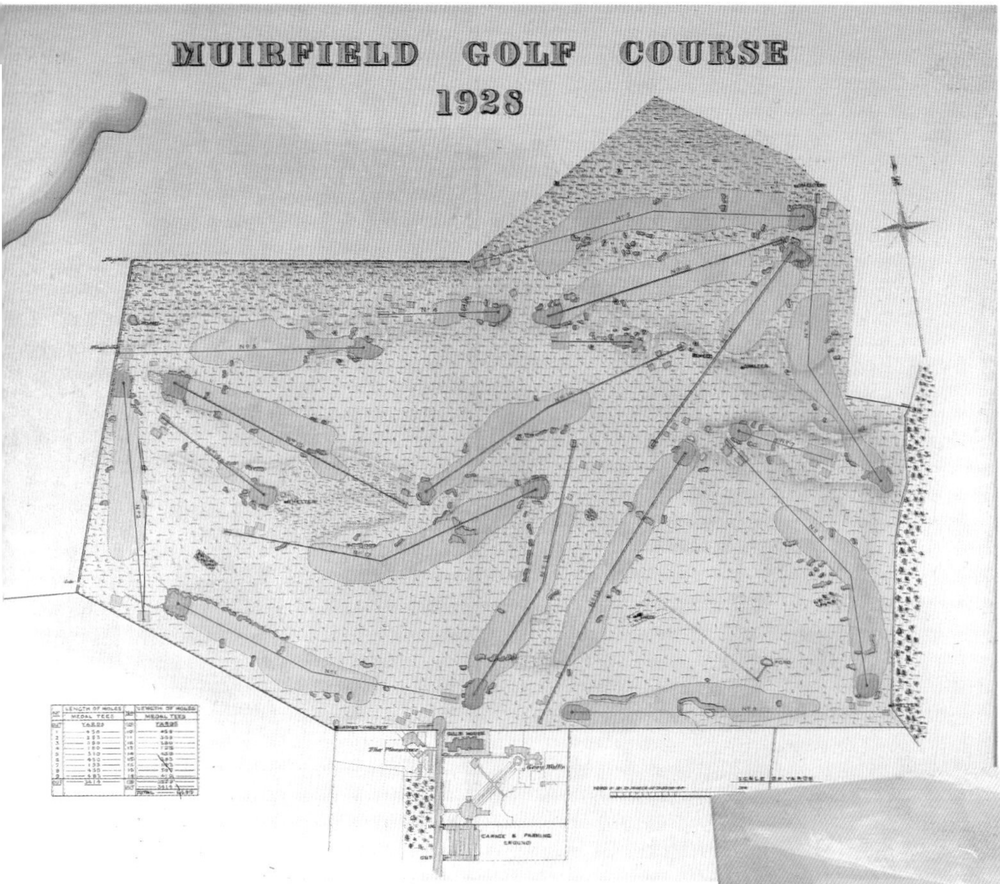

MUIRFIELD GOLF COURSE
1928

MUIRFIELD GOLF COURSE
1891

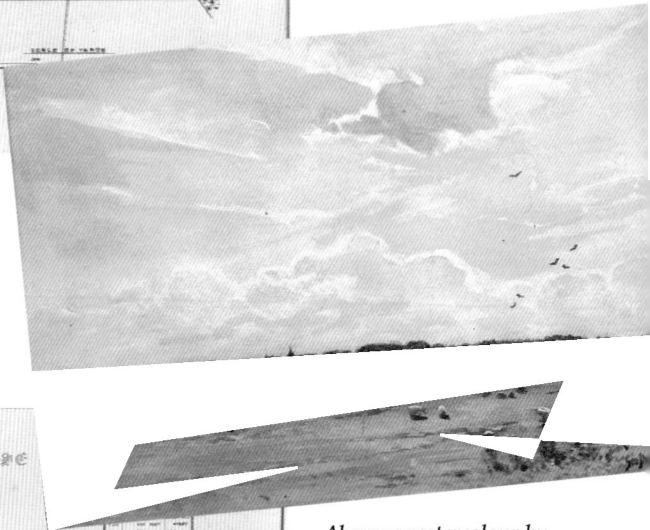

Above: a watercolour by George Straton Ferrier of Muirfield in 1893, looking from the links southwards towards the newly built clubhouse

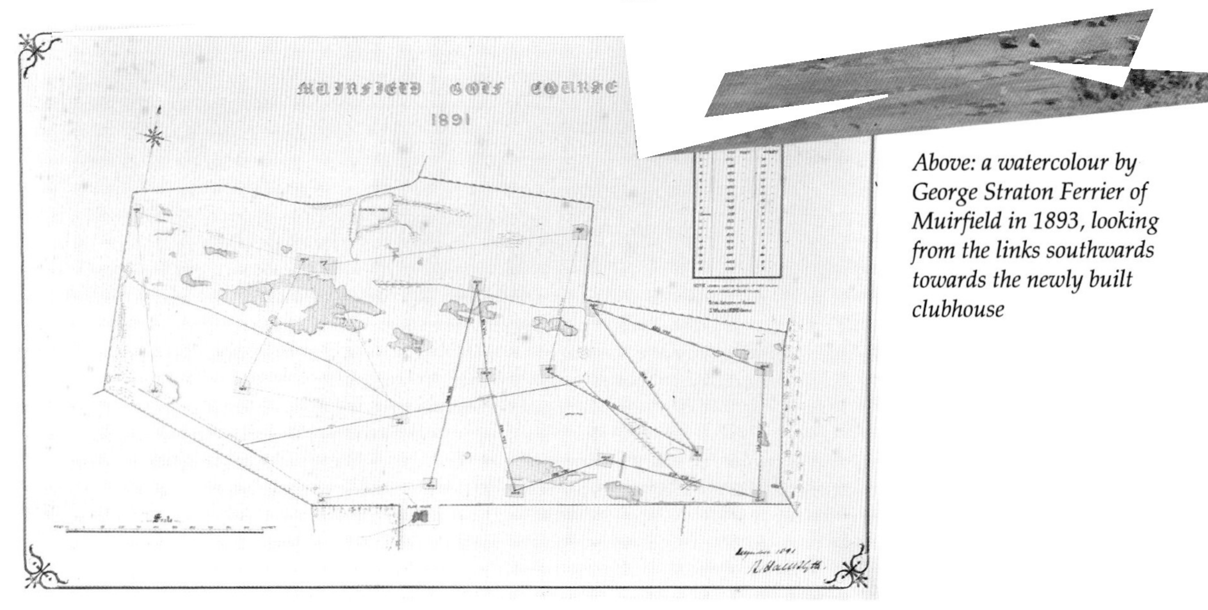

7 The Honourable Archivist– Archie Baird

IN the cartographical field, Archie Baird, the Honourable Company's archivist, will admit to what he modestly describes as one small claim to fame: the exposure of a fallacy in the history of golf course architecture which had given every indication of lingering in perpetuity. The fallacy in question? That Old Tom Morris, when concerned in the laying out of Muirfield, originated the concept of two nines with the tenth tee by the clubhouse as opposed to those so-called Stone Age links which tended to run straight out and straight back.

It was when he was arranging the various framed maps of Muirfield in chronological order preparatory to hanging them in the locker-room that Baird realised that the golfing historians were mistaken: 'It was not until 1928 that two nines as such finally evolved at Muirfield. In the beginning, there were eight holes running clockwise round the outside with the other ten more or less higgledy-piggledy within that outer rim.'

Three successive plans of the course at Muirfield – bottom left the original course of 1891 with, right, the 1920 layout, and, top left, the 1928 course, which remains substantially the same today, minus over 100 bunkers!

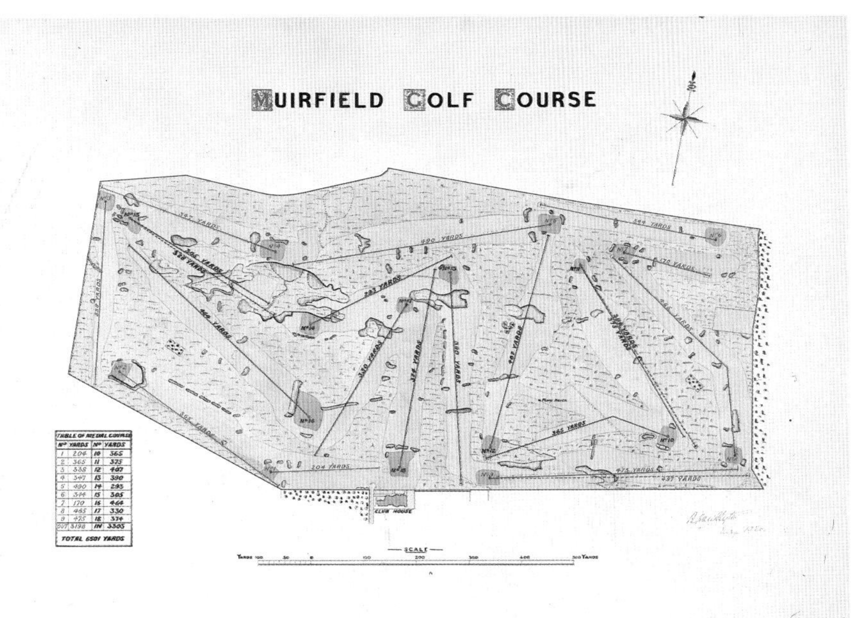

Archie Baird

Only Royal Birkdale on the current Open championship rota has a ninth hole which comes back to the clubhouse although it is, of course, a feature of golf course architecture which is becoming commonplace among the newer courses. 'It was,' points out Baird, 'a concept which, in itself, told you much about the difference between the American idea of golf and ours, especially in bygone days. Over here, most golfers would think in terms of a round in the morning, lunch and another round in the afternoon. In the US, partly because of the difference in the weather in many parts of the country, they would play a leisurely nine holes, very likely as a four-ball, have a meal and then saunter forth for the second nine.'

One of the display cases in the clubhouse created by Archie Baird. The portrait is of the 'Gigantic Biggar' of Thomas Mathison's 'heroi-comical poem in three cantos' The Goff *(1743), some lines of which are quoted below. Other items include the 1744 Silver Club presented by the City of Edinburgh, the first* printed *edition of the original rules (1744) and a printed copy of Mathison's poem*

'North from Edina on Fortha's sounding shore, Here Caledonian chiefs for health resort, confirm their sinews by the manly sport ...'

Baird was no stranger to America even in the days when he had only the mildest passing interest in the Royal and Ancient game. In 1939, at the outbreak of war, a man whom his grandfather had befriended suggested that Archie and his brother, Roger, come and stay with him. Initially based in California, Baird had studied for two years at an agricultural college in New Mexico when the US military began making overtures. The teenage Scot 'resisted their advances' and made for Canada where it was possible for him to enlist in the RAF as a prospective fighter-pilot.

Demobbed, he returned to Edinburgh, where he had been born into a family who, for three generations, had been veterinary surgeons. He studied at Skerries College, emerging with Higher English and Lower Spanish. This would not have been enough to gain entrance to the Royal Dick Veterinary College had it not been for a sympathetic principal. Willie Mitchell had known both the father and the grandfather and, in keeping with his profession, was prepared to back the bloodline. Both Archie and his brother repaid his faith, duly qualifying with Archie returning to the small animal practice which his mother had courageously run for many years.

He turned to golf as the ideal way to unwind after frequently working from eight in the morning until ten at night, six days a week, in what was in those days very much a labour of love. When he joined Gullane in 1954 – the club he was to captain in 1976–78 – there was no entrance fee and the annual subscription was a mere eight guineas.

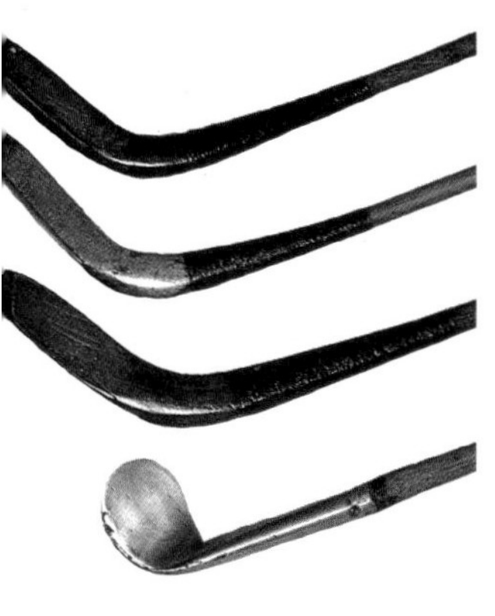

The heads of some early clubs in the Honourable Company's collection, including an iron club used for negotiating cart ruts on Leith Links

Discovering that none of his four children wished to continue in the family tradition, Baird found the work becoming a burden, much of his sense of purpose having gone. He placed an advertisement in a veterinary journal offering his practice for sale. Replies flooded in from all over the world. In fact, he sold out to a bidder who resided in the self-same city; an applicant who could safely be entrusted with the century-old practice. He was free to play golf to his heart's content. Even today, when his handicap is in double figures where once it was a stuffy seven, he averages over three hundred rounds a year. Still more to the point, he was also now at liberty to delve still more diligently into the East Lothian golfing inheritance.

Way back when he was first married, not long after his graduation, he and Sheila, a doctor, were living in an basement flat in York Place and attending assorted lane sales in search of suitable furniture at prices within their pocket. It was while doing so that he chanced upon a lot in a sale which was to change the course of his life. An old canvas golf bag from which peeped an array of long-nosed hickory-shafted clubs caught his eye. Removing the dust, he made out the inscription, 'W. Park, Musselburgh'. 'These,' he said to his wife, 'must have been made by your great-grandfather, Willie Park.' Tickled by the family link (Willie Park, the first of all the Open champions, had won the title four times) he coughed up five shillings for them. Once home, he got to thinking: 'They were made by a craftsman, they were signed and they were over a hundred years old. You didn't have to be a genius to work out that they were, almost certainly, worth an awful lot more than five bob!'

He started visiting the junk shops in Edinburgh and found them fertile soil for long-nosed clubs, rapidly acquiring Philp and McEwan models. His interest now thoroughly aroused, he began to look for books which would tell him more and found the city's antiquarian bookshops an even richer source than were the junk shops. 'Soon I had specimens of all the early clubmakers and every golf book on the subject published before 1900 which I could reasonably hope to acquire.'

In his RAF days, he and a chum, who was bound for the Edinburgh College of Art, had headed for Paris on an ancient motor-bike, an unholy machine which Baird had bought from a man of the cloth in Wales for £4.10d. They had £10 each in their wallets and all the tea and coffee they could cram into their haversacks. For a month Baird was dragged round the galleries of the French capital until, almost in spite of himself, he began to know something about pictures and enjoy them. It was to stand him in good stead in his second coming, as a golf collector. With the east coast of Scotland a veritable treasure trove, he picked up pictures for £50 which proved to have a market value of £10,000. Indeed, there was one on sale at £50 which Sheila got for £45 which shortly was worth £12,500 – the concession having been made on the strength of a slightly cracked frame!

Once, when Gullane was covered by snow for five long weeks and her hyperactive husband was getting more and more under her feet, Sheila suggested that he write a book. At that moment she was, one suspects, thinking wistfully of something along the lines and length of Gibbons' *Decline and Fall of the Roman Empire*; but even before the snow had melted, *Golf on Gullane Hill: a Celebration of 100 years of Gullane Golf Club* was ready for the printers.

Not long before the 1980 Open at Muirfield, having by then retired as a vet, Baird leased the old caddie-car shed at Gullane, did it up and founded the Heritage of Golf Museum. It was officially opened on the eve of the championship by that avid golf historian, the 1984 US Masters champion, Ben Crenshaw.

A portrait sketch by Charles Lees of one of the Honourable Company's captains (W.M. Goddard 1852). Note the grid lines drawn on the background for scaling up the picture – it was a preliminary sketch for 'The Grand Match'

Any vision he may have had of charging 50p a head to thousands of visitors over the year soon evaporated, and nowadays he opens only by appointment for genuine enthusiasts. Those who have not bought anything will often drop a donation into the box, but mostly he finances it by buying and selling clubs, many of which he has restored himself. How on earth had he learnt to do that? 'When you have performed a hysterectomy on a cat, putting a new grip on a golf club is no great feat!'

Unlike some other museums, he also does valuations and investigations for appraisal, and for those services he does charge a modest fee. But though he makes sure that it pays for itself, the museum is primarily – as he wryly acknowledges – his addiction writ large.

There are around two hundred members of the British Golf Collectors' Society. Baird himself, whose own harvest includes not only old clubs, books and pictures but balls, ceramics and silver, considers Yorkshire's Peter Crabtree pre-eminent as an authority on clubs relating to the featherball era. However, when clubs appertaining to the gutta-percha ball and the rubber-core are also taken into consideration, there is generally held to be none in these islands who knows more than Baird himself. He has the signal distinction of being one of the ten directors of the American Golf Collectors' Society. The other nine are all based in the US whereas his parish is the whole of Europe.

He believes, of course, that he has been uncommonly lucky to live in what was for long the cradle of the game for, though he knows such an opinion is highly contentious, he will defend to his last golfing relic the right of Leith Links and Musselburgh to take precedence over St Andrews for much of the feather-ball epoch. 'The reason why St Andrews overtook both in importance,' he will go on to explain, 'was that the golfers from the original Leith Links and Bruntsfield Links had, for a variety of reasons, to move on to pastures new. The golfers of St Andrews stayed put.

'Nor is it widely appreciated just how few golfers there were in the days of the feather-ball simply because it was so expensive that not all that many were prepared to meet the cost. Even at the close of the feather-ball's reign, there were only 15 courses all told and most of them were down the east coast.'

A member of Muirfield since 1977, he confesses that he did not realise just how rich the club was in golfing artefacts until Paddy Hanmer, on demitting office as the Honourable Company's secretary, embarked on a general clear-out. 'I couldn't believe what there was jumbled here, there and everywhere in the clubhouse. There were books stuffed away in old tea-boxes – books of which even the duplicates were worth a five-figure sum. Moreover, I spotted a beautiful bookcase, of Chippendale class, which Paddy and his predecessors had used as a glorified tip for their stationery and what have you. A bookcase which, when I got hold of a piece of string and measured it, proved a perfect fit between the fireplace and the left-hand wall in the smoking-room.

'That little library safely established, I was *persona grata* and urged to go ahead. The entrance to the clubhouse comprised an alcove to the right with a stand full of abandoned and disreputable umbrellas while, on the left-hand wall, there were coat-hooks most of which boasted some old, bedraggled head-cover. Not very inspiring. We cleaned it out and turned it all into the display you see today which does so much to give the visitor more than a whiff of the Honourable Company's unique history.'

Two of the club's most valuable golfing heirlooms, the John Taylor portrait and the Robert Maxwell, would have been prohibitively expensive to insure. Consequently, both were already on permanent loan to the National Portrait Gallery, though the copies still hang within the clubhouse portals.

'Mind you, if it were up to me,' exclaims Baird, who is assuredly not without his pragmatic side, 'I should sell the originals. With the proceeds, I would build a new clubhouse down at the corner of Archerfield where the club own some wonderful golfing terrain between the wood and the sea. Real Birkdale country in very little need of landscaping. I'd keep the present holes, of course, and perhaps the clubhouse as well but it could be a magnificent course, eminently capable of coping with the changing demands in terms of length, spectator facilities and so on of a modern Open championship. But whenever I mention it to the past captains, they always say the same thing – "We've got a perfectly good club as it is, Archie."

'And each time they say it, my retort is equally unvarying: "Dammit, if our ancestors had thought like that, we'd all still be scratching about on Leith Links!"'

8 Keeping Muirfield Green – Chris Whittle

FOR Chris Whittle, it was love at first sight. Ever since he had turned his back on his earlier venture into banking in favour of greenkeeping, he had lived for the day he would have charge of an Open championship course. As Muirfield unfolded before him on that afternoon in the summer of '88, he knew that he had found the promised land. The only snag was that he had still to get the job. He had sent in his application more in hope than expectation: 'It seemed a very long shot yet still worth the cost of an envelope and stamp.' But, having seen the links, he would, had the post gone to another man, have felt jilted.

He need not have worried. By the autumn, he was installed and, after three weeks in tandem with his predecessor, David Kirkaldy, he was in command. Furthermore, he was rejoicing in what was for the Honourable Company a brand new title, that of Course Manager. He and Kirkaldy – a former lieutenant of the legendary Logan – had hit it off at once but no two greenkeepers necessarily see a course with the same eye. The Honourable Company had been having terrible trouble with moss on the greens. To Whittle, that could not have been more indicative of scalping had it been not a red flag but a Red Indian arrow protruding fom the hole. He wanted a better head of grass although, as he explains, there is a delicate balance to be struck. The moss, prevalent in the area and thriving in the climatic conditions, had invaded the greens because the fertility level was too low. Yet, if the fertility level were allowed to get too high, it would just as damagingly change the type of grass.

Where the greens had previously been cut three times a week – on Mondays, Wednesdays and Fridays – Whittle has had them cut during the growing season on all seven days. That has been good for them and much to the benefit of those members who play most of their golf on a Sunday.

Not every early summer morning at Muirfield is as idyllic as this, but the greenstaff are out on the course whatever the weather

Whittle has a stimpmeter, the latter-day device for measuring the speed of the putting surfaces. He has had the practice putting-green – which, he stresses, is no different from the greens on the links – rolling at 11½ feet, but the pace he deems appropriate to Muirfield (shades of Charles Lawrie) is a little slower than that. The stimpmeter has not left the cupboard for a couple of years because, as a spirit level would soon confirm, the Muirfield greens offer few places where it is possible to get the flatness of roll necessary for a pertinent stimpmeter reading. A 12-handicapper, he gauges the pace of the putting surfaces by his own touch and eye, playing them as a golfer. He was greatly gratified when he had the greens running at just the speed he wanted for the 1992 Open.

As he points out, there are other factors which affect the pace of a green – whether, for example, it is out of the wind or tilts away from the sun. But it does help the consistency that, with the exception of the tenth, which was altered in the 1950s, all the greens have the same base of approximately nine inches of sand loam. The sand loam beneath the tenth is stonier but, though the grass seems, strangely, to grow a little faster, the texture and pace are very much the same as the other greens.

Fertiliser is sparingly used on the greens, twice a year and very lightly even then. They are, though, perhaps four times a year given a top dressing of Muirfield's own sand and soil – dead bunker-facing and other unneeded turf having been mixed with sand and left for four or five years to mature.

As for the fairways, Whittle wanted to get away from the thinness of growth which was causing them all too readily to dust and on which a ball was apt to sit uninvitingly 'between the grass rather than on top of it'. He raised the cutters to three-quarters of an inch. The grass at Muirfield is fescue and bent, but there are patches of Yorkshire Fog grass and annual meadow grass which are uncommonly difficult to eradicate though not too hard to control through cutting and scarifying. Whittle suspects that they date back to the days before the coming of the European seed laws in 1974 – laws which stipulated minimum germination and purity rates.

Once a year, usually in November, the club hire a verti-draining machine which simulates the levering action of a hand-held fork in letting in air. It is used, as required, on fairways, tees and paths, and has been an unqualified success.

The fairways are also overseeded with a 'very linksy' mixture concocted specifically for the needs of Muirfield in terms of drought tolerance and minimal watering and fertilising. Verily, the three witches over their cauldron in Shakespeare's *Macbeth* did not take more pleasure from getting the ingredients exactly right than do Whittle and the Sports Turf Research Institute's David Boocock. In addition, the fairways are fed liquid seaweed extracts, the aim always being to grow grass with the traditional look of Muirfield; natural grass rather than the bright green, immaculately striped, lush Augusta sward.

For the 1992 Open, Whittle's first at Muirfield, the fairways – save for the third, which authority sought to narrow – were left at the width at which the members play them and the rough graded no differently. A ten-feet band cut at one and a half inches; beyond that, another belt of between five yards and ten at five inches; and, after that, jungle. There are parts of the links where it is more sparse but, generally speaking, the rough has a luxuriant growth more pleasing to a greenkeeper than to the jaundiced eye of the wayward golfer: 'Rough,' exclaimed Doug Sanders, of the admittedly somewhat exceptional 1966 Open, 'in which you could mislay your caddie, never mind lose your ball.' But, of course, it is the very richness of the growth which allows a degree of definition, with regard to where the fairway ends and the rough begins, which is often unobtainable on sundry other links.

Some years ago, when the Open was looming at Royal Troon, Gary Player begged the golf correspondent of the *Scotsman* to use his influence to ensure that the bunkers were not belatedly filled with new sand. 'Half an inch of sand is enough,' opined the man so often hailed as the world's greatest bunker player.

'I read what Gary Player had to say,' remarked Norman Fergusson,

Muirfield is renowned for its deep and steep-faced bunkers. Periodically the bunkers have to be rebuilt – a task requiring considerable expertise – see page 86.
Right: the plan for the new irrigation system introduced in 1993 (Plan © Sports Turf Services, Newbridge, Midlothian)

Royal Troon's head greenkeeper, 'but keeping the depth of sand to no more than half an inch could be bit tricky because, as far as I know, there is nothing but sand between here and New Zealand!'

Of course, as the mischievous Fergusson knew perfectly well, what Player was really referring to was not the compacted sand but the upper layer which a club would cut through in playing a bunker recovery.

'No more than an inch and a half,' nods Whittle, 'but don't forget that the length of the bunker-rake's teeth comes into it. Again, as the sand dries out, it loosens and can rise to as much as five inches. What we do then, obviously, is water it.'

The Honourable Company have their own sand quarry below the fifth hole. When they put in new sand, they first shape it and then tread it down. For the last six weeks before an Open and probably longer, no new sand is added. Blown sand is a particular problem and no time is wasted in brushing it back into the bunkers – not just because it would look untidy but because, if left, it could scorch and smother the grass. The turf bricks for the grass faces of the bunkers are grown and cut in Muirfield's own on-site turf nursery and, where feasible, the surrounds of the bunkers cut with three-wheeled ride-on machines. Previously, fly-mowers were used even on the least precipitous inclines, leading to complaints that the bunker banks were too soft. Now they are reserved for the faces which are virtually vertical. Whittle claims that the greenkeeping staff at Muirfield – nine including him – are the best in the world when it comes to bunkers. Why? 'Because they get so much practice!'

Alone of the courses on the Open championship rota, Muirfield,

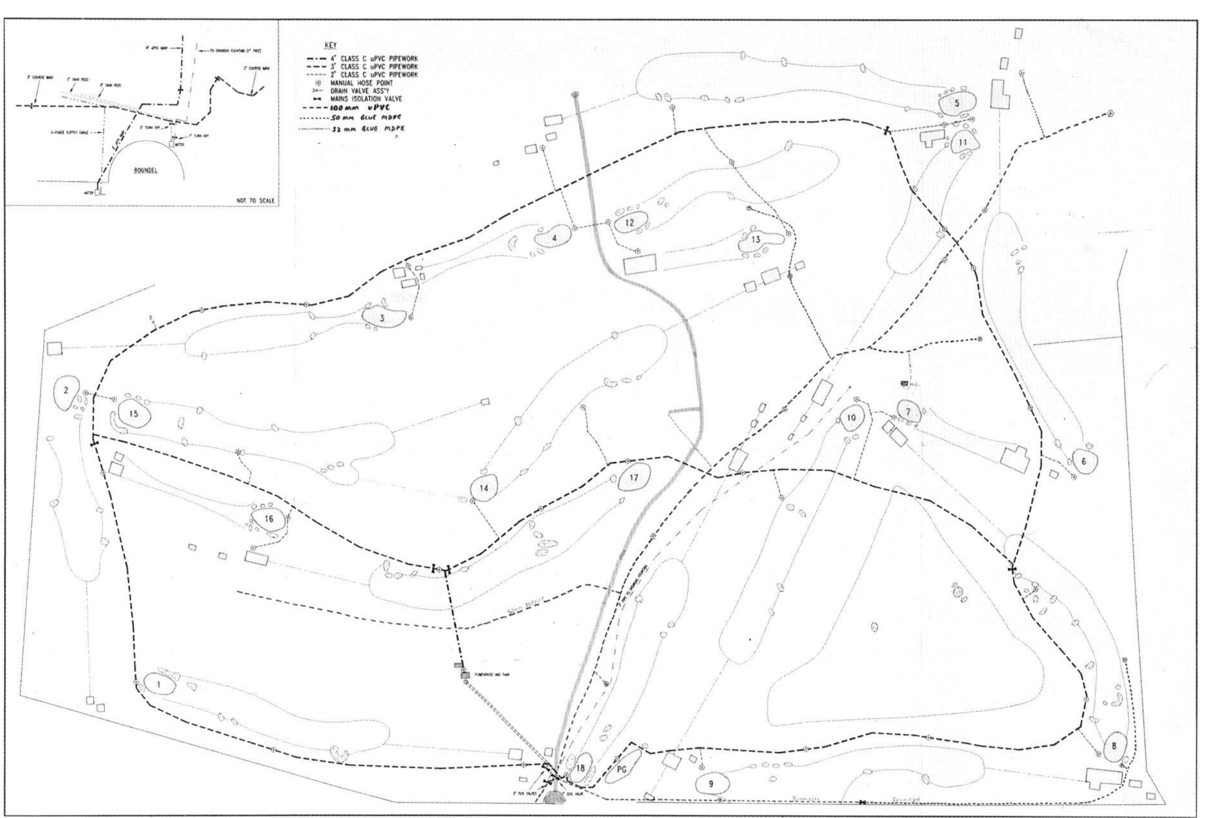

amazingly, has as yet no automatic watering system; not so much because of the cost – between £200,000 and £400,0000 – but because they now have instead what Whittle calls the ultimate in pipe watering. They used to have some 30 hose-points whereas, under Whittle, they have 51. They now have, too, their own storage tank. Thus the pressure is constant where, when they drew directly from the town mains, the pressure was fine at night but dropped during the day.

While serving his apprenticeship at Formby, Whittle, who had left school with seven O-levels, attended classes in Wigan on such subjects as turf culture, botany and irrigation. He has encouraged his staff at Muirfield to take relevant courses at Elmwood College in Fife and Oatridge College in Broxburn. Intelligent and articulate, he is deeply steeped in his craft, what with a brother, a cousin and an uncle all in the profession. His idol remains Scotland's Jimmy McDonald, whom Whittle served first at Formby and then at Royal Lytham before spending seven years as the head greenkeeper at St Annes Old Links. McDonald, in the weeks before an Open, will be wide awake in the small hours of the night at the merest patter of rain on the roof, and Whittle similarly lives his calling.

'The members of the Honourable Company understand golf in general and links golf in particular,' he reflects gratefully. 'They don't make stupid remarks about the course because they know what you are trying to do. The layman might be surprised at the difference which that makes. Muirfield is a very special place, as Augusta is; a place, mainly because it is in the shelter of Gullane Hill, with its own micro-climate. It is seaside but the direction of prevailing wind is such that, unlike Birkdale and Lytham, there is seldom, if ever, a taste of salt on the lips.'

Chris Whittle and his team laying new turfs to reface a bunker

The Muirfield Bunkers

IN 1928 there were 224 bunkers on Muirfield. With advances in modern technology rendering many tactically obsolescent, the number had shrunk to 148 by the time Nick Faldo won the 1992 Open though a new splash bunker at the eighth has subsequently been added.

Jack Nicklaus said of the bunkers at Muirfield that they were 'all visible and the most fastidiously built bunkers I have ever seen, the high front walls faced with bricks of turf fitted together so precisely you would have thought a master mason had been called in'.

They are sufficiently punitive to have had Seve Ballesteros vowing in deep midwinter to practise his sand-play as never before for the 1992 Open. He was only too well aware that bunker-play had been a decisive factor in many a Muirfield Open, Gary Player getting up and down in two from greenside bunkers 11 times out of 12 in winning the 1959 Open.

On the eve of the Walker Cup that same summer, the great American amateur, Harvie Ward, was still struggling to recapture his old form and was disarmingly frank about how poorly he was playing. None the less, he took exception to one damning newspaper article prior to the match. 'It was reported the other day,' he complained, quite fiercely, 'that I was in 30 bunkers. That was not true.' Just as the scribe responsible was beginning to redden, fearful that hearsay had lied, Ward snorted, as a man with all the sands of the Sahara behind him, 'A libellous understatement!'

The Honourable Company would be the last club on earth to go in for instant tradition, scattering bogus names like confetti. One bunker, however, which does have a name is Simpson's, called after its creator, the

This picture gives a good idea of the task facing the unfortunate golfer who finds his ball under the face of a Muirfield bunker

golf course architect, Tom Simpson. It is in the middle of the fairway at the long ninth awaiting the second shot. It would, promised Simpson, in submitting the plans, be the most hated bunker on the course and the most feared.

The bunkers – beautifully groomed and immaculately manicured – gather and even if they do not move in with the bowler's run, one knows what the cricketing golfer meant who declared that it had been 'like batting against a crack fielding side'. One can see him now, brushing the sand out of his hair one summery noon following his maiden Muirfield round and wailing piteously, for he was normally none too bad a golfer, 'I have just made my first ever hundred before lunch!'

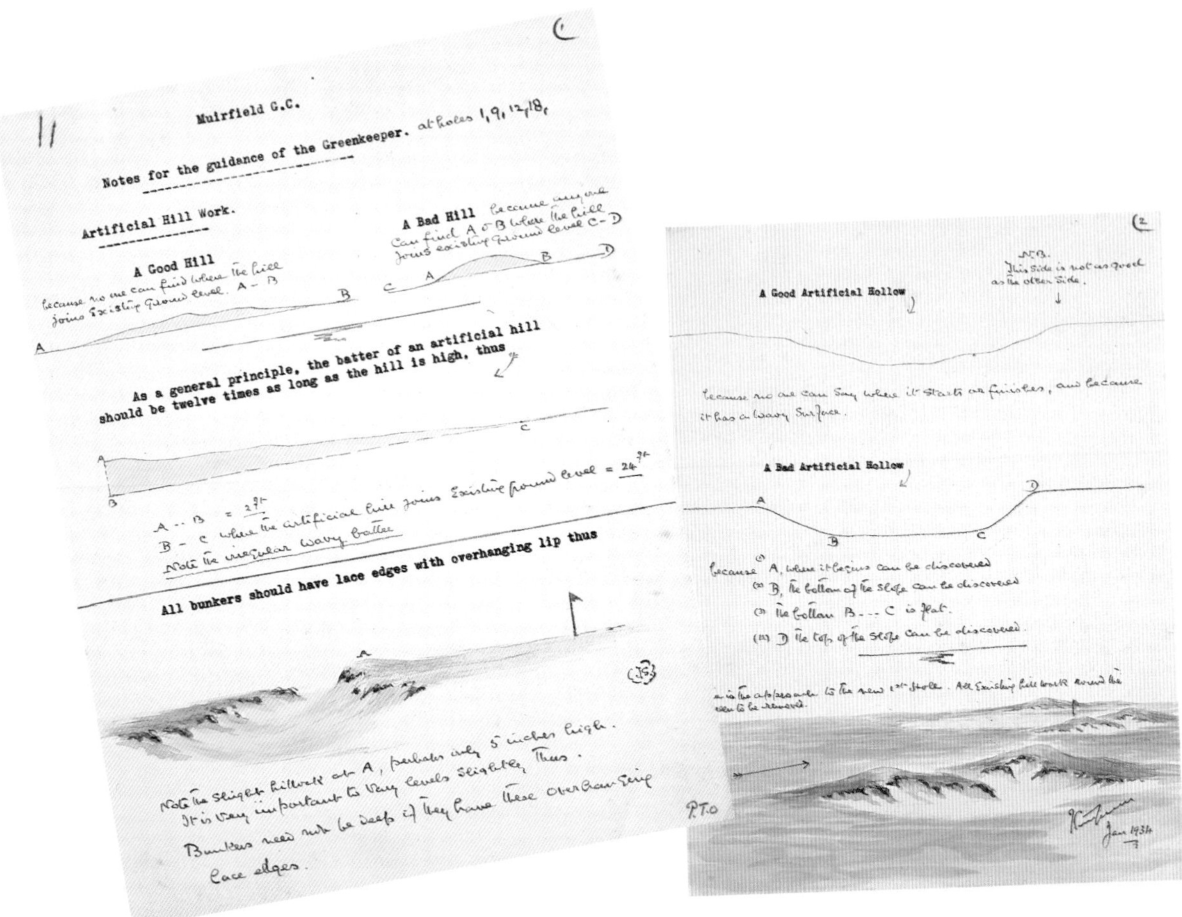

Muirfield G.C.

Notes for the guidance of the Greenkeeper. at holes 1, 9, 12, 18.

Artificial Hill Work.

A Good Hill because no one can find where the hill joins existing ground level. A – B

A Bad Hill because anyone can find A & B where the hill joins existing ground level C – D

As a general principle, the batter of an artificial hill should be twelve times as long as the hill is high, thus

A – B = 2 ft
B – C where the artificial hill joins existing ground level = 24 ft
Note the irregular wavy batter

All bunkers should have lace edges with overhanging lip thus

Note the slight hillwork at A, perhaps only 5 inches high. It is very important to vary levels slightly, thus. Bunkers need not be deep if they have these overhanging lace edges.

P.T.O.

A Good Artificial Hollow

N.B. This side is not as good as the other side.

because no one can say where it starts or finishes, and because it has a wavy surface.

A Bad Artificial Hollow

because (1) A, where it begins can be discovered
(2) B, the bottom of the slope can be discovered
(3) the bottom B – C is flat.
(4) D the top of the slope can be discovered.

Jan 1934

Two pages from Simpson's illustrated notes 'for the guidance of the Greenkeeper' which expound his theories on 'a good hill' and 'a bad hill', etc. The sketches are dated January 1934

'In all my life I have never heard anything as lonely as the cry of the peewit in that twilight on the rolling Muirfield course, nor was I ever so lonesome.'

O.B. Keeler, Bobby Jones's Boswell, after Jones had been beaten in the quarter-finals of the 1926 Amateur championship by the young Scottish amateur, Andrew Jamieson.

The striking similarity in the swings of Leslie Balfour-Melville and Henry Cotton during the phase when Cotton, in search of greater length, was allowing his left heel to rise

Robert Maxwell on Muirfield

THE COURSE. – I did not know the original course. One outstanding feature of Muirfield from the first I knew it up to the time it was reconstructed by Harry Colt was that it was a cross-hazard course, as indeed practically all the old courses were. St Andrews was the unique exception so far as I know. I think the chief criticism of the course was the putting greens. The texture of the grass was considered rather wiry or bristly, not true seaside, and the greens themselves knobby rather than undulating and therefore not true. As a matter of fact I always believed that if a ball were hit true it ran true but a slight mis-hit was greatly accentuated.

With the great increase of players the course, even after two alterations before 1914, was apt to become congested, especially in the centre about the 13th green and 14th and 18th tees. With the purchase of the course with very considerable additional ground it was considered advisable to 'modernise' (a dreadful word and much abused) and the leading Golf Architect was called in. The result is practically the present course. I sometimes wonder if fashion will again change and courses will go back to cross-hazard. They are certainly more spectacular and I think players get a bigger thrill from a 'carry' than being able to get on a green by hitting what old Andrew K. would call a 'dirty swithering shot'. Also having to approach and chip over a bunker was no mean strain.

Since we became members I have no doubt the course as a whole is vastly improved, due to drainage and modern machinery and a large staff, but certainly neither the present generation nor their successors can enjoy happier memories of Muirfield than ourselves. But possibly actually the strongest feature of the Honourable Company is esprit de corps. Long may it continue.

9 A round over Muirfield

An aerial view of the first fairway and green, with the second hole in the distance. (This and all the following photographs in this chapter were specially taken for the club by Glyn Satterley during the 1992 Open)

Overleaf: the twelfth green, looking west over the fourth hole towards Gullane Bay, with Arthur's Seat and Edinburgh in the distance

Hole 1 447 yards (409m) par 4

'One of the scariest opening holes in golf' in the opinion of Tony Jacklin. The first tee on any golf course has connotations of its own and at Muirfield the player, possibly with the prevailing wind hard in his face, peers out at a fairway narrowing in an Open championship to under 20 yards between the bunker on the left and the graded rough on the right. A tee shot held left helps to set up the second to a green bunkered on the right and then to the left rear.

Looking back down the first fairway towards the tee.

Hole 2 351 yards (321m) par 4

Especially at first sight, the most tempting par 4 on the links; a hole where, in the 1966 Open, the newly crowned Amateur champion, the teenage South African, Bobby

Cole, had a two. Again the tee shot should favour the left, thereby easing the approach to a green of ticklish contours whose right flank is pocketed by bunkers. 'Maybe,' suggested that considerable golf course architect, Jack Nicklaus, 'you need a hole such as this after that demanding opening hole. In other words, in assessing it, you have to consider whether it is the right hole in its place on the course.'

A side view of the second green showing the boundary wall which runs down the left (west) side of the hole

Hole 3 379 yards (346m) par 4

Now comes the first of three successive holes running in the same direction. It is the longest such stretch on a course which frequently changes its angles to the wind in contrast to so many of those so-called Old Testament links with their long haul out and long run home.

Particularly with a following wind, many will choke down to an iron lest they find sand off the tee. Once more the place to be in the fairway is down the left, this time to allow a view of the green through the pass running between the obstructive hillocks.

Hole 4 *180 yards (164m) par 3*

The hole where, in the 1972 Open, Brian Barnes – like Italy's Dino Canonica in 1966 – had an ace, the shock of which brought the strapping Scot a seven down the long fifth. The green is a jealously protected plateau and it makes good sense to be up because the retribution behind the green is relatively merciful. Certainly by comparison with the right-hand bunker into whose malevolent depths so many who underclub plummet . .

The fourth green, looking back to the fourth tee on the left. The fifth tee is on the raised bank on the right of the picture

Hole 5 *559 yards (511m) par 5*

With the new back tee, the fifth had taken over from the seventeenth as the longest hole on the links by the 1972 Open. The angle of the drive is affected, though only slightly, by the tee alteration. The line nowadays is arguably to the right of the second bunker on the left rather than straight at it, though it remains necessary to avoid the shoal of bunkers down the right out of sight of the tee. The tee shot kept left facilitates the second, which should be struck to cash in on the right-to-left slope heralding the green. In the 1972 Open, Johnny Miller sank a beautifully flighted spoon for a two; the deuce of a deuce.

The green of the long fifth hole with the Firth of Forth in the background

Hole 6 *469 yards (429m) par 4*

A new tee, 30 yards to the left of its immediate predecessor, meant that the hole was more than 30 yards longer for Tom Watson's Open than it had been for Lee Trevino's, though otherwise the overall yardage of the links remained almost exactly as it had been in 1972. The staple tee shot, the most awkward on the course to the eye of Nicklaus, is to the right since, in addition to bunkers – both visible and hidden – clinging rough awaits the over-ambitious drive. There is a deceptive dip just short of the green and many a man has taken one club too little for his second.

Hole 7 *185 yards (169m) par 3*

The siting of the tee for Nicklaus's Open stretched the hole by some 30 yards and, into the prevailing westerly wind, the hole has become a much more hostile proposition. Where judgment of distance is concerned, the more culpable sin is to be short. There is a caddies' tale that the slope of the green is but an optical illusion, that almost every putt on the seventh green is, in fact, straight – but a brief experiment conducted before the 1972 Open with the secretary of the Honourable Company and the then captain rapidly exploded that myth.

The view from the tee to the flag stretches into the far distance towards the Forth and one recalls the Championship committee of 1972 stoutly resisting the temptation to erect a spectator stand immediately behind the green, convinced that it would rob the hole of its traditional challenge by furnishing a backcloth and – uncharacteristically for Muirfield – artificial definition.

Below: Fred Couples getting out of trouble at the short seventh

Opposite: Gary Player putting on the ninth green

Hole 8 *444 yards (406m) par 4*

In cricket parlance, there is, in terms of bunkers, a packed off-side field. The total number of bunkers on Muirfield, incidentally, came down from 165 in 1972 to 151 by the 1980 Open, simply because some had become obsolete or, as John Salvesen, the then chairman of the Championship Committee put it, 'fossilised'.

Farther right are the buckthorn trees indignantly planted to close the route taken by the always inventive Walter Hagen in his 1929 Open triumph. In his television match versus Nicklaus, Gary Player out-Hagened Hagen by driving on to the practice ground, but the practice ground is now out of bounds and not just because a competitor's ball might easily be scooped up along with the rest by the ball-collecting machines on duty at an Open.

The stroke to the green, over cross-bunkers, is partially blind while, at the far left-hand corner of the putting surface, a bunker pouches those who are a fraction strong.

Hole 9 *504 yards (461m) par 5*

One of the legendary holes of golf, usually offering an intriguing study in tactics. Many have opted, down the

years, to play short of the fairway's most slender neck. Against a west wind, the green is virtually out of reach in two. To the left is that infamous out-of-bounds wall; to the right, bunkers, obviously in collusion, keep a hungry eye on the second shot. Even down the middle, there is Simpson's, a pest of a bunker. It is part of the lore of the links that a pitch landing short of the green at the ninth is apt to have less run than it would at any other hole on the course.

In 1972, as Nicklaus, six shots off the pace at the start of the last round but now in the lead, shaped on the eleventh green to a putt which would bring him his sixth birdie, a great roar from the ninth green greeted the putt Trevino had holed for an eagle. Nicklaus backed away from his putt then, as he settled to it again, came another roar from the same green as Jacklin matched Trevino's eagle. Once more Nicklaus addressed that putt – and in it went.

Nick Price plays left-handed from close to the boundary wall along the south side of the ninth fairway

Hole 10 475 yards (434m) par 4

'A great hole' in the words of Nicklaus. 'One of my all-time favourites.'

Bunkers to starboard help steer the drive left. The sec-

ond lies over cross-bunkers; and, for those who come up short, the chip is normally aimed to land on the putting surface to thwart the sloping ridge short of the green. In 1966, the tenth killed Arnold Palmer, among others, but that year the billowing rough was so deep it prompted Doug Sanders' oft-quoted and immortal reaction when first he set eyes upon it: 'Give me the lost-ball and hay concession and you can keep the prize money!'

In 1972, however, the rough was graded, with the first 15 feet at two inches, the next 15 at approximately four, and only thereafter was it allowed to grow unchecked. As the 1980 Open approached, John Salvesen, chairman of the Championship Committee and a member of the Honourable Company for more than two decades, showed himself very much of the 1972 school of thought: 'The shot that pitches in the rough on the fly deserves all it gets. That is what your real rough is for; but the shot that just runs off the fairway does not merit the same punishment. That is where your semi-rough comes in . . .'

Hole 11 *385 yards (352m) par 4*

A blind drive. A bunker stationed on the right suggests a

Opposite: the tenth tee with the backdrop of Greywalls Hotel

Below: Tom Watson plays his approach to the eleventh green

drive left of the guideline which, with the flag often tucked in behind the bunkers on the right of the green, opens the approach. Bunkers jostle the green's rear.

The hole, 363 yards in the 1966 Open, was stretched to 386 yards in 1972, with the carry from the new back tee over the hill a little matter of 195 yards. Which is why the then chairman of the Championship Committee, the late Charles Lawrie, decreed that, in the event of a heavy head-wind first thing in the morning, the new tee would not be used that day.

Here, in the 1980 Open, in the last round, Tom Watson, having taken five at the tenth, hit the shot of his round, a five-iron which, in the old phrase, bored a hole in the wind to end four feet behind the flag.

Hole 12 381 yards (348m) par 4

Like the fourteenth, a better hole when the wind is from the west – though, interestingly, Nicklaus has opined that a west wind, if anything, makes the course play more easily since it shortens both the long fifth and the par five seventeenth. Save for the siege-guns – or, in conditions plainly conducive to length – the tee shot should be sited on the left-hand bunker. The sweep of the ground complicates the stroke to a green where the hole positions are more than usually significant. The real connoisseurs among the swarming galleries of an Open avidly note the day's pin position.

Below: Looking from behind the eleventh green with the twelfth hole on the right of the picture

Hole 13 152 yards (139m) par 3

'A gem,' to quote Nicklaus once more.

The short thirteenth is uphill to a long, slim green in a basket of dunes. The bunkers to either side up the green sire satanic permutations of stance and lie, aim and ele-

Wilson
Wilson
J&B
PARAMINS

Left: playing from the thirteenth tee to the elevated green

Right: looking from behind the thirteenth green back towards the tee, with the twelfth green on the right

vation, but legend has it that Hagen deliberately hit into a bunker rather than risk bequeathing himself a long and glassy downhill putt. In 1948, Charlie Ward went one better in solving that particular problem by holing his tee

shot, the late King George VI being among his greatly gratified gallery.

Hole 14 449 yards (410m) par 4

In contrast to 1966, the tee now in use is the one mounted in the dunes, a little to the right and forward of the one which was employed that year. The drive should be down the right rather than otherwise. There is a fringe of bunkers looking across to a notably strategic trap on the starboard side. A bunker, little but lethal, lurks on the right of the green, and those who have run through the back have mostly had cause to rue the occurrence.

Olazabal driving from the fourteenth tee

Hole 15 417 yards (381m) par 4

The hole was lengthened by over 20 yards for the 1980 Open. By Muirfield's standards, a reasonably straightforward tee shot. It is a course which basically sets a premium on accuracy from the tee, it being worth noting that, in winning the 1948 Open, Henry Cotton hit 52 out of 56 fairways.

The green did not earn the name of the Camel's Back for nothing, but at least the greens at Muirfield are traditionally fast and true, dressed as they are with sand and fertiliser but not compost, and better able than most nowadays to stand up to the day's traffic.

In the 1992 Open, in the fourth round, Nick Faldo, having held a four-stoke lead, boarded the tee trailing America's John Cook by two strokes, a devastating transformation in the space of just seven holes. The five-iron he piloted to within three feet of the hole, a wonderful amalgam of courage flight and roll, was the epitome of a champion's response.

Panoramic view of the fourteenth hole. The fourteenth green is in the centre of the picture, looking back to the tee on the right. Behind is the thirteenth hole. In the foreground is part of the seventeenth fairway with its hazardous bunkers

Hole 16 188 yards (172m) par 3

An exacting short hole, where the lie of the ground – in particular, the dip before the green – makes the choice of club a teasing decision. A pesky greenside bunker is poised timelessly at two o'clock, while the green's tantalising slopes are hardly calculated to soothe nerves still

Faldo hits his crucial approach to the fifteenth in the final round of the 1992 Open. The ensuing birdie three helped him to victory (see page 154)

jangling from the Camel's Back.

The first Open at Muirfield played with the 1.68 ball was Watson's Open in 1980 but Trevino, in 1972, switched sizes, as players could then legally do, from hole to hole according to the shots likely to be required. Less well known is the fact that Player, in helping himself to a priceless brace of birdies at the thirteenth and sixteenth in his final round in 1959, played both those downwind par threes with the big ball.

Though it was here that Peter Butler holed in one in the 1973 Ryder Cup, the shot with which the hole will be forever associated was the one Trevino sank from a bunker in the third round in 1972, the ball hitting the flagstick in full flight and bringing him a two where he might so easily have taken five.

Hole 17 550 yards (502m) par 5

It was here in 1948 that Roberto de Vicenzo holed his two-iron for an albatross; a hole where, en route to victory in the last round in 1966, Nicklaus hit a superb three-iron and matching five-iron. But the ghosts which will never leave the hole are those of Trevino and Jacklin; the former holed almost heedlessly a horribly difficult little

Right: looking back to the tee of the short sixteenth from behind the green

Below: playing from the sixteenth tee

Looking down the fairway from behind the seventeenth green

chip against the lie of the grass to rescue an improbable five and trigger the three putts which cost the Englishman a six that Open, and one shudders to think what else besides in the years that have passed.

The drive should be directed right to evade not only the visible bunkers on the left but also the secretive pots. The pimples – otherwise known as the ex-captains' graves – which used to protrude among the aforesaid pots, have been obliterated, being, in any case, of no great antiquity.

The second over the cross-bunkers is to a heavily defended green alive with – in the words of Frank Penninck, an erstwhile English Amateur champion and golf course architect – 'fiendish contours'.

Hole 18 448 yards (410m) par 4

'Probably the best hole on the best Open championship course in Britain' is how Nicklaus sees this famed finishing hole, the definition and the degree to which you get what you hit at Muirfield appealing to American golfers in general.

In 1948, Cotton, from that renowned right-hand

The view from the clubhouse windows of the eighteenth green and fairway

bunker, with its distinctive grass inset, took two to emerge, though ultimately holing nobly for nothing worse than a five. In 1959, Player bunkered a drive that failed to fade as intended; hit a six-iron from sand 100 yards up the fairway; another six-iron short of the flag; and, finally, took three putts. In 1966, Nicklaus, after a vintage one-iron, banked a three-iron perfectly against the right-to-left wind on his way to a flawless four. And, in 1972, Trevino, loitering on his way to the last tee to avoid dwelling on the shot, left himself off his triumphant drive only 145 yards to the green, his eight-iron settling seven feet past the flag.

Faldo putting on the eighteenth

Three acquisitive bunkers nod expectantly to their lone colleague across the fairway, the line from the tee being, according to Muirfield habitués, the door of the distant caddie shed.

The eighteenth was already a classic from the old championship tee, but the new back tee built for the 1972 Open, like those of the fifth and seventeenth (but unlike those changed tees at the sixth and fourteenth) was constructed out of deference to the power of the modern player armed with contemporary equipment, the basic aim, successful or otherwise, being to give the player of today roughly the same problems with his second as faced his not too distant forebear.

Olazabal playing his second shot to the eighteenth green with the backdrop of the clubhouse

10 Portrait Gallery

Alexander Stuart

'OF Andy Stuart, so long Alex Stuart Junior,' wrote Stair Gillon, 'little must be said because he might be angry and think I was writing with the pen of the flatterer.' Alexander Stuart was captain in 1892 in succession to Colonel Anderson who had had charge of the migration to Muirfield. Not long turned 30, Stuart was in office during the construction of the club's new home.

No less an authority than Horace Hutchinson ranked him, among the amateurs of the day, next to John Ball, Johnny Laidlay and, without undue modesty, Horace himself. Bernard Darwin, by way of supporting Hutchinson's contention, borrowed a passage from a Badminton book on the St Andrews swingers: 'Oh duffer! Ill will it fare with you if you strive to emulate their supple elasticity. This is but the fruit of a boyhood spent golf club in hand. Swing with their young insolent fearlessness – it is but a caricature. Look rather at Mr Alexander Stuart . . . His is a free, long, supple swing, indeed, but formed upon quieter methods. There is more repose – less fascinating dash, maybe; but more apparent absence of effort. His is the safer style for your model.'

Winner of the last winter medal at Musselburgh, Stuart – who had reached the semi-final of the 1888 Amateur championship at Prestwick and won the inaugural Irish Open in 1892 – retired early from championship golf. Nonetheless, despite the increasing attraction which the Highlands and field sports held for him, he remained a fine player and in a class of his own in the golfing domain of Bench and Bar. 'His ease of style, his power and reserve, and his touch and finish' had all, suggested Gillon, promised greater achievement. But, conceded that Honourable Company scribbler, his record was still a proud one in respect of medals won. What, to Gillon, had set him apart had been 'his control of the masterful committees, over which he presided in the most critical years of the club's whole history'. Gillon spoke eloquently, too, of Stuart's more personal contribution 'in knowledge of the game and of links – all leavened with much common-sense and in the true spirit of sport.'

Stuart was a member for more than man's allotted span, 72 years in all, and, averred George Pottinger, 'during all that time, there was no more engaging or popular figure at Musselburgh or Muirfield. The portrait, showing him in the captain's evening-dress, which hangs in the smoking-room, is convincing evidence of the genial, quizzical sense of humour recorded in contemporary reports.'

B. Hall Blyth, captain 1880-81

P.H. Don-Wauchope

THOUGH he was overshadowed by his elder brother, the incomparable A.R. Don-Wauchope, P.H. Don-Wauchope was similarly known less as a golfer than as a rugby player. He made his international début against Ireland at Raeburn Place in 1885. A.R. also a member of the Honourable Company, was at stand-off, the first time a pair of brothers had formed a half-back partnership in international rugby. To cap a memorable day for the clan, Andrew, with a typically brilliant side-stepping run, scored the final try in a Scotland win.

At Muirfield, however, P.H. (Patrick Hamilton) has gone into the archives as the man who, in something of an emergency, came up with a plan to extend the original course – primarily conceived by Old Tom Morris – by some 600 yards. What had brought about the crisis was that on a Thursday in April 1894 (Thursday being then the usual day for Honourable Company competitions), R.H. Johnston had won the spring medal with a

79, going out in an unpropitious 48 but coming home in 31.

The reaction was unflattering: namely, that if John Herbert, as the members called him, could cover nine holes in 31, then by no stretch of imagination could Muirfield continue to lay claim to the mantle of a championship course. Johnston was reckoned to get by only on concentration and a cricketer's eye, the tendency to cut his shots being exacerbated by his becoming increasingly muscle-bound. 'In the whole gamut of his game,' one writer added, in case anyone hadn't quite got the picture, 'there was not one truly-hit golfing stroke.' In the terminology of today, Johnston obviously had a skin of surlyn rather than balata for, far from being cut to the quick, he remained an amicable and highly popular Recorder. When he died in 1910, it was the members who made the supreme sacifice, out of respect for his memory, cancelling the dinner scheduled for the following evening.

P.H.'s course-changing scheme came before the committee on 5 December 1895 and the amended links, which would shake the custodians of today's Open championship courses, was ready for the Open of 1896. It was won by Harry Vardon, whose success, as a gauge of the validity of the test, was understandably held to be at the other end of the spectrum to Johnston's.

B. Hall Blyth *(by George Pottinger)*

HALL BLYTH (Captain, 1880–81; Recorder, 1888–96; and a Trustee from 1894 onwards) was a civil engineer and, though keen, was never a scratch player. He triumphed in the famous cross-country match in 1880, against Willie Campbell, which was played from Point Garry, North Berwick, to the High Hole at Gullane. Campbell opted for the shore line and played over North Berwick, Archerfield and the ground that eventually became Muirfield, before reaching Gullane. Hall Blyth elected to play on an inland route through Dirleton and, although longer, this was much the simpler course. Hall Blyth won easily over the six-mile distance and his opponent came early to grief on the rocks.

Hall Blyth served on numerous committees concerned with golf clubs throughout East Lothian and he usually got his way. A tall, powerfully built man, he had a loud voice in which he boomed confident opinions and defied challenge. He wore a Dragoon's moustache and affected something of the air of a martinet. To see him, attired in checks almost as loud as his voice, referee a championship match and hear his resonant rulings was said to be unforgettable. His appetite was famous. He used to apply the gouge to the Stilton with the same vigour that he brandished his niblick in a bunker – leaving a similar cavity. But he also seems to have inspired some admiration – and perhaps some reluctant affection – and he, more than anyone else, is responsible for the present clubhouse and the Muirfield Green.

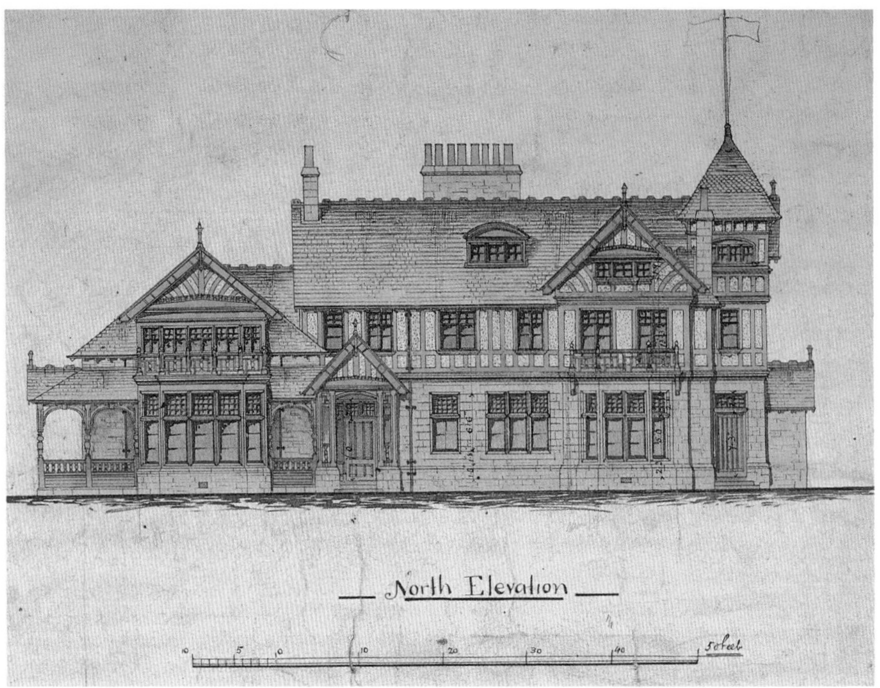

This original drawing for the Muirfield clubhouse was recently found in the archives of Blyth & Blyth, the civil engineering firm founded by Hall Blyth. They kindly presented it to the Honourable Company. Note the balcony running along the front at first-floor level

Guy Robertson Durham

EVEN Idi Amin, who was given to awarding them to himself, might have envied Guy Robertson Durham his collection of medals: 23 from the Honourable Company, 19 from Gullane and one, the Silver Cross of St Andrews, from the R & A.

The product of endless hours of practice? Well, not exactly. Just once, on a morning at Muirfield when he was due to partner 'Squiggles' Mackie in a match against the prospective Scotland team, did Robertson Durham decide to break the habit of a lifetime and hit some balls. Not too many, for he did not want to overdo it. Three to be precise. Dropping them beside the right-hand fairway bunker at the eighteenth, he let fly for the home green with his trusty five-wood – and holed out. Satisfied that further practice was unlikely to bring any marked improvement, he picked up and pocketed the other two and returned to the clubhouse. Which, even by the standards of the Honourable Company, was style.

Plus one at his best, he reached the last eight in the 1949 Amateur championship at Portmarnock, losing to Max McCready who went on to defeat the American, Willie Turnesa – Willie the Wedge – in the final.

On the strength of his achievement in qualifying for the 1948 Open, Robertson Durham was one of the 32 amateurs in the field for the *Daily Telegraph* Amateur–Professional Foursomes. He and Arthur Lees beat Alf Perry, who had won the 1935 Open at Muirfield, and the Welsh Walker Cup player, Tony Duncan, by 8 and 7 before succumbing in the quarter-finals.

Never capped, he was a Scottish trialist and, of course, for 31 years, a Lorettonian stalwart in the Halford Hewitt. They never won but thrice they reached the semi-final with Robertson Durham's happiest memory an 8 and 7 rout of Harrow's Leonard Crawley and Eustace Crawley, the former an erstwhile English Amateur champion.

A natural games player, Robertson Durham played rugby, cricket and hockey for Loretto, won the school mile and made the shooting team. A particular facility for playing on the left wing saw him win his hockey colours at 15, two goals in the blood match with Fettes doing the trick. Three years in the cricket XI, he was a batsman who came in at No. 5, took guard on the leg stump and thereafter, as P.G. Wodehouse might have said, never spared himself in his efforts to do the ball an injury. It was, though, to his days in the unbeaten Loretto First XV of 1941–42 that he looked back most fondly.

Indeed, at the end of the war, he played at openside wing-forward for the British Army in France and came out of the forces with ambitions to make his mark with Edinburgh Wanderers. His father, however, decreed unequivocally that he had to choose between rugby and golf, and golf won.

He had served with the Black Watch, holding seven ranks from private to major, not excluding unpaid lance-corporal, and was twice wounded on active service with the 51st Highland Division. On the second occasion, shortly before the crossing of the Rhine, they were in a house during street fighting when a 'tattie-masher' – otherwise known as a German grenade – came in through the window and rolled to the feet of this erstwhile Loretto outfielder.

He gathered with an alacrity which would have delighted his old cricket master but, in the days when he was firing the ball in from the boundary at Newfield, there had been a conspicuous absence of machine-gun fire. Now, with the bullets pinging off the walls, his left-armed return was a mite untidy, coming back into the room off the window-sill. His left hand took the brunt, necessitating a sizeable skin graft. 'I had,' was his laconic reaction, 'a bad grip before that encounter and I still had a bad one after it!'

In those *Daily Telegraph* foursomes, Arthur Lees had gazed upon Robertson Durham's very personal species of two-handed grip and wondered; but, by the time they had seen off Perry and Duncan, he had been prepared to take a tolerant view: 'You have a strange grip, Mr Durham, but it doesn't seem to do much harm.' Not fulsome perhaps but quite reassuring all the same.

Golf was in Guy Robertson Durham's genes. Jim, his father, had captained Oxford University in 1909 and 1910 and both he and his brother, Alex, had played for Scotland. Alex's daughter, Min, won the Scottish Ladies' championship.

Alex won three Honourable Company medals but, where Guy's own handsome haul even included three Grant Cups – in other words, the aggregate over the spring and autumn medals – Jim, try as he might, could never add even one to the 33 medals he garnered from Gullane and Luffness. His frustration hardly had the global impact of Lee Trevino's inability to win the US Masters or of Arnold Palmer's and Tom Watson's to capture a US PGA championship but, in such realms, all golfers are the same under the skin and it plagued him all his days.

Like his son, Jim was captain of both the Honourable Company and Gullane as was Guy's Uncle Alex. In fact, the four score years in which there has always been a Robertson Durham on the membership roll of the Honourable Company contain a double which would light up any family photograph album.

In 1929, Alex Robertson Durham, as captain of the Honourable Company, presented the Open championship trophy to Walter Hagen, and 43 years later, Guy handed over the same historic jug to Lee Trevino. Unique? One does not know but it may well be.

G.R.D., as he often referred to himself, reckoned that Muirfield changed very little over the post-war years other than that, here and there, it was lengthened or tightened. Even so, he calculated that, by comparison with 1946, it was some three and a half strokes harder.

Though he estimated that he had lost some 30 yards in his last five years, he had no truck with metal woods, carbon shafts and the like, the same nine clubs peering from his bag as were to be observed when Britain still had an empire. 'I have always hit a five-iron farther than a three-iron and so there is no point in my carrying a two, three or four-iron, let alone a one-iron.'

The *pièce de résistance* was his venerable hickory-shafted, wry-necked putter, his fifth limb: 'It's a bad day when I don't hole at least one putt from off the green and, as long as I have that putter, the 30 yards I have shed don't matter too much.' Over the years, he had no fewer than 14 holes in one.

A retired stockbroker – he was a dealing partner – he played a goodly portion of his golf over the neighbouring Gullane. He was amazed that, for all that each would always be characterised as a links, the turf is so very different: 'Gullane will start shipping water if the rain is heavy enough. I have seen water lying in the bunkers at Muirfield but I cannot, for the life of me, recall any flooding on either the fairways or the greens.' So much for Andra Kirkaldy's 'just an auld water meadie!'

Right: Freddie Tait playing his beloved pipes at Balmoral in 1896, from an illustration in John L. Low's book, F.G. Tait – A Record, *published in 1900*

Below: Guy Robertson Durham (left) presents Jack Nicklaus with a copy of Pottinger's book on Muirfield which, he said, had already been posted to him in Ohio but had been returned marked 'addressee not known'

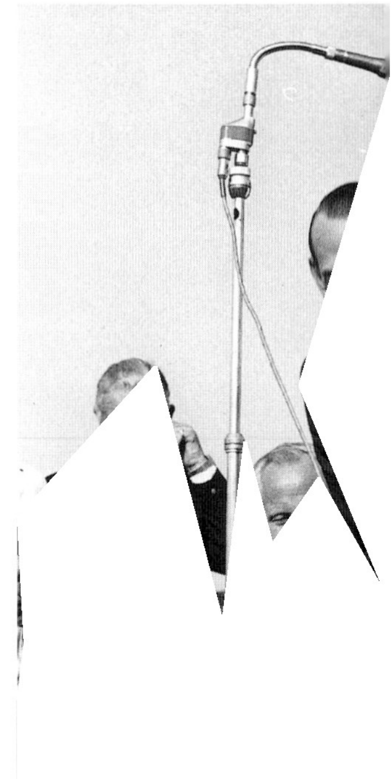

Freddie Tait

FREDDIE TAIT was elected a member of the Honourable Company in October 1899 but he was never to play in a medal. At the age of 30, serving with his regiment, the Black Watch, Lieutenant Tait died on active service in the Boer War. 'I do not think,' declared Bernard Darwin, 'I have ever seen any other golfer so adored by the crowd – no, not Harry Vardon or Bobby Jones in their primes. He liked the thrust and parry of match-play and regarded score-play as no more of a game than rifle shooting. He loved in particular the foursome and, when he played in one, was always most particular to consult his partner on any possible point of tactics. Moreover, he had, as it seems to us, that almost parochial sort of patriotism which wants above everything else to see the Englishman beaten.'

For all that he never played in an Honourable Company medal, he held the amateur record at Muirfield with a 73 in the Open of 1896 in which he finished third, winning the Amateur Medal. Twice Amateur champion,

he was renowned for his long hitting. One drive of his, at the thirteenth on his beloved Old Course at St Andrews, made with the gutta-percha ball, travelled 341 yards. The ground had frost in it but there was no wind and the real point was that the carry was reckoned at around 250 yards. Writing of it to another, Tait said: 'I enclose you a cutting from the *Daily News* of Monday, January 16th, by Andrew Lang, on a drive made by me on my twenty-third birthday. No doubt you will say, as the governor said: "Stuff!, Humbug!" But the fact still remains. The governor will be very much annoyed about the article, as he wrote not very long ago an article to *Golf* proving conclusively that it was impossible to carry more than 190 yards on a calm day.' In fairness to Professor Tait, it should be added that he had not then made his important discovery as to the effect of underspin on the flight of a golf ball . . .

An Edinburgh Academical, Freddie Tait – a crack shot and gifted cricketer – was a rugby forward who, in the opinion of Ian McIntyre, president of the Scottish Rugby Union, was 'one of the very best forwards playing in Edinburgh if not in Scotland. I cannot understand to this day how he was passed over in the selection for the Inter-City.'

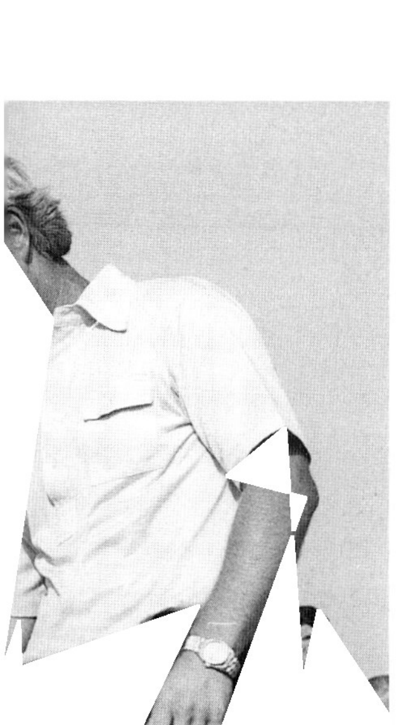

Like another Honourable Company soldier, Major David Blair, Tait thrice won the St George's Challenge Cup. He usually had the measure of the first Open champion at Muirfield, Harold Hilton, but was on the wrong side of the debit and loss account versus that other man of Hoylake, John Ball. Their most memorable match was at Prestwick in 1899 – Tait's last championship before he sailed for South Africa, never to return. At one time in the morning he was five up but he lost to a three by Ball at the 37th. Darwin reported that: 'The Hoylake supporters in a body retired to the clubhouse after the 36th hole. They could endure no more and waited, with their heads presumably buried in cushions, till someone came to tell them what had happened.'

Darwin liked to end any account of Tait with those words of Andrew Lang: 'I never heard a word said against him except a solitary complaint. That, in the lightness of his heart, he played pibrochs round the drowsy town at the midnight hour. What would we not give to hear his pipes again?'

Bill Miller

WHERE, long ago, he would have won the honour out on the course, in more modern times the captain of the Honourable Company is invited by his predecessor after consultation with past captains. The nomination then has to be ratified at the club's AGM. In 1980, the incumbent was Bill Miller and one would wager that it was more than just a happy accident that, in a year when the Open returned to Muirfield for the twelfth time, the captain was a man already deeply steeped in the staging of the great championship.

The image of the Royal and Ancient committee men at the time of an Open is of ruddy faces above the statutory blazers and rosettes. Many of those countenances, though, would have paled at the very thought of undertaking the unique double which stood to the name of William

Mitchell Miller that year in the domain of officialdom.

Chairman of the R & A's championship committee in the successful mounting of the Open at Royal Lytham and St Annes in 1974, at Carnoustie in 1975 and at Royal Birkdale in 1976, Miller occupied in 1980 what was generally recognised as the chief executive office of the R & A – chairman of the General Committee. Throw in the odd other office such as his role as co-chairman of the World Amateur Golf Council – the body responsible for the running of the World Cup, alias the Eisenhower Trophy – and it was not difficult to understand how his own handicap had lapsed.

In his schooldays, first at Ardvreck and then at Rugby, and during his nine years as a regular soldier in the Grenadier Guards, Miller had dabbled in a variety of sports and had, in fact, been a useful enough full-back to understudy, in the London Scottish First XV, the celebrated Scottish international, Keith Geddes. But more and more, golf took precedence. In his military career, he had to play his golf where he found it with, among his more vivid memories, a match played on the nine-hole course at Tripoli where the greens were compounded of oil and sand over a concrete base.

As ADC to General Horatius Murray, he found himself making up a four. The other two members were Lord Louis Mountbatten and a member of the Honourable Company in the future Brigadier Billy Steele who, in pre-war days, had beaten the then amateur Bobby Locke at Muirfield by 3 and 2, playing the four holes from the thirteenth in 2, 3, 3, 3. A polo player rather than a golfer, Lord Mountbatten had not wielded a club in years but the majestic drive he struck far down the first fairway was with Miller for the rest of his days. On the strength of that round, he mused, 'I should say Lord Mountbatten was a completely natural sportsman who, had he been born into a different family, might have reached the top in one game or another.'

With the army contracting, Miller (by then a major) decided to become a stockbroker, his last memory of services' golf being of an army championship at Muirfield in the mid-1950s when the winner was an as yet unhonoured and unsung young subaltern, Second-Lieutenant M.F. Bonallack.

Bill Miller, captain of the Honourable Company 1980-82

Once two handicap at St George's Hill, and the possessor of a winner's medal from the Halford Hewitt – albeit a somewhat bashful possessor, since he had been out of form that week and did not play in the final – Miller calculated that, in 1976, his final year as chairman of the Championship Committee, he had been away from home on R & A business for exactly a hundred days. His wife, Susan, was herself enmeshed in that she was at that time the R & A's appointed physiotherapist for the Open championship – mercifully, perhaps, since it helped to make her more understanding than might have been many another long-suffering spouse.

In the past quarter of a century, few members of the Honourable Company became better known to the golfing world at large than the zealous Miller. One of the rewards of R & A office for such an enthusiast is that many of the game's greats become personal friends. What is more, the angle from which an official like Miller habitually sees golf's household names can be more than a little different from that of the general public or even the majority of the press. In support of which contention, Miller would tell of how he was the committee member travelling with the second-

THE POOL

It was John Chiene, brother of the 1962–63 captain, George Chiene, who invented the Muirfield pool. It operates on Wednesdays, Saturdays and Sundays, members merely phoning in to have their name included among those from whom the secretary, with the aid of his computer, will concoct the day's foursomes matches. He will ring the changes to ensure that different people play with and against each other while simultaneously striving to provide well-balanced matches. It has become one of the Honourable Company's most popular features.

last match on the final day of the 1968 Open at Carnoustie when Gary Player was being hounded down the finishing stretch by Jack Nicklaus.

'What are you trying to do to me?' Player had wailed in mock protest as Nicklaus thumped his ball aboard the short sixteenth, a great stroke. 'I'm trying to beat you, what do you think I am trying to do?' Nicklaus had retorted, with a nice brand of bemused amusement.

And yet, which is why it became Bill Miller's signature story with regard to his years in office, when they came to the eighteenth with just two strokes separating them, it was Nicklaus who interceded on Player's behalf on a point of law.

At lunchtime that day, Miller had had the sudden thought to seek the advice of Stewart Lawson, chairman of the R & A Rules Committee, on the precise ruling where the marks left on the green by the plugging of an old hole were concerned. Lawson, a veritable fountain of knowledge on such matters, had replied that, oddly enough, it was something he had just been discussing, because it happened to be one of the few points on which the R & A and the United States Golf Association were still at variance. In contrast to the USGA, the R & A treated it as just a rub of the green.

With just such a disused hole on his line on the home green, Player asked if Miller could repair the scar for him and Nicklaus heard Miller respond in the negative. 'That's not right,' objected Nicklaus at once, citing a similar experience he had had shortly before in America and the very different answer he had received from so revered an official as Joe Dey. Because of that previous conversation with Lawson, Miller – at what could otherwise have been an exceedingly sticky moment – was able to explain with a firm confidence exactly what the position was and both players, plainly appreciating that he knew what he was talking about, readily accepted the verdict.

But, apart from intoning a silent prayer of thanksgiving for that final item of eleventh-hour homework, Miller came from that last green marvelling that, at such a time, Nicklaus should have had thoughts for the other man, of justice rather than of his own fast-fading chances.

'They were both Old Boys of Muirfield,' Miller would add, smiling, 'in that both had won the Open there for a first time. Back in the eighteenth century, they did not have to bother with quite such niceties but somehow I think that the promulgators of the Thirteen Articles would have approved.'

Jim Draper

JIM DRAPER who, after losing to Arthur Perowne in the quarter-finals of the Amateur championship at Hoylake in 1953, defeated Prestwick's Bill Gray by 4 and 3 to win the 1954 Scottish Amateur championship at Nairn.

A native of Biggar and a graduate of Edinburgh University, Draper, secretary of a whisky firm in Markinch, made his internationl début later that summer in the Home Internationals at Royal Porthcawl.

James Logan

JAMES LOGAN – or, as he was more commonly known, Shay Logan – spanned six Opens at Muirfield from Alf Perry's win in 1935 to Tom Watson's in 1980. What was more, save for the war years, he had been a greenkeeper in East Lothian since 1927 – first under his father, the head greenkeeper at Gullane, and then at Muirfield.

'Logan has been truly superb,' exclaimed Charles Lawrie, when chairman of the R & A championship committee for the Open of 1972. 'He knows the local conditions and the course as a man might know his own flesh and blood. If I deserve any credit it is for having had sufficient sense to leave it up to him.'

Logan always had his own views. 'Contrary to what many think,' he once told the writer, 'frost and snow are good for a golf course. The frost makes the ground rise, breaks it up, removes the need to aerate it while the snow is a protective blanket which keeps the heat in. All you need to know then – provided you have not been so stupid as to pile on the manure over August, September and October which is the quick road to fusarium – is when to roll it.' And how do you know that? 'Why, you feel it through your feet just by walking.'

'God,' Logan was fond of asserting, 'is the best greenkeeper.' Which was his way of saying that you must appreciate when to let nature take its course and not be carried away by modern fertilisers and artificial watering.

Yet, if God were the best greenkeeper, one could never escape feeling that Logan had to be close behind and, as to getting his own way, it was probably a dead-heat. Even Gerald Micklem, who did so much for golf but who was a sometimes less than benevolent despot, met his match in Logan. Micklem was chairman of the R & A championship committee for the Open of 1966 when the rough was so deep that Harold Henning took one look and staggered weakly back to bed. 'It's virtually ungraded,' protested Harold the Horse, 'and even if you are only two yards off the fairway you require a fully-fledged search warrant!'

On the evening of the championship even Micklem got cold feet and made his way to Logan's home where the great man, no doubt with the aid of a dram or two, was relaxing, satisfied that he could do no more. As Guy Robertson-Durham told the story, Micklem, muttering that perhaps it was a little too severe, commanded him to cut the rough back here and possibly there. 'Not on your nelly, Mr Micklem,' quoth Logan, 'You asked for it and you've got it!'

Reid Jack driving in the 1959 Walker Cup and, right, his scorecard of 68 in the 1959 Open

Reid Jack

REID JACK'S championship days were long gone by the time he became a member of the Honourable Company and, indeed, because of other commitments, his time at the top was renowned for its quality rather than longevity. Born in Cumbernauld in 1924, he won the Scottish Amateur championship at Muirfield in 1955 and the

N CHAMPIONSHIP 1959

RABLE COMPANY OF EDINBURGH GOLFERS.
MUIRFIELD

A.M. DAY PLAYER R. REID JACK

Score for Hole	Hole No.	Score for Hole
4	10	4
4	11	3
3	12	4
3	13	3
5	14	5
4	15	5
4	16	2
4	17	4
4	18	3
TOTAL OUT 35	TOTAL IN	33
	TOTAL OUT	35
MATCH No. 10	2/14	68

AYER'S SIGNATURE
RKER'S SIGNATURE

Amateur itself in 1957, having reached the semi-finals the previous year.

Lightly built but a lovely stylist, he always looked class, a swing founded on the eternal verities readily handling the torque of hickory in an exhibition match against the steel shafts of the much more mechanical Ronnie Shade. In the 1959 Open championship at Muirfield, wherein he had rounds of 71, 75, 68, 74, he finished fifth, a placing not bettered by any amateur since the Second World War. An Eisenhower Trophy player in 1958, he played in the Walker Cups of 1957 and 1959, his matches with Billy Joe Patton, who had himself come third behind Ben Hogan and Sam Snead in the 1954 US Masters, ranking among the highlights of his career.

Playing top at Minikahda, he was five up on Patton at lunch but lost on the 36th green after an afternoon in which Patton's powers of recovery from his wilder shots would have startled a Seve Ballesteros. Though Great Britain and Ireland had already lost by the time the match ended, Jack gained a measure of revenge by defeating Patton by 5 and 3 at Muirfield in 1959. It was nowhere near as dramatic as their previous meeting but a match compelling in its contrasts.

One will not easily forget Jack's measured rhythm set against a player with a swing so fast as to rekindle the story South Africa's Dale Hayes used to tell of a teaching professional who promised him. 'Come to me for just six lessons and I'll slow your swing to a blur ...'

Peter Burt

IN the Spring Medal on 1 May 1993, Peter Burt, with the aid of three 2s, won with a 69 which matched the score with which Major David Blair had won the Winter Medal in 1961. Where Blair was a Walker Cup golfer, Burt, Chief General Manager of the Bank of Scotland, was off a 5 handicap at the time of his 69. But he had been as low as 1 and had won both the Willie Park putter at Musselburgh and the Haddington Open, both 36-hole events.

Thrice in a winning Merchistonian team in the Queen Elizabeth and once in the Halford Hewitt, Burt has the unusual distinction of having figured in the winning of the County Cup with three different clubs – Longniddry, Gullane and the Honourable Company.

Blair: 3 4 3 3 4 4 2 5 4 = 32 Out
5 5 4 3 5 4 3 4 4 = 37 Home

Burt: 5 4 4 2 5 4 2 4 5 = 35 Out
5 3 4 2 5 3 3 5 4 = 34 Home

Helen Ramanauskas

A cross dangles from the chain around the neck of Helen Ramanauskas but for many years, give or take an apostrophe, the Lord's Day to her connoted not a Sunday but a Monday. For that was the day of the week at Muirfield when, in the great legal tradition of the founding fathers, the Law Lords of the Honourable Company played their golf. After 29 years at Muirfield, first as a house table maid and then as the assistant stewardess, Mrs Ramanauskas, though now retired, is deeply steeped in the Honourable Company as seen from her angle. Nor has any captain, from John Rattray to Douglas Foulis, been more protective of the reputation and renown of that golfing body.

Her first Open was that of 1966 and it remains her favourite to this day, not least because of a gesture by the winner, Jack Nicklaus. 'After he had won, and the prize-giving was over, he came back into the clubhouse and shook hands with each of the staff, thanking them. When you think of all he had won, it was a lovely thing for him to think of doing and, perhaps because of it, he has always been my favourite golfer.'

'Pure gold,' declared Captain Paddy Hanmer, bracketing Helen with her great friend, Connie Gourlay, another cherished servant of the club who is soon to retire herself. Helen herself would always want the former cashier, Helen Gordon, similarly included in such accolades, and Gordon's predecessor, Jenny Straiton, who did a great deal to keep the club ticking over in the war years.

Rob Macgregor

IN seniority among past captains, Rob Macgregor is now second only to the octogenarian, James Dallmeyer, who held that office in 1952–53. 'Jimmy Dallmeyer,' reminisces Macgregor, 'had a truly wonderful swing and, when I first encountered him, which was when I was at Cambridge and he was playing for Royal Worlington, he must have been scratch or close to it. Though he was quite unaware of it, he was known as Bollinger in those days because that was his favourite tipple, but the nickname lapsed. The Second World War followed in which he commanded the First Regiment of the Lothian and Border Horses. He was taken prisoner but escaped and ended up with a very distinguished war record.

'He was one of the great club members and the captain who introduced the New Year's Day Frolic when everyone brings a prize and everyone takes one home even if it is the one he brought himself! It is played as a Stableford and, for the purpose of the Frolic, Jimmy laid down a par of his own devising. The four par 3s are played as such but every other hole is a 5 with the exception of the second and the eleventh which are played as 4s. That par for the Frolic holds good to this day and it is also used for the consolation Stableford following the Captain's Weekend.'

Macgregor had been a golf Blue in his Cambridge days, being one of three members of the team who, on Macgregor's twenty-first birthday, matched their best ball against Henry Cotton in a match at Ashridge – a match which, understandably, has remained vividly etched in his memory.

A gunner in the Cambridge OTC, he was called up and was serving with the 135th North Hertfordshire Yeomanry, Field Regiment RA in Singapore, when he was captured by the Japanese. He was a PoW for three and a half years, compelled to help build the Bridge on the River Kwai and to work on the railway. It was a grim experience by any yardstick but he still

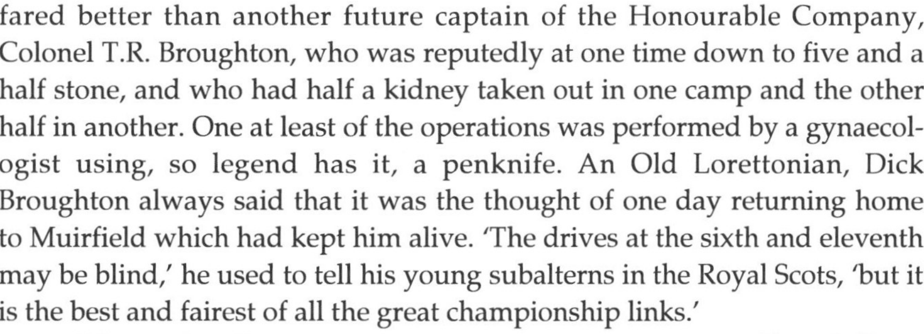

Left: Helen Ramanauskas serving a customer in the dining-room at Muirfield

Below: Rob Macgregor, captain of the Honourable Company 1968-70

fared better than another future captain of the Honourable Company, Colonel T.R. Broughton, who was reputedly at one time down to five and a half stone, and who had half a kidney taken out in one camp and the other half in another. One at least of the operations was performed by a gynaecologist using, so legend has it, a penknife. An Old Lorettonian, Dick Broughton always said that it was the thought of one day returning home to Muirfield which had kept him alive. 'The drives at the sixth and eleventh may be blind,' he used to tell his young subalterns in the Royal Scots, 'but it is the best and fairest of all the great championship links.'

Educated at Cargilfield and Rugby before going up to Clare College, Cambridge, Macgregor came back to Scotland after the war. A member of the Honourable Company since 1940, he was captain in 1968–70 and nowadays is a much revered elder statesman. The better players of his day included such as Squiggles Mackie, Charles McQueen, George Chiene, Henry Turcan, David Middleton and the Scotland cricketer, Logan McClure, not to mention Ian Considine, who reached the last eight of the 1949 Amateur at Portmarnock, and Melville Bucher who was a Scottish international. 'But in the department of good golfers,' he states, unequivocally, 'the outstanding members' member was Guy Robertson-Durham. He was very long but it was his short game, his putting and his pitching and chipping, which won him most of his matches – that and the fact that he was a marvellous competitor.'

There is more than one version of the events preceding the day Robertson-Durham played with King George VI but the best perhaps – and the one authenticated by his widow, Kate – has Guy returning home to find that the R & A's Tom Harvey had been on the phone to tell him he would be playing the next day with Bob McLaren, who was the Honourable Company's captain, Harvey himself and the monarch.

'Wake me in the morning,' Guy instructed his father, 'because I am playing with the King.'

'Don't be so damn stupid, Guy,' replied his parent, impatiently. 'Go to bed and sober up.'

Confronted by a choice of the Honourable Company's spare set and McLaren's own clubs, the King, to McLaren's chagrin, helped himself to the latter. Thus armed, the sovereign was soon displaying the same eye for a ball and games sense as had had him partnering Louis Greig in the men's doubles at Wimbledon. 'He could,' reckoned Robertson-Durham, 'have been very good indeed if he could have given the same time to it as the Duke of Windsor.'

A traditionalist who regrets the passing of the Honourable Company's ballot box and the institution of a handicap prize where formerly there was just a sweep and the scratch medals, Macgregor, who still plays twice a week, never forgets that it is not always the best golfers who make the best members. 'Bill Milligan – Lord Milligan – was a character any club would have loved to have had and the stories attached to him are legion. Such, for instance, as of the day he, as usual, took a taxi to Drem, preparatory to catching a train home to Edinburgh. But he was a great beer drinker and, to his increasing consternation, the train had no corridor. He had to get out at Longniddry urgently and finish the journey by bus.'

A showcase in the dining-room which houses most of the Honourable Company's collection of ancient clubs and balls and some silver trophies. The woods were made by McEwan and Philp. The silverware was the first prize in the 'Great Golf Tournament' played at St Andrews in July 1858 and won by Robert Chambers Jnr

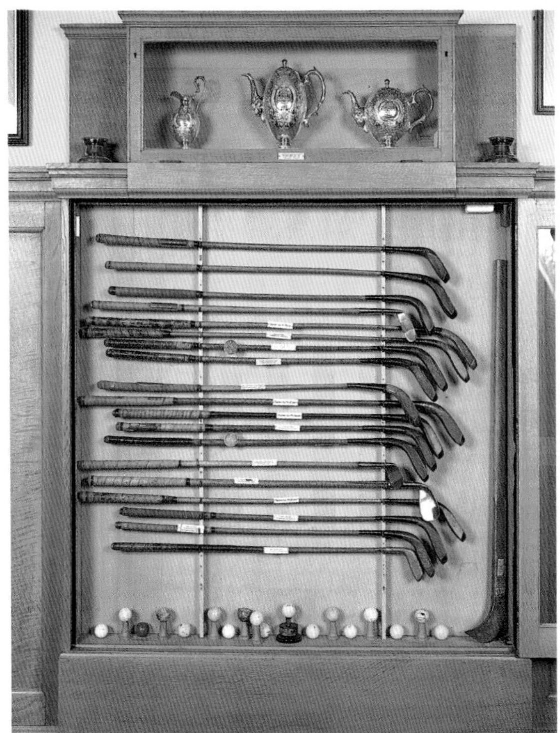

11 A captain for all seasons – Douglas Foulis

CAPTAINS of the Honourable Company nowadays are elected for one year but, unless something untoward has happened to leave the membership unexpectedly dissatisfied, the normal term is two. It is a measure of Douglas Foulis that, having been captain when the 1992 Open was at Muirfield, he has been asked to remain in office for a third year to take in the club's 250th anniversary.

With bat and boot, ski, sail and shot, he has been another of the Honourable Company's innumerable all-round sportsmen but, plainly, golf and the affairs of the Honourable Company have come to occupy many of his leisure hours, the ring of the telephone on golf club business punctuating even his professional life. He is chairman and managing director of Hunter and Foulis – a book-binding firm which, though it would have to give best to the Honourable Company in terms of antiquity, can trace its own antecedents back to 1857 and a tiny close, Strichen's Close, off Edinburgh's Royal Mile. It is a family concern. His father was chairman and managing director before him, though not his immediate predecessor, and the visitor leaves even today with, for all the modernity, a whiff of Old Edinburgh and the impression of a staff affectionately led, not driven.

Left: the dining-room, looking towards the bar at the south end. The windows at the north end of the room overlook the course. Portraits of the captains, from 1749 to the immediate past captain, look down from the walls

The passage from the locker-room to the smoking and dining-rooms accommodate some additional lockers

At Loretto in the 1940s, Foulis won his rugby and cricket colours as, respectively, a full-back and opening batsman, and was captain of shooting. He has been, too, a more than competent skier, yachtsman and archer.

He left school in the war years and at once volunteered for the army, being commissioned in the Royal Artillery with whom he served in India. His regiment were due to move on to Japan but the atom bombs got there ahead of them and they returned home shortly before India's partition. Demobbed, he did a short course at Edinburgh University before joining Hunter and Foulis, beginning on the factory floor and working in each department and on each machine in turn. There followed two years in London and the United States, broadening his experience in respect of his calling. During his sojourn in the south, he played most of his golf at Berkhamsted of which the trees, conspicuous by their absence at Muirfield, are his abiding memory.

During his four years in the army, he had toyed with the notion of becoming a regular soldier, and it was not all that long before he had enlisted in the Territorial Army. Several of his fellow officers were members of the Honourable Company and, in 1956, he himself was elected a member.

At his best, he was four-handicap at Gullane and five at Muirfield. Today, his handicap at Muirfield is 14, a mark these days in full accordance with the handicap regulations where, in the past, each member's handicap was arbitrarily assigned to him by the secretary in conjunction with the captain.

The spring and autumn medals, held on a Saturday, are major

occasions within the club, invariably attracting a good entry. The over-60s, unless competing for the medal itself, play on the Sunday. In contrast, many of the monthly medals draw a field of maybe no more than half a dozen, and even those members will probably be mainly interested in marking a card for handicap purposes. The primary importance of the handicaps is the part they play in the dinner matches, the four-ball encounters which are the very heart and soul of the Honourable Company's golf.

The club committee comprises the captain and treasurer, the secretary, who is *ex officio*, and six committee members, two of whom demit office every year to make way for replacements, though they can be re-elected at some future date. The committee meet every two months but the captain and secretary are frequently in almost daily communication.

Some years ago, a £500 levy (which took effect retrospectively) was placed upon those on the waiting-list, less with a view to raising money which could be profitably invested than to make sure that those who remained on it were serious applicants. Even so, a prospective member can expect to wait more than 20 years before coming up for election.

The entry list is currently closed with the membership at its maximum of 550 full members and 75 overseas members. In addition to some non-playing members, who no longer golf on account of age or infirmity, there are six honorary members – HRH Prince Philip, Duke of Edinburgh, KT; Colonel T.B.A. Evans-Lombe, OBE; His Grace, the Duke of Hamilton; Captain P.W.T. Hanmer, RN retd; Colonel C.J.Y. Dallmeyer, DSO TD; and T.R. Macgregor.

The days of the black ball – not much bigger than a marble and made of wood – are gone. Now, more prosaically, a would-be new member, having been proposed and seconded and the relevant form filled in and lodged, is considered initially by the secretary and captain who check for what is termed 'gross error'. If, in other words, he is obviously totally unsuitable then, in order to spare all concerned unnecessary embarrassment, those who have put him up are quietly advised that it would be unwise to proceed further. If, however, the prospective member gets over that first hurdle, nothing else will happen until he has moved far enough up the waiting list to be within a couple of years of possible election.

Right: the original part of the smoking-room with its imposing portraits of St Clair of Roslin, John Taylor, Robert Maxwell and Sir Alexander Keith, and the bookcase containing the golfing library. Below right: the new extension of the room provides a magnificent panorama of the links as well as extra space. Far right: a corner of the locker-room with its series of plans of the course (see pages 76, 77)

A list of would-be members who have arrived at that stage will be circulated and that is the time for those who wish to support the application to write in and those who have some objection to do likewise. All such correspondence is, of course, confidential in that it goes no further than the secretary, captain and committee. Again, one of the main objects of the exercise is to avoid anybody being subjected to avoidable discomfiture. The publicity surrounding those whose membership ambitions were unfulfilled has been of their own making, not the club's.

After all of which, always providing he has the appropriate support, the golfer will be elected in the fullness of time. But, until not much more than a decade ago, it was all very different, climaxing in the famous – or infamous, depending on your standpoint – ballot box and black ball procedure.

The list of candidates for election would be brought to the notice of the membership and, twice a year or more, the committee would meet in

the Edinburgh Chamber of Commerce, latterly in Hanover Street but before that in Charlotte Square. There would be a separate, named ballot box for each candidate and those ballot boxes would stay open on a given evening for 90 minutes between 4.45 p.m. and 6.15 p.m. A member who wished to cast his vote would come in and, selecting the relevant ballot box or boxes, take one of the wooden balls and insert his hand through a hole. The left-hand drawer was the 'Yes' vote, the right-hand the 'No'. He had no need of a googly for no one could see his hand. At quarter past six, the door would be closed and the secretary would open the ballot boxes – the 'No' drawer first – under the eye of the captain and committee that all might be seen to be open and above board. So many 'Yes' votes nullified one 'No' vote.

Just once in living memory, in the days when the captain was the immensely popular Colonel T.R. Broughton, did the committee unofficially exercise their own discretion, discounting what appeared to be a lone sniper's barrage of black balls. A new member, and a young one at that, had arrived shortly after the ballot boxes had closed but was allowed to vote, the committee looking out of the windows to ease his abashed hurry but hearing a ball being dropped in each of the ballot boxes. When they opened them, there was one black ball, and only one, against every single name. They decided that the only logical explanation was that the fledgling member, in his confusion, had each time holed out in the wrong compartment!

Above: the bar in the dining-room and the cash/reception desk
Opposite: the main display case for the club's trophies including three of the four Silver Clubs presented by the City of Edinburgh. Also included in the display are trays of the vast number of medals won by Robert Maxwell

A little sadly for those who love quaint traditions, that time-honoured process was discontinued as being, with the twenty-first century in sight, an anachronism. A visitor can still inspect a ballot box and balls in the clubhouse, but most were purchased as souvenirs of the old ways by members who had themselves survived that particular inquisition.

The entry fee in 1994 is £860, the annual subscription £430 while, for visitors, it is a charge of £50 for a round, £70 for the day. The Honourable Company, most of whom would no doubt vote for the party which has long claimed to be that of law and order, have for many years given a discount not just to the services but to the police. For them, the fees are £26 a round, £42 for the day.

The membership is changing as society itself changes. The legal profession, the medical, the services and the farming community are still heavily represented but there are more nowadays from the realms of business, commerce and investment. As to visitors, be they societies or otherwise, they are best advised to write at least a year in advance explaining just what they would want. With regard to individuals, they should give their handicaps while it is always a help if there is an accompanying letter from their own club. 'We take people as people,' reflects Foulis, 'and we wouldn't know if some chap might be a spy or something worse.'

Once more, with the aim of preventing any embarrassment, the impending visitor will be furnished with a paper explaining the form in relation to such things as dress and meals. A lady visitor, notes Foulis, must play her golf with a man with both having to apply in good time and the usual manner. She will find new ladies' changing facilities which were installed for the 1992 Open in what used to be the assistant secretary's office.

Members' wives pay only a nominal green fee of £2 and are made very welcome, but there are no lady members as such. Foulis and many other members of the Honourable Company recognise that the day could come when the law of the land will compel all golf clubs to open their doors to both genders but they will cross that bridge when they come to it. Not that they have not hugely admired some of the golf they have seen at Muirfield when they have happily played host to such international events as the Curtis Cup and the Vagliano Trophy. As P.G. Wodehouse observed, a woman is only a woman but a hefty drive is a slosh – but when, in the 1984 Curtis Cup, the members saw the two in blessed union in the person of Laura Davies, even the staunchest male chauvinist could scarce forbear to cheer.

'Don't you know that I would rather be permitted to call you Mary than do the first hole at Muirfield in two?' P.G. Wodehouse's Mortimer Sturgis endeavouring to convey, in *Sundered Hearts*, the depth of his feelings to Miss Somerset whom he erroneously believes to be the Ladies' Open champion.

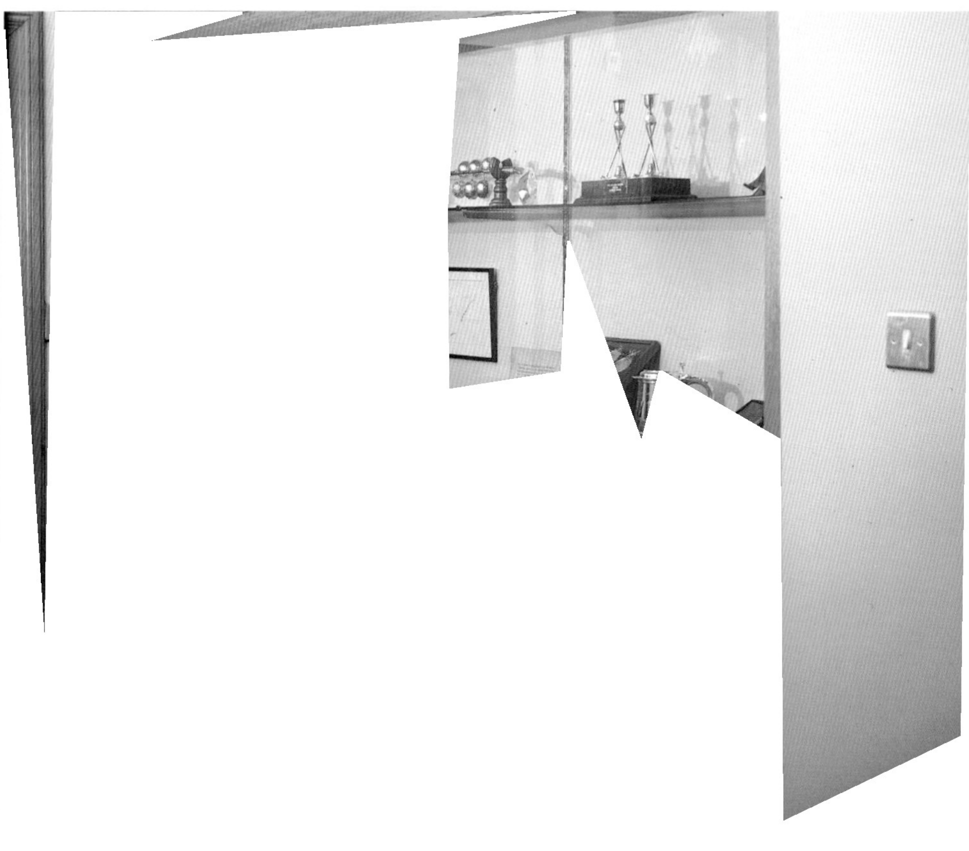

12 *Twelve Open Champions*

Harold Hilton (1892)

AS the world is reminded every time the Open returns to Muirfield, 'Just an auld water meadie' was Andra Kirkaldy's contemptuous dismissal of the Honourable Company's links after the 1892 Open. But Andra had been sorely tried. Scottish professionals had won the first 30 Opens as of divine right. Now, for the second time in three years – sandwiching the win of Andra's brother, Hugh, at St Andrews in 1891 – the Open had been captured by an amateur and, what was worse, a Sassenach, Harold Hilton. In the circumstances, 'an auld water meadie' may well have been but the expurgated version.

In matching the feat of his Hoylake contemporary, John Ball, at Prestwick two years earlier, Hilton had resorted to last-minute cramming. Obliged to earn his living in an office in Liverpool, the 23-year-old Hilton had rather less time for golf than Ball. He travelled to Muirfield overnight and, by way of preparation, had *three* practice rounds on the Tuesday. 'Suicidal', shrugged the pundits. He opened with a 78, then sagged further with an 81, scoring which was blamed on his superabundance of holes on the eve of battle. He trailed the leader, Horace Hutchinson, by seven strokes, and, but for the fact that this was not only the first Open in which admission was charged but the first over 72 holes, that would have been that.

A chain-smoker who 'played magnificent strokes without bothering to take the cigarette from his lips', Hilton sought always to settle early so as 'to miss no chance of avoiding the pressure of the crisis' but, especially in stroke-play, he could fight. A 72 catapulted him to within two strokes of the new leader, Ball. When they teed up for the last round, Ball's triumph at the expense of Hilton in the final of that summer's Amateur was fresh in many minds and not least in those of the two players. But this was to be Hilton's afternoon as Hilton himself must have begun to suspect as, outward bound, he twice sank a chip. He was round in 74 for a total of 305 which was not bettered until Harry Vardon's 300 at Prestwick in 1903.

As an exponent of the spoon, Hilton was considered by many to be without peer and he was a master, too, of improvisation and buzzing backspin. His full-blooded swing was graphically depicted by Bernard Darwin: 'Imagine a short man (five feet six inches in height) with a long club placing his feet with meticulous care with regard to the line and then rather sitting down to the ball. The waggle is careful and restrained; then suddenly all is changed; he seems almost to jump on to his toes in the upswing and fairly fling himself at the ball. There is no doubt at all that he is on his toes at the moment of hitting . . . In the old days, when caps were smaller, his cap always fell off as the club came through.'

The doctrine according to Hilton came to us across the years from Ernest Holderness via Laddie Lucas, the latter a Walker Cup left-hander whose right hand and arm are his stronger. 'Hilton used to say,' Holderness told the young Lucas, 'that when he was playing well, he always felt he was hitting the ball with the back of his left hand – like a backhanded shot at tennis or racquets played with the left hand. Using the left hand,

A sketch done 'on the spot' by A. Donnelly at Muirfield's first Open in 1892. Centre is A.J. Balfour (the Prime Minister) with Hall Blyth on his right. Old Tom Morris with his beard and pipe is on the extreme right, while in the foreground is 'Fiery' the caddie. Note the old windmill

Previous page: putting on the thirteenth green on a practice day for the 1992 Open

Harold Hilton, 'Hoylake's son', was one of four amateurs to win the Open

and keeping the *back* of the head over the ball at impact – not allowing it to come up with the shot – these were the two things Hilton told me he was conscious of when playing his best golf. His two fundamentals.'

Hilton, who latterly could number the aforesaid Andra Kirkaldy among his admirers, won the Open again at Hoylake in 1897 and four British Amateur championships. As for his lesser victories, they were, said Darwin, 'as the sands of the sea'. But what ultimately sets him apart is that he is the only Briton to have won the US Amateur, which he did at Apawamis in 1911, when he was over 40. That summer he did the double, taking the British Amateur at Prestwick.

In the final at Apawamis, though, versus Fred Herreshoff, he hit one of the worst shots of his life at the 37th but his ball ricocheted off a rock on to the green. Perhaps, as Bobby Jones believed, the outcome of a championship really is already written in the stars before the first shot is struck.

Harry Vardon (1896)

HARRY VARDON, whose six Opens remain a record, won the first of them at Muirfield in 1896. J.H. Taylor came to the championship bidding to make it three in a row and was not to know that the man who denied him in a 36-hole play-off was destined to pass with him into golfing history as a member of the Great Triumvirate.

'When I arrived on the last tee,' Vardon wrote, 'I was set with an extremely difficult problem. I required a four to gain a victory outright and a five to tie, which would give me the right to play off with him for the championship. The last hole at Muirfield at this period was a testing one, requiring as it did a good drive and a real good brassie to reach the green. There was, however, a very bad bunker guarding the green and while there was very little difficulty in securing the necessary five, which would enable me to tie, I might very easily take a six in my attempt to reach the green with my second shot. Thoughts flash through the brain with a lightning rapidity at such a moment and to me this was an occasion of the utmost importance. The final decision, however, was to a large extent the result of allowing my eyes to wander among the spectators in front of me. I caught sight of my friend, James Kay of Seaton Carew, making frantic efforts to attract my attention. He was pointing with his hand to the ground this side of the bunker.' Vardon took the advice, which he had not solicited, played short and holed out in five to tie with Taylor on 316.

There being a tournament at North Berwick on the Friday, the play-off was delayed till the Saturday and that gave the championship a twist of twists. Vardon, who was one day to become so pitifully prey to the yips, was a good enough putter in his youth but he had not been at his best on the Muirfield greens and was worried about the play-off. In the corner of Ben Sayers' shop at North Berwick, his eye fell on an ancient cleek. He asked one of the assistants 'to put a new stick in it' and, with that implement, he won the play-off with a 36-hole aggregate of 157 to Taylor's 161. But, strange to relate, he never used it as a putter again.

The former gardener who, as a small boy in Jersey, had begun by playing by moonlight with self-made clubs and large white marbles called taws, was soon the automatic favourite in every event he entered. In his element with the gutta-percha, which he much preferred because it demanded clean hitting – he took hardly any turf even with his famous push shot – he was so unfailingly consistent in his striking as, in the words of Andra Kirkaldy, 'to break the heart of an iron ox'. But even Vardon lost out when, over the Old Course, St Andrews, he took on the better ball of the Honourable Company's Leslie Balfour-Melville and J.E. Laidlay.

Harry Vardon in trouble at the ninth hole at Muirfield in the 1912 Open

The US Open champion in 1900, he favoured a bent left arm which did not straighten till the start of the downswing. When questioned, he would content himself with murmuring mildly but with a mischievous menace, 'I *like* playing against golfers with a straight left arm.' Bernard Darwin was not taken by his action when first he saw it because it offended the accepted canons. For one thing, his right elbow flew. But that was what they were to say of Jack Nicklaus and he, too, turned out to be a bit useful.

Darwin was won over with a vengeance and now Vardon – who, in spite of having suffered so badly from tuberculosis, 'came within an eyelash' of winning the 1920 US Open at the age of 50 – is seen as the father of the modern swing. Using the overlapping grip which acquired his name, Vardon took the club straight back with the hands leading and lifted it quite sharply into an upright plane. It was far removed from the old St Andrews swingers and gave him unusual height on his flight, enabling him to drop the ball in softly left to right.

He could be very long and his accuracy gave rise to that old chestnut about his being unable to play the same course twice in a day because his drives in the afternoon finished in his morning divot holes – an obviously apocryphal tale which yet had a prosaic latter-day professional grumbling, 'If he was *that* accurate why did he not just avoid them?'

Bobby Jones observed that where, with his 'stronger' grip, his hands were fractionally ahead of the ball at impact, Vardon's were perceptibly behind, the club being whipped through rather than pulled.

Vardon's rhythm was smooth and graceful, Horace Hutchinson noting that he played with clubs which were shorter and lighter than those used by the other players of his day. By all accounts, if he were away from home and did not have his clubs with him, he would often borrow a set of clubs from a lady member – not something which would have been easily done at the Honourable Company. However, members of the Honourable Company, from Singing Jamie Balfour and before, would have been as one with him in his oft-quoted retort to a lady preaching temperance: 'Moderation in all things, Madam, but I have never lost to a teetotaller in my life!'

James Braid as seen by 'Spy' in the 'Vanity Fair' supplement

James Braid (1901 and 1906)

THE first-born of the Great Triumvirate and the first to win five Opens, Braid was the son of an Elie ploughman. Vardon and Taylor had already won three Opens apiece when Braid, who had been a runner-up to Harold Hilton in 1897, teed up at Muirfield in the summer of 1901, the first year when the entry for the Open exceeded 100. Having won the preceding Musselburgh Open with the then remarkable tally of 140, he was in the best of spirits but not overconfident. On his own admission, Braid liked to feel 'a little nervous' before a championship.

Letter from Leslie J. Taylor on behalf of his father J.H. Taylor (then in his 92nd year) to D.J.R. Mackay, dated 17th June 1962 (All of the latter-day Big Three – Arnold Palmer, Jack Nicklaus and Gary Player – now wear contact lenses):

Dear Mr Mackay,

On behalf of my father, J.H. Taylor, I would like to thank you for the letter you recently wrote to him. I very much regret to say that my father has not been able to reply personally to his letters for the past six months as he is now enfeebled and finds letter writing entirely beyond him. Physically, he is pretty fit considering he is now in his 92nd year and gets about fairly well. As regards your enquiry concerning the eyesight test and the photograph given to your father by the 'Triumvirate' and Alex Herd, I am pleased to say that I can help you. For 25 years I was assistant to my father at the Royal Mid-Surrey Golf Club and heard him relate this most interesting story on several occasions whilst talking to members about the old days of Braid, Herd, Vardon and himself.

The facts, as I well recall my father telling them, are as follows. The four were, after a day's golf, walking along an Edinburgh street when Alex Herd complained that he had putted badly and said that he had not sighted the ball clearly on the greens and wondered whether it was due to his liver being out of order or to his eyesight becoming in any way

Yet, as Bernard Darwin said of him, no player 'unless it be Padgham today has worn so calm a mask as Braid . . . All human emotions seemed temporarily wiped from his face and this complete tranquillity made a notable contrast with what has been called the "divine fury" of his hitting. He lashed at the ball as if he would kill it, and at long intervals he was capable of a terrific hook.' In truth, he hooked his opening tee shot at Muirfield over the wall and so began the 1901 Open with a five.

But, if he were wont to make more mistakes than a Vardon or a Taylor, he was, in Darwin's estimation, their superior in terms of his ability to recover: 'Not merely could he move mountains by sheer strength but he was master of every kind of shot, delicate or ferocious, when in trouble, in particular the "explosion" shot from a bunker near the pin.'

He took 43 to go out that first day before battling successfully with a westerly wind on the homeward journey to be back in 36 – a recovery which left him two shots to Vardon's rear. After a second-round 76, the two were tied in what was by then a two-horse race, with Taylor seven shots adrift. Vardon was the odds-on favourite going into the third round but Braid, whose putting was so suspect in his early years that he preferred to use a cleek, putted well enough that morning to foil the forecasts. His 74 left him five ahead.

By the time he came to Muirfield's by now notorious eighteenth in the last round, Braid could afford, as the golf writer, Tom Scott, noted, 'to indulge in a little flourish. He lashed into a long drive, and bent into the succeeding cleek shot with equal ferocity. The shaft splintered and the head of the cleek flew off by itself. But the ball had flown straight and true for the centre of the green and Braid, with two putts and no pressure on him at all, was champion; the final link of the Great Triumvirate was in place.'

impaired. This aroused the interest of the others, especially my father, who suggested that they all went together and have their eyes tested by a really competent man.

Furthermore, in very non-technical style, I well recall what my father used to say was the result of their visit. Briefly, the one who had anything approaching perfect sight was Harry Vardon, with Alex Herd a good second. My father's right eye was very weak (he used to address the ball with his head turned slightly to the right) and James Braid's sight the weakest of all. As regards the latter, it was a sort of standing joke between the other three never to concede a short putt to Braid as they considered it to be his golfing 'Achilles heel'. Also, at past 60 years of age, when he was still playing very fine golf indeed, he confided to my father that he then never saw the ball in flight after he had hit it.

James Braid receiving the Gold Medal at the 1901 Open championship

Braid was 31 at the time, his late arrival being due to parents who had steered him from school into joinery. In their view, the life of a craftsman was more respectable than that of a professional golfer. But joinery had paved the way for clubmaking and it was while working in that capacity for the Army and Navy Stores that he played at Sandwich in 1894 in his first Open. He finished tenth and, though he did not make the journey north to St Andrews the following year, halved with J.H. Taylor, the 1895 champion, in a match which in effect decreed that his future lay in the professional game. He was given a post of his own at Romford, the following spring, while his legendary association with Walton Heath began in 1904.

When Ross Whitehead joined him as an assistant, Braid took him out to the eighteenth and had him set up on the grass upslope of the cross-bunkers. The left shoulder was thereby raised much higher than the right, the whole position a precursor of what was later to be known as the K address. 'Now that,' advised the great man, 'is the feeling I want you to have every time you address the ball.'

James Braid at Muirfield in 1901. Note the 'open' stance at address

Having collected the second of his five Opens at St Andrews in 1905, Braid won again at Muirfield in 1906. His 300 aggregate was nine shots fewer than it had been five years earlier – something which doubtless had more than a little to do with putting surfaces which that venerated sage, Horace Hutchinson, rated 'excellent'.

There were whispers, on the eve of the 1906 championship, that the days of the Triumvirate were over. Yet they came, as ever, to the fore, with Taylor the leader at the end of the first 36 holes and still ahead after the third round. At this point, he was a shot ahead of Rowland Jones and three clear of both Braid and Vardon. In the fourth round, all but Braid fell away: Taylor had an 80, Jones an 83, Vardon a 78. Whereupon Braid closed with a 73, with his playing of the eighteenth a joyous as opposed to nerve-jangling affair as he finished four ahead of Taylor, five clear of Vardon.

Braid won his five Opens – only one of them with the gutta-percha – in the space of ten years and all of them in Scotland. America never saw him, partly because he disliked the idea of so long a voyage but also because he viewed the New World with the same suspicion as he viewed plus-fours, refusing ever to don anything so trendy. However, in a message of hope to all mankind, Braid who, at the age of 57, reached the final of the *News of the World* PGA championship, spoke of having gone to bed one night a short hitter but woken up a long one.

Alas, Darwin, in a dampener tantamount to telling the children on Christmas Eve that there was no Santa Claus, opined that what Braid described as the greatest mystery he had encountered in golf was no miracle at all but all down to Braid's procurement, for 18p, of a driver with a longer shaft and flatter lie which had formerly belonged to the six feet four inch John Berwick.

A descendant of Charles Darwin, apologised 'Bernardo', had to prefer the scientific explanation but the barrister he once was should have detected the flaw in the argument. That Braid, a clubmaker himself, would never have missed the connection had it been pertinent.

Ted Ray (1912)

THIS 'huge, lumbering figure of a man', as he has more than once been described, emerged from the layered shadows of the Great Triumvirate to win the Open of 1912. His 295 aggregate was a figure which reflected refinements in terms of clubs and balls even if Vardon, who finished in second place, four shots to his rear, would spend much of the week talking nostalgically about the merits of the old gutty as opposed to the new hard-cored ball. 'Ray', in the incisive summation of Bernard Darwin, 'was unquestionably the player of his year and always a formidable one, not to be judged by any too nice and pedantic standards.'

Ray knew well enough what they said of him. 'I have always,' said he, 'been known as unorthodox. But I am not so unorthodox as some may think . . . My method is one which might with advantage be adopted by the generality of golfers. The underlying principle of my style, if it may be called style, is that of attacking the ball without taking too much account of grace.'

He could not resist spelling out his irritation at those golfers who, in making a tee shot, looked as if they were 'posing for the camera instead of playing for results . . . I have seen them bring the club over their left shoulder at the finish of a swing by the deliberate act of lifting it there. That is no use at all. Wherever the clubhead finishes, it must get there entirely by its own momentum. In fact, the finish is of no consequence, except in as far as it indicates the completeness of the follow-through.'

Since his hard-hitting philosophy – 'the faster the clubhead flies through, the more likely is the ball to be cleanly hit' – was coupled with a touch of sway and heave, Ray was prone to the odd disastrous shot. Indeed, as far as the cartoonists were concerned, he was forever attempting an escape à la Houdini from an impenetrable forest of whins and bents.

But if Ray's rhythm was not that of a slow waltz, it was there just the same, and, at Muirfield, he was steadiness personified. Again, his short-game had about it the sensitivity of a gentle giant, lighting his play on and around the greens throughout all four rounds. After opening scores of 71 and 73, he held a two-shot lead over Vardon, with Braid one further back. Round three saw his pursuers falling away, with Vardon, after his 81, blaming the 'kick' of his new-fangled rubber-cored ball – 'a monstrosity' – for the two sixes on his card. Vardon came back in the fourth round with a 71 which had him thinking, for ever more, that the 1912 Open should have been his, but Ray, to his credit, held him off to finish a shot ahead of him.

He abhorred the very word 'theory' but he knew a lot more about the golf swing than many supposed, recognising that there was no greater killer in respect of length than what has come to be labelled the reverse pivot. Similarly, he preached against the straightening of the right leg on the backswing which so many advocated in favour of keeping both knees flexed. Doing so, he asserted, facilitated both the correct shoulder turn on the backswing and the movement into impact.

His Open championship triumph at Muirfield had golfers everywhere lapping up the advice which Ray bestowed on the fellow who asked, in all seriousness, how he could best find more length. Namely, 'Hit it a bloody sight harder, mate!'

Some four score years later, the kindred spirit that was Long John Daly was reminding his caddie, on his way to winning the 1991 US PGA championship at Crooked Stick, for which he had started the week as ninth reserve, to declaim 'Kill!' to him on every tee. Was that Ray, who himself won the 1920 US Open, one heard chuckling or just the wind in the trees?

Walter Hagen (1929)

IN winning in 1929, just a fortnight after the British had beaten the Americans in the Ryder Cup, Hagen had three rounds of 75 separated on the second day by a record 67. Percy Alliss's 69 of the day before became, literally as well as idiomatically, yesterday's news. It was a not untypical performance, for Hagen made a habit of leaving everyone else in the shade. Like Henry Cotton, who was pictured shaking his hand after that 67, he had style, with his way of life setting new standards for professionals who, up until then, had looked for little more out of life than a few extra yards off the tee.

Left: Ted Ray after his victory in the 1912 Open

Muirfield, to Hagen, was situated in Scotland's Arctic circle – 'the water actually froze in the pails on the tees'. Nor would the greenkeepers of the day have been too enamoured of The Haig's description of their methods though, to modern enthusiasts, it is intriguing that it was the Americans who were fretting at how fast the greens were. 'They never artificially altered those greens,' claimed Hagen. 'The idea is to play them as nearly to their natural state as possible. So these fellows just run a close mower over what little grass has dared to show its head after the sheep got through and shaved it off clean. Leo [Diegel] watched them disgustedly,

Photographed in Aberlady: left to right: C.R. Smith (Elie), James Braid (5 Opens), Ted Ray (2 Opens, 1 US Open), J.H. Taylor (5 Opens, 2nd US Open), Harry Vardon (6 Opens, 1 US Open)

noting the slick, smooth surface. "Why don't you iron it now?" he asked.'

Hagen's 67 – out in 33, back in 34 – was a round in which he capitalised on the inviting, early conditions. 'Oh what a beautiful morning!' he was moved to exclaim at the end of it. However, those who watched the four rounds of the championship were taken more with the opening holes to his third round.

'From the start,' wrote Darwin, 'he played like a conqueror. He dealt with the storm like an artist and his touch on the windswept greens was beautiful. His start, 4, 4, 3, 3, 4, 4, was perfect for six holes, and he had added to his lead on both Englishmen [Alliss and Mitchell].'

He finished the day four ahead of the former and five clear of the latter. It surprised him not at all. 'I'd spent plenty of effort and study to conquer that style of weather, since that disastrous finish I'd made in my first British Open in 1920.' Having opened with a wind-tossed 85, he that year had come 53rd out of a field of 54. His ploy was one of using clubs

Right: Walter Hagen driving from the first tee in the 1929 Open

The American invaders of our Open – Leo Diegel, John Farrell and Walter Hagen

Below: panorama of the spectators watching Hagen win the 1929 championship

with less loft and to hit his approach shots with a long roll in mind. 'I played a number of strokes of ordinary mashie-niblick and mashie length with much straighter-faced irons.'

Hagen's last round was nothing less than a triumphant procession. He holed a good putt for a three at the second and, to use Darwin's words, 'went careering joyously along until he was two under fours for seven holes'. Then, after going to four under at the eighth, he embarked on 'a holding-on phase'. It included a six at the ninth where he hooked his second hard up against the wall but, in a typically extravagant and unexpected touch, produced a left-handed club from his bag, 'much as a conjurer produces a goldfish out of a hat'.

Out in 35 and ten ahead, he enjoyed having the stage to himself homeward bound. His finish took in two bunkers in the last four holes and a missed tiddler at the last. If it was not quite the dashing close he had in mind, nothing could detract from the exaltation he felt at what was ultimately a six-shot winning margin over Johnny Farrell. 'In my other three British Open championships,' he would recall, 'there was just one stroke between me and the runner-up.'

The prizemoney – £100 – was, to Hagen, neither here nor there and, indeed, he gave it to his caddie. 'The real pay-off for us in those days was the glory of adding that championship to our records and of getting names on the mug.' He had won from a field which contained the US Ryder Cup team and such formidable transplanted transatlantic Scots as Bobby Cruikshank, Tommy Armour and MacDonald Smith. Furthermore, he had, in his own phrase, taken a terrific shellacking from George Duncan in the Ryder Cup at Moortown, trounced by 10 and 8.

For all his flash exterior, his quiet reverence for the Open never wavered: 'In spite of all the new fields to conquer offered our present-day golfers, I still hold that no golfer is a true champion until he has played and won the great British Open cup . . . until he conquers those windswept seaside links.'

Hagen always brings to mind the lady who said that Shakespeare was all right but there were too many quotations. Such has been the mileage enjoyed by so many of his quips. As, for example, 'I never wanted to be a millionaire – I just wanted to live like one.' Or his advice, since we only pass this way once, to stop and smell the flowers; or his rejoinder to a reproachful reminder, as he partied far into the night before the final day of

the 1929 Open, that the highly strung Leo Diegel, who was leading by two strokes, had been in bed for hours, 'Yeah – but he's not sleeping!'

Big Jack some folk still call Jack Nicklaus though he is not that tall and, in the same way, though Hagen was only about five feet ten inches in height, Damon Runyon always referred to him as the Big Fellow. 'He seemed,' said O.B. Keeler, 'to dilate at impact.'

He had a wide stance and while Darwin thought him a better iron player than wood, Keeler took the opposite view. His showmanship and powers of recovery were legend and Bobby Locke used to tell how it was from Hagen that he learned how to putt with topspin. There was something of a sway in his free, slashing swing but, as with Ted Ray, much of it took place after the ball had been hit.

He was, above all, a compulsive competitor, Bob Harlow, his manager saying of him, 'If Walter got in a game of tiddly-winks with a couple of kids on the nursery floor, he would try as hard to beat them as he did to win the Open in Britain.'

'I love to play with Walter,' remarked Bobby Jones. 'He goes along, chin up, smiling away; never grousing about his luck, playing the ball as he finds it. He can come nearer beating luck itself than anybody I know.'

Henry Cotton uses the orthodox overlapping grip, with a glove to emphasize a firm grip with the left hand. Note the right forefinger crooked round the shaft, giving an impression of tremendous power

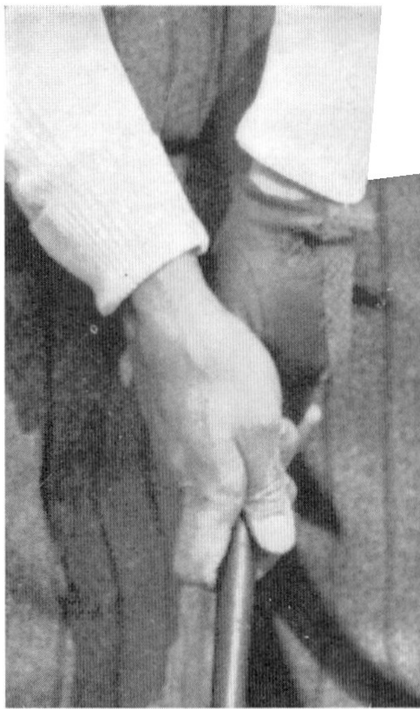

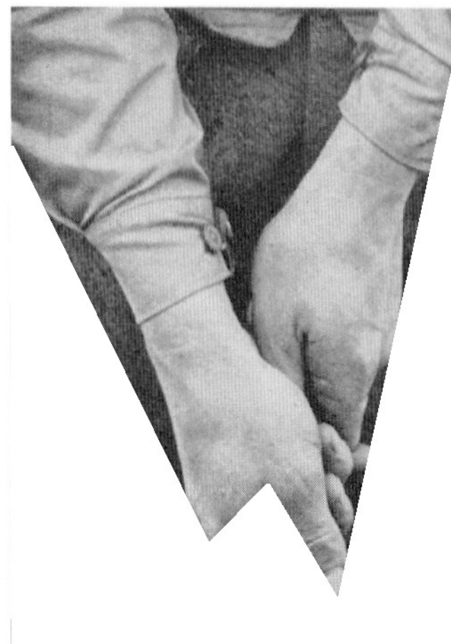

***Alfred Padgham** – an orthodox example of the standard overlapping, or 'Vardon' grip. More right hand than Perry, but less than Cotton*

Alf Perry (1935)

AT 66-1, Alf Perry was scarcely the cynosure of all eyes. Nor was his performance in the qualifying rounds – he made it with only a couple of strokes to spare – such as to have anyone taking a second look. Yet, with a total of 283, Perry would win with strokes to spare from a field which included not only the defending champion, Henry Cotton, but such as Lawson Little, Macdonald Smith and Charles Whitcombe. A two-club golfer at the age of six – his father had given him a brassie and a niblick – Perry had been forced to improvise, learn all the shots. Not only that, but he was always sufficiently ambidextrous to have the beating of many a club golfer when playing left-handed.

He went into the final round on 211, a shot ahead of Whitcombe. The latter, piquantly, was the man from whom he had derived his own distinctive grip with the right hand well under the shaft – a hooker's grip which, in his opinion, accounted for much of the 'dig' he got into his shots with his forceful punch of a swing. At the first on the last afternoon, he drove into rough and then, having recovered, took four to get down from not all that far off the green to open with a six. Not the most auspicious way to begin a round which, one way or the other, was going to be the most important of his life. It goes without saying that most felt it spelt the end of the man whose swing, in the words of Bernard Darwin, was 'sound and true – but a little bucolic' and whose clubs featured an assorted miscellany of steel and hickory shafts.

Having shrugged off that hiccup, Perry homed in on the flagstick – to him, the focal part of the game. 'There's only one way to play golf,' he would say. 'There's the pin and you've got to go for it!' Closing 4, 4 with a spoon thumped without ceremony aboard the eighteenth, he was round in

__Alfred Perry__ adopts the grip that is usually calculated to produce a hook, with the left hand right over the shaft. No doubt which is the master hand here. The right plays no part in taking the club back

__Cyril Tolley__ – the old-fashioned 'two-handed' grip without either interlocking or overlapping. The general position of the right hand exactly duplicates that of Padgham, but the left is rather more on top of the shaft

72 to win by four shots from Padgham.

There was one scribe of the day who would pen that Alf Perry 'came from nowhere and then went back there', but such a jibe was somewhat unfair. Though he made little impact in his three Ryder Cup appearances, Perry came to Muirfield having already reached the final of the *News of the World* Match-Play championship. Three years after his Open championship triumph, he had four successive rounds in the 60s over Wentworth's West course in capturing the Dunlop Metropolitan and won two other tournaments besides. Then in 1939, which is what so many forget in denigrating his admittedly unforeseen 1935 victory, he came close to winning the Open again, finishing joint third after a last-round 76.

Darwin felt that the eccentricity of his grip so riveted the eye as to detract from what, for want of a better word, he termed the 'roundness' of his forcing style. 'He attacks the ball,' declared Darwin, 'with the greatest dash; his club comes right through and he pitches and putts with the almost insolent confidence of a small boy with his master's iron on a caddie's miniature course. About his game, as there was about Ray's, there is something which looks a little uncertain until the results are scrutinised.'

The modern champion, often after holding court afresh for the world's assembled press, tends to take off the following morning in a private plane for his next venue. Perry's departure from Muirfield was as untrumpeted as his arrival. The deposed champion, Henry Cotton, gave him a lift to the station at Drem and the next morning, at 7.30 sharp, Perry was back on duty in his role as the club professional at Leatherhead.

Henry Cotton (1948)

WHETHER his old caddie, Ernest Hargreaves, was right and he missed only one fairway out of 56 or, as history has always had it, he failed to hit four, there is no question but that Henry Cotton's superb driving was central to his victory in the 1948 Open. It supported perfectly the assertion of the noted golf scribe, Pat Ward-Thomas, that Cotton never drove better than when the fairways were narrow and the rough punitive. Muirfield that year could not have been set up better for his particular assets, though the subtle borrows on the greens got to him in the first round of the championship, rapidly destroying the new-found putting method in which he had the ball well back in his stance and the bulk of his weight on the right side.

In 1935, Alf Perry's Open, Cotton had arrived as the defending champion and the firmest favourite since the heyday of Harry Vardon. He had opened with a 68 but thereafter subsided. Still further back, the 1929 Open at Muirfield had been the first for which he had qualified for the last two rounds and he had had the chastening but instructive experience of four rounds paired with the eventual champion, Walter Hagen – Cotton having an 80 followed by an 82 on the last day as Hagen, keeping the ball below the wind, had a brace of 75s.

Illness had seen Cotton invalided out of the RAF and, at Hoylake in 1947, when Fred Daly won, he had dissipated a promising position as his strength and stamina gave way. Consequently, Cotton who – like Peter Thomson in the years to come – started thinking about the next Open the moment the current one ended, had taken himself off to America to get what he deemed the right kind of food. The nutritionists and dieticians of the 1990s would maybe have thrown up their hands in horror at what Cotton was doing to his cholesterol level, but those who had not seen him for some time were at once impressed on his return by how much fitter and stronger he appeared to be. Even so, since in those days everyone had to face the two qualifying rounds and he needed to conserve his energy, Cotton followed his usual practice of resting on the Sunday before the curtain rose.

In the qualifying rounds, he at once threw down the gauntlet, returning an admirably constructed 69 over Muirfield. At the eighth, as he laid a long iron hard by the flag, he had found his mind going back to 1929 when Hagen, already two under fours after seven holes in the final round, had got a wonderful three by following his preconceived tactical plan. To the chagrin of the members, Hagen had deliberately driven into the right rough where it had been trodden down by the spectators. He had thereby so shortened the hole that, by the time of the 1935 Open, the Honourable Company had retaliated by planting buckthorn bushes in Hagen's landing area! Much to the Haig's amusement.

A 69 at Gullane on the second day saw Cotton lead the qualifiers by two strokes but, in the championship itself, he started inauspiciously by driving into a bunker. Otherwise he was playing beautifully from tee to green. Alas, his month-old putting style gave way, Cotton taking three putts three times in four holes from the fifth. He was out in 37 and a five at the tenth followed. However, his putter did its stuff at the eleventh where he holed for a birdie three and, before it was safely back in the bag, it had been kissed by Cotton's wife, the inimitable Toots. He was home in 34 to emerge with a 71 and that night lay equal sixth, on the same mark as the pre-championship favourite, Australia's Norman von Nida.

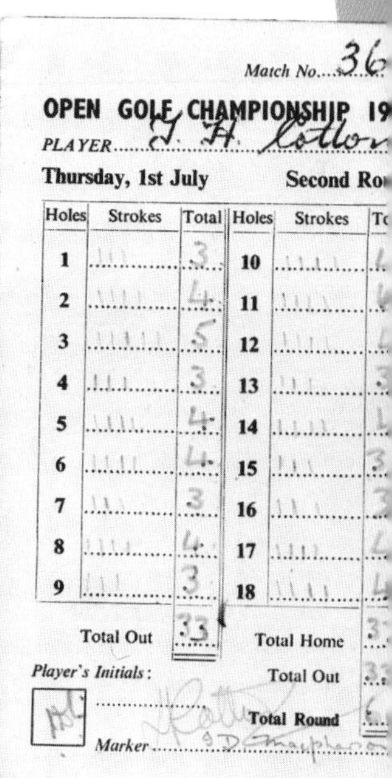

Match No. 36

OPEN GOLF CHAMPIONSHIP 19

PLAYER T. H. Cotton

Thursday, 1st July Second Ro

Holes	Strokes	Total	Holes	Strokes
1		3	10	
2		4	11	
3		5	12	
4		3	13	
5		4	14	
6		4	15	
7		3	16	
8		4	17	
9		3	18	

Total Out 33 Total Home

Player's Initials: Total Out

Total Round

Marker

The next day was one of the red letter days of a great career from the moment he was formally presented to King George VI – with whom, ironically, he had already played sundry rounds. Home in two at the long ninth, he holed for an eagle to be out in an appropriately regal 33. He kicked for home with three threes in four holes from the twelfth, a burst culminating in the sinking of a swinging 47-footer at the fifteenth. He was round in 66 and, of his play that day, in admittedly benign conditions, Bernard Darwin penned: 'Neither I nor anyone else has ever seen him play better, more calmly, or more confidently.' It is part of the folklore of East Lothian that King George VI saw all 66 strokes but Cotton always maintained that the King watched only the last nine holes, lest he be thought just too partisan.

Teeing up for the 36-holes of the last day, Cotton, on 137, led by four strokes from Charlie Ward and Sam King, with Arthur Lees and Flory van Donck a stroke to their rear. As dangerous a quartet as Alf Padgham, Roberto de Vicenzo, Norman von Nida and Fred Daly were hard on the heels of Lees and van Donck. Even so, Percy Boomer, who knew Cotton and Cotton's game better than most, had no hesitation in proclaiming, 'Only one man can beat Henry and that's Henry himself.'

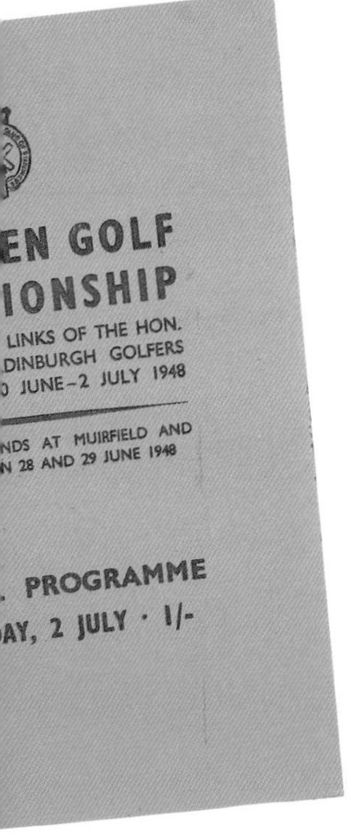

Top: King George VI with, on his left, Von Nida and, on his right, the captain R.M. McLaren and Dai Rees (1948 Open)

Left: the scorecard of Henry Cotton's 66

Cotton was off early and seemed very much at ease until suddenly, with his putting once more awry, he dropped a stroke at seven successive holes from the fifth. Turning in 39, he had fives at both the tenth and the eleventh and, at that juncture, Toots gave tongue. Whatever she said – and it was unlikely to have been 'Don't you worry' – it had the desired effect, Cotton hauling himself back from the brink by holing a 12-footer at the twelfth. His supporters' cheers were more tentative than triumphant, but when he struck his tee shot to six feet at the short thirteenth and sank 'a bending, borrowing little putt', the crowd went wild. Cotton was back in control, his rhythm restored, his 36 homeward-bound giving him a 75.

Cotton still led but now Padgham and King were within two strokes. But though out in 37 to King's 36, Cotton looked to have taken an unshakable grip on the title by the time he came to the last tee wanting a four for a 71. His final drive was symptomatic of what had gone before, bisecting the fairway, but his second found the island bunker, with its grass inset, to the right of the green. His ball was close enough to the face to threaten his recovery and, at the first attempt, he left the ball in the sand. Since this was long before the days of leaders out last, neither he nor anyone else knew how much or how little that lapse would matter. Years later, Toots would speak of how, having escaped at the second time of asking to within not much more than three yards of the hole, he fastidiously dusted the sand from his attire and then, having satisfied himself as to the line and weight of the putt, holed out unerringly.

For Bernard Darwin, it was an incident which contributed to the contrasting calm on the morrow as he looked out across the links. 'One of the things that never ceases to strike me,' said Darwin, writing on the Saturday morning, 'is the sudden contrast between the tumult and shouting of the championship and the tranquillity that succeeds it . . . The tents and ropes are still there, but are rapidly vanishing and, out of the window at which I am sitting, not one human being is to be seen in all that green expanse.'

Darwin, not always one of Muirfield's staunchest admirers, would write that he had never seen a better-run championship. 'Everything went with wonderful smoothness. There was a very big crowd indeed – I almost gave up trying to see on the last afternoon – and yet it was so well shepherded and stewarded that it impeded no one and caused the very minimum of delay. And if the crowd helped to make the championship the great success it was, so did the course itself. It was in beautiful order. I believe that not so very long before it had been dry and bumpy and glassy, and the authorities had been tearing their hair. The rain had mercifully come to the rescue and by the time play began nothing could have been more verdant and velvety, a joy to look at and walk on, and doubtless to play on . . .'

Those who pointed to how there were no top Americans in the field were reminded of Carnoustie in 1937 where Cotton had won the second of his three Opens from the full might of the American Ryder Cup side. An immaculate stylist, he could hardly have been more of a contrast to the last Open champion sired by Muirfield, Alfred Perry, whose swing, observed Peter Lawless, was 'a naturally slashing one embracing unorthodoxies not so much condemned in modern text books as unmentioned'. Cotton, the

American golf writer, George Trevor, once opined, 'might have walked out of a Leonard Merrick novel. Dapper, suave, polished, Cotton is a far cry from the seamy-faced, leather-skinned, shabbily-dressed, old-time British professional. He buys his clothes on Savile Row, his boots from Peel, and selects his golfing ensembles with fastidious attention to detail. He prefers grays, fawns and beiges but has the nerve to flaunt a dash of colour when he feels in the mood for gaiety. His slacks are creased to a razor's edge. Physically, there is a suggestion of the Latin about this tall, svelte, limber chap with the swarthy complexion, dark, lustrous eyes, and aquiline nose. He could double for Valentino in profile . . .'

Above: Henry Cotton driving in the 1948 Open and, below, the 23-year-old Gary Player in the 1959 Open

Lord Deedes, in making the address at the memorial service for Cotton which was held on 16 March 1988, marvelled at the manner in which his subject, who died knowing that he was to be knighted, had shaped his own lifestyle in a world where the class system gave little credence to the professional sportsman. 'It called for great strength of mind – as well as blistered hands – to seek pre-eminence in that world then. Not only to seek pre-eminence but to change it . . . Every British professional golfer since has been heir to an estate which Henry Cotton created and bequeathed to them.'

Cotton had won at Muirfield by five strokes and yet, for all the convincing margin, he always said afterwards that he thought that night that he would never win the Open again. In fact, he was not well enough to defend his title the following summer and was never again to finish higher than fourth.

It was often said of Cotton, as it was to be said of the next man to win the Open at Muirfield, Gary Player, that he was a 'made' golfer. Each, though, had already shown himself to be no mean games-player before golf claimed him for its own, Cotton having been a budding footballer and cricketer and Player a talented scrum-half and very useful off-spinner. But both – the latter on the former's advice – worked tirelessly not just on their swings but on their golfing muscles.

Laddie Lucas, the Walker Cup left-hander who, along with such other leading amateurs as Scotland's Hector Thomson, Jack McLean and Eric McRuvie, had played all four rounds of Perry's Open, has an analytical eye and is among the most compelling of golfing theorists. In a foreword to Peter Dobereiner's highly readable biography of Cotton, Lucas, who had won the Amateur medal in that 1935 Open, wrote of how, in the mid-1930s, Cotton 'still took the club back well inside but, as it moved up toward the top, he began, he said, to get his hands up and into a more upright and open position with the left wrist under the shaft and the clubface itself well open, i.e. with the toe pointing downwards. He confided that he had to be conscious at the top that his hands were "up and forward" with the shaft of the club not so much across the top of the back as forward almost above the neck. From this upright and open position at the top, he contended he could hit the ball "as early as you like without any fear of hooking it".' After this change, in the opinion of Lucas, there was not, in the late 1930s, 'another contemporary striker, British or American, to touch him'.

Cotton was, of course, the ultimate hands man and, to train them, invented all manner of drills. One night at a cocktail party in Portugal's

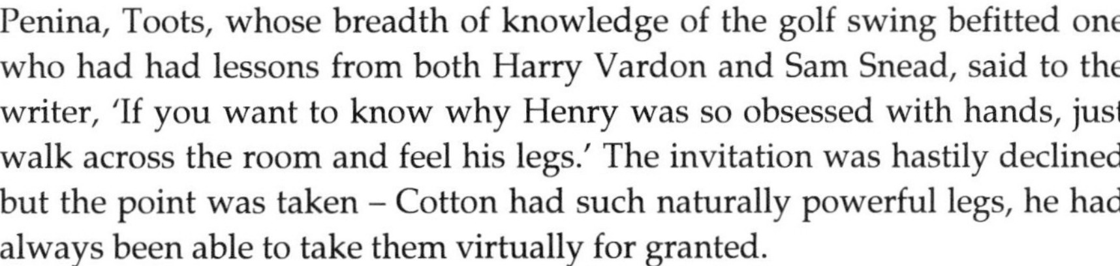

Penina, Toots, whose breadth of knowledge of the golf swing befitted one who had had lessons from both Harry Vardon and Sam Snead, said to the writer, 'If you want to know why Henry was so obsessed with hands, just walk across the room and feel his legs.' The invitation was hastily declined but the point was taken – Cotton had such naturally powerful legs, he had always been able to take them virtually for granted.

Grooved though his own action was, he experimented ceaselessly. He even stuck two balloons up his jersey the better to understand the problems on the distaff side of those with a big bust – an apparition which, in his days at Temple Golf Club, caused a professor of anatomy, who thought he had seen everything, to shank clean across the neighbouring fairway.

Gary Player (1959)

THEY still tell in rugby circles of how, in 1974, before the Fourth Test against the British Lions, the South Africans called upon Gary Player to give a team talk to the beleaguered Springboks. 'You must play until you drop,' urged golf's Black Knight. 'Until you think you are going to die. You won't die,' he concluded, reassuringly, 'but if anyone does, I'll look after his dependants . . .' Vintage Gary. The Springboks did not win but they drew, the only match on the entire tour in which the Lions were not victorious. That same summer, Player had won the Open for a third time, his other successes being in 1968 and 1959. The first of those titles, at Muirfield, was a prime example of the refusal to accept defeat which he was seeking to instil into his rugby-playing compatriots.

After qualifying just two shots behind Peter Thomson, Player had had an anti-climactic start to that 1959 championship – a 75. 'Even the man who would finish last [R. Haydon of Woodbrook] was tied with me,' said Player, who brooded sombrely on the fact that he had had the worst of the weather but did not let an injustice he could do nothing about get into his golf. None the less, it rankled that Henry Cotton, on the wrong side of 50, had got home at the fourteenth with a drive and three-iron whereas he himself, a mere two hours later, had needed a drive, spoon and wedge.

Yet the wind which tugged at his swing had tightened his resolve. From that round on, he played every stroke 'as if it were the only one which mattered'. On the second day, he had a 71 which left him in a share of twentieth place and had his badly disappointed mentor, George Blumberg, offering a consolatory, 'Don't worry, Gary, I promise I'll come over every year until you win.'

But Player himself had not begun to give up on 1959 and, moreover, he was by now handling the wind a lot more happily. Harold Henning, and not just because he stood to win £600 from a wager if his countryman won, had pointed out to him that, in attempting, say, to hook the ball at the tenth where it was blowing left to right, he was fighting the wind, not harnessing it. Player listened to the voice of experience.

A 70 on the morning of the third day took him past nine of the players who had stood between him and the lead. He was now lying tenth, just four shots off the pace, with Fred Bullock and Sam King being by then the front runners on 212. Out in 34 on the last day, Player was conscious of both a quickening pulse and a loose impediment in one eye. The former he had to cope with himself but the latter, which had its origins in the hayfever which had had him rubbing his eyes, was removed by a medical man who rolled up his eyelid with a matchstick and blew – Player having sunk a ten-footer for a birdie at the tenth with that watering optic shut.

After birdies at the short thirteenth and sixteenth holes where, on each occasion, he switched to the 1.68 as was then permissible, Player was six under fours and needing two more fours to equal the course record of 66. 'I knew if I could do that I was home and dry.' But Player's last two holes were among 'the most nerve-wracking of my life.' He holed from 20 feet for a four at the seventeenth but then, at the eighteenth, the fade he had attempted from the tee failed to materialise and he was bunkered. A six-iron from the sand, another six-iron and three putts later, he had amassed a six which he feared would cost him the championship. There followed a two-hour wait before van Donck and Bullock came up the last needing birdies to tie. Player, by then watching from an upstairs window in the clubhouse, saw Bullock come to grief in the bunker he himself had caught earlier. Finally, van Donck, chipping to tie, was wide of the hole. 'When that happened,' said Player, 'I whooped like a dervish. I had won the Open.'

'At Muirfield,' Player was to claim in taking stock of his career, 'I just knew the title was mine. As far as I was concerned, my name was in the book even before the tournament started.' Maybe so, but he had not looked that convinced amid the aftermath of his closing double-bogey. He denies that he was in tears. But, having been back to his North Berwick hotel for a cold bath and change of clothing – Henning, back at the course, was keeping him abreast of the shifting fortunes by phone – he returned to pace in anguish up and down the road outside Muirfield with Blumberg.

''Tis not in mortals to command success. But we'll do more, Sempronius. We'll deserve it.' Player had cut lucrative American tournaments from his schedule in order to give himself plenty of time to focus on the smaller ball and to switch from First Flight to the Slazenger clubs he was contracted to play in Britain. He came with two weeks in hand and was at once enmeshed in awkward negotiations with the secretary, Colonel Evans-Lombe, who, having no intention of creating a precedent which might upset the membership at large, refused him permission to play. A heated Player pointed to how, in such circumstances, Ben Hogan would have turned round and gone home. 'It would be the same for anybody,' maintained the secretary, unmoved. There followed what Player termed 'an unnecessary argument' – and thereafter a compromise. He would be allowed 18 holes a day, while he could spend the rest of his time at Gullane where he would, in any case, be having to qualify.

This was not satisfactory in the eyes of this particular perfectionist and scarcely enough to enable him to familiarise himself with greens, bunkers and winds from every angle. His frustration built up until, one evening, he slipped out for a further nine holes at Muirfield. He had reckoned without the Colonel's vigilant eye. For four days, Player's accomplice, his caddie, was banned, just in case the little South African

OPENS AT MUIRFIELD

1892
H.H. Hilton (R. Liverpool)
78 81 72 74 305
J. Ball jun (R. Liverpool)
75 80 74 79 308
H. Kirkaldy (St Andrews)
77 83 73 75 308
A. Herd (Huddersfield)
77 78 77 76 308
J. Kay (Seaton Carew)
82 78 74 78 312
B. Sayer (North Berwick)
80 76 81 75 312

1896
H. Vardon (Ganton)
83 78 78 77 316
J.H. Taylor (Winchester)
77 78 81 80 316
F.G. Tait (Black Watch)
83 75 84 77 319
W. Fernie (Troon)
78 79 82 80 319
A. Herd (Huddersfield)

Player lines up a putt in unmistakable style at the 1992 Open

At the 1974 Amateur, Sandy Sinclair, a Scottish international golfer in his own right, told a story which should perhaps be prescribed reading for all intending spectators. He had been watching the 1959 Open and had opined that Player had not only played a bad chip but had played it with the wrong club. A member of the gallery, seemingly recognising an authority when he heard one, turned round and asked politely if Sandy knew how Player was doing.
'He's six under fours,' explained Sinclair.
'Then why,' came the bitter retort, 'don't you bloody well shut up!'

1901
J. Braid (Romford)
79 76 74 80 309
H. Vardon (Ganton)
77 78 79 78 312
J.H. Taylor (Richmond)
79 83 74 77 313
H.H. Hilton (R. Liverpool)
89 80 74 77 320
A. Herd (Huddersfield)
87 81 81 76 325

1906
J. Braid (Walton Heath)
77 76 74 73 300
J.H. Taylor (Mid-Surrey)
77 72 75 80 304
H. Vardon (South Herts)
77 73 77 78 305
J. Graham jun (R. Liverpool)
71 79 78 78 306
R. Jones (Wimbledon Park)
74 78 73 83 308

golfer thought he had got away with it. Subsequently, Player was to confess that, once he got to know them, he had 'found the members and staff at Muirfield to be charming people.'

Away from the course, he was making the acquaintance of his two-month-old daughter, Jennifer, whom he had not seen before. She had arrived with Player's wife and together they settled happily into the Marine Hotel in North Berwick, an establishment which Player would call 'the best I have stayed at in Britain' – and where, as he returned in triumph for a celebratory dinner, the band struck up 'Sarie marais'.

Tom Scott and Geoffrey Cousins, who compiled their history of the Open in tandem, wrote: 'That the South African, Gary Player, would win the Open was regarded by everyone as a certainty. It was sad, therefore, that his first victory was in one of the worst and least interesting of modern championships . . . You had Gary Player, who had come to Britain as a shy little boy with a flat swing and a burning desire to be champion, achieving his ambition. You had old favourites coming within an ace of victory and you had an amateur [Reid Jack] making a serious bid with two last rounds of 68 and 74. But having said that about the 1959 Open, you've said it all.'

No mention in all of that of Player's bunker play which had his caddie marvelling that here was something he had never thought to see – someone even better out of sand than Norman Von Nida. Possibly more than any other of the great bunker players, Gary Player attacks his shots out of sand but then his pitches, chips and putts all embody a very definite hit. In 1978, when he won the US Masters, the Tournament of Champions and the Houston Classic in rapid succession, he was stroking his putts rather than, as Vivienne, his wife, used to put it, stabbing them. It was not long, though, before the old rap was back in his putting action: 'That was the method in vogue when I came on the scene, favoured by such lethal putters as Billy Casper and Bob Rosburg.' As for his closed stance on the green, he had, as befitted a good South African, copied that from Bobby Locke.

Player was just 23 when he won at Muirfield but already, of course, there was that pronounced forward press with the kick in of the right knee, the width of arc founded on a very straight left arm, and a lateral movement in the clearing of the left hip and the drive into impact reminiscent of his idol, Ben Hogan. From the first, Player, by far the smallest of the latter-day Big Three of Player, Jack Nicklaus and Arnold Palmer, hit the ball hard. By relentless exercising, this fitness fanatic found an additional 15 yards which, over two full wooden shots, is a lot more than it sounds.

Jack Nicklaus (1966)

JACK NICKLAUS had made his first bid for the Open at Troon in 1962, a disastrous attempt which saw him finishing in a share of 32nd place with rounds of 80, 72, 74 and 79. 'Spectators who watched me,' he ventured, 'must have been wondering how on earth I had ever managed to defeat Palmer a few weeks before in our play-off for the US Open.'

The following year, he had led before, to use his own words, 'snatching defeat from the very jaws of victory by bogeying both the 71st and 72nd. All the good golf I had played was tossed away. I finished a stroke behind Bob Charles and Phil Rodgers.' It was a collapse which had him wondering if he had wasted what might be his only chance to win the Open – a feeling which was reinforced at Birkdale the following year when he ended in a share of twelfth place.

He had felt all along that he and Birkdale were not cut out for each other but, in planning his Muirfield trip in 1966, he was as one preparing to meet an old friend. 'I knew it, and I knew it well from having played in the 1959 Walker Cup. Muirfield, with its splendid turf, its moderate undulations, its honest "inland" character – it was my kind of course.' Yet he was shocked when he arrived a week before the championship. He hardly recognised this old friend: 'It looked less like a golf course than a wide expanse of wheat whipping in the wind.' Gerald Micklem explained how they had grown the rough in order to tighten the course and keep it in line, in severity, with the other courses on the Open championship rota.

Nicklaus, after gaping aghast at fairways no more than 20 yards wide, decided that he would like it rather than lump it. 'I don't know what lay behind this stroke of intelligence, this sudden burst of maturity, but I think it must have been Muirfield itself. The memory of the 1959 Walker Cup was still fresh in my mind. I had never stopped looking back to it, not only because that match had changed me from a good junior golfer into a good golfer, but also because that whole week at Muirfield had personified sport at its best . . . people at their best, the world at its best. It was Muirfield, and if anyone could handle it I could. After all, I was an old Muirfield man.'

Over four days in which he unsheathed his driver no more than 17 times, Nicklaus set a new record with his second-round 65 to have a one-shot lead at the halfway stage over Peter Butler. Phil Rodgers, Kel Nagle and Harold Henning were three behind. On the Friday, there was a stiff, westerly wind and Muirfield was asking very different questions. Nicklaus turned in level par but he had four bogeys in his last five holes to be home in 39 for a 75. In the meantime, Phil Rodgers had come home in 30, Arnold Palmer in 32. 'The whole tournament,' remembers Nicklaus, 'was turned round. Rodgers was now the leader on 210. I was two behind him, Doug Sanders three, Palmer only four . . .'

Come the Saturday and Nicklaus quickly had matters in hand, sinking a 25-footer for a birdie at the first even as Rodgers opened with a bogey. He turned in 33 and, after pinning down his par at the wind-tossed tenth, was comfortably out in front again, with Dave Thomas three to his rear.

In a position to add another shot to his lead at the eleventh, after punching his approach seven feet from the flag, Nicklaus left his first putt 15 inches short and missed his second, the ball curling out of the hole. He began to worry and 'to play jittery golf' but, after the solid long putt which paved the way for his three at the sixteenth, he returned to thinking about winning the tournament rather than losing it.

With Thomas and then Sanders finishing on 283, he would need to finish with a birdie and a par. No one ever did what had to be done more impressively: a lovely three-iron and five-iron shrivelled the long seven-

Right: Jack Nicklaus with the famous Open claret jug in 1966

1912
E. Ray (Oxhey)
71 73 76 75 295
H. Vardon (South Herts)
75 72 81 71 299
J. Braid (Walton Heath)
77 71 77 78 303
G. Duncan (Hanger Hill)
72 77 78 78 305
A. Herd (Coombe Hill)
76 81 76 76 309
L. Ayton (Bishop's Stortford)
74 80 75 80 309

1929
W. Hagen (USA)
75 67 75 75 292
J. Farrell (USA)
72 75 76 75 298
L. Diegel (USA)
71 69 82 77 299
A. Mitchell (Private)
72 72 78 78 300
P. Alliss (Germany)
69 76 76 79 300

1935
A. Perry (Leatherhead)
69 75 67 72 283
A. Padgham (Sundrige Park)
70 72 74 71 287
C. Whitcombe (Crewe Hill)
71 68 73 76 288
W. Lawson Little (Presido, USA)
75 71 74 69 289
B. Gadd (Brand Hill)
72 75 71 71 289

1948
T.H. Cotton (Mid-Surrey)
71 66 75 72 284
E. J. Daly (Balmoral)
72 71 73 73 289
N. G. Von Nida (Australia)
71 72 76 71 290
J. Hargreaves (Sutton Coldfield)
76 68 73 73 290
C. H. Ward (Little Aston)
69 72 75 74 290
R. de Vicenzo (Argentina)
70 73 72 75 290

1959
G.J. Player (South Africa) 75 71 70 68 284
F. van Donck (Belgium) 70 70 73 73 286
E. Bullock (Prestwick St Nicholas) 68 70 74 74 286
S.S. Scott (Roehampton) 73 70 73 71 287
C. O'Connor (Dublin) 73 74 72 69 288
J. Panton (Glenbervie) 72 72 71 73 288
R.R. Jack (Dullatur) 71 75 68 74 288
S.L King (Knole Park) 70 74 68 76 288

1966
J. Nicklaus (USA) 70 67 75 70 282
D. Thomas (Durham Forest) 72 73 69 69 283
D. Sanders (USA) 71 70 72 70 283
G. Player (South Africa) 72 74 71 69 286
B. Devlin (Australia) 73 69 74 70 286

teenth; a one-iron, his club of clubs that week, was the prelude to a three-iron cut into the right-to-left cross-wind, the ball alighting softly on the home green just 25 feet to the right of the flag.

It had been among the most memorable of all Opens. For one thing, it was Tony Lema's last. That man of lithe and liquid, oddly feline grace was, in the opinion of Jack Nicklaus himself, 'just about the prettiest player of the '60s.' Not that you would always have known it to listen to that laconically humorous soul. He had arrived at Muirfield not all that long recovered from an elbow injury. 'How soon,' began the press interrogation, 'did your swing come back after you started playing again?'

'Right away, I'm afraid,' reflected Lema, shaking his head sadly. 'I was afraid it would and it did!' Less than three weeks later he was dead, killed in a plane crash.

With the fairways so often but slender ribbons between swaying seas of rough, Arnold Palmer – Nicklaus's pre-championship tip for the title – had found it maddeningly claustrophobic and inhibiting. Eventually the Legend of Latrobe – the man to whom, more than any other, the Open owed its renaissance – resolved to 'stop pitty-pattying', ripped a third-round 69 out of the old links and finally expired in the grand manner, it being said that the left rough at the tenth still throbs to this day from the thrashings of the great man's death throes.

With the fairways flanked by such penal retribution, there was about those who had completed their rounds successfully something of the relief and reaction of airmen returned from a mission. Yet, for all the wailing and gnashing of teeth, there had been some dramatic scoring. On the second day, Peter Butler had a 65, equalling the lowest ever round returned in the Open and breaking Henry Cotton's course record – the Maestro, in congratulating him, remarking, tongue in cheek, that the course was 'nothing like tight enough!' The serene and implacable Butler explained that he had been dissatisfied with his form almost all season but that he had recently studied some action pictures taken at an earlier tournament. 'I could see at once what was wrong. I was getting into a shut position at the top.' Hence his 65; but the next day, alas, Butler subsided to an 80. Back to the dark room . . .

Then there was that 70 of Rodgers with a scoreline which was pure Wimbledon – namely 40-30. Rodgers had been a focal point all week, putting split-handed with a longer than standard shafted putter wedged securely into position against a larger than standard stomach.

Nicklaus's win saw him join Gene Sarazen, Ben Hogan and Gary Player as the only men to have won all four of the majors. By the time he returned in 1980 for what was his fourth Open at Muirfield, he needed to win the Open just one more time to have been four times round the modern Grand Slam before anyone else had been twice. A statistic worth not only an honoured place in any golfing handbook but even in Ripley's *Believe-it-or-Not* . . .

It was a measure of how much his victory at Muirfield meant to him that he named a course after the links just as Gary Player had named a house and James Braid a son – the last mentioned being no doubt suitably grateful in later years that the Open that year had not been played at Gog Magog.

Lee Trevino (1972)

ON the first tee of the final round, Lee Trevino had turned to Tony Jacklin, who was lying on 208 to his 207. 'Well,' said he, 'Nicklaus might catch one of us but he ain't going to catch us both.' Jack Nicklaus that summer had already won both the US Masters and the US Open and was therefore still on course for the Impregnable Quadrilateral of the second half of the twentieth century – all four majors in the one season. Six shots off the lead with a round to go, he played such superb golf for five-sixths of the fourth round, a golfing Colossus in vintage vein, that he was actually ahead of the pair when he was playing the eleventh and they the ninth.

But he heard, as peals of impending doom, the successive roars as Trevino and Jacklin both eagled the ninth. By the time they reached the penultimate hole, they needed nothing more exotic than a couple of pars apiece to beat Nicklaus who, having failed to get a four at the long seventeenth after a four at the par 3 sixteenth, had by then posted a 66 for a five-under-par tally of 279. Let Jacklin, who still bears the unhealed wounds, tell the story of the seventeenth: 'Trevino hooked his drive off the tee into a bunker. I hit a perfect drive and then put my second just short of the green with a three-wood. Meanwhile, Trevino had played sideways out of the bunker, hit his third into the left rough, his fourth over the green *and he had given up.*'

Though he had thought his chip was a good one when it came off the blade, Jacklin had left himself with a 16-footer. But he was not unduly alarmed for now Trevino was playing five. 'He simply took a club out of the bag,' spelt out Jacklin, in a biography penned by Liz Kahn. 'Never lined it up – took one look and hit the chip just like you would when you want to get the job over. And, incredibly, it went into the hole.'

Jacklin's immediate but fleeting reaction was that he would hole his putt and still go to the eighteenth tee a stroke ahead. Instead, he took three stricken putts. He had been paired with this wise-cracking warlock for two days and taken everything he had thrown at him but now he was as a man hexed. Badly shaken, he followed with a broken bogey at the eighteenth to finish in third place. A third place which, as far as he was concerned, felt worse than last.

Arnold Palmer met Jacklin as he came off the home green and said, 'Whatever you do, try not to let it affect the way you think.' Jacklin tried; but even now he describes that incident as 'the most significant thing which happened to me in golf. By tenfold, it was the worst shock I've ever had on a golf course. It was such an important event, it was in the one tournament that means more to me than any other in the world, and the only saving factor was that I'd already won an Open. If I'd never won one, then it would have been even worse.'

Trevino would admit that he had not given that *coup de grâce* of a chip his full attention, but he made the point that the shot was ticking with a lifetime of pitching and chipping practice: 'Yes,' he admitted, 'I was mad when I chipped at the seventeenth . . . mad at having hit the ball over the

Above: Lee Trevino putting and, below, Tom Watson driving in the 1992 Open at Muirfield

1966 contd.
K.D.G. Nagle (Australia)
72 68 76 70 286
P. Rodgers (USA)
74 66 70 76 286

1972
L. Trevino (USA)
71 70 66 71 278
J. Nicklaus (USA)
70 72 71 66 279
A. Jacklin (Potters Bar)
69 72 67 72 280
D. Sanders (USA)
71 71 69 70 281
B.W. Barnes (Fairway Driving Range)
71 72 69 71 283

1980
T. Watson (USA)
68 70 64 69 271
L. Trevino (USA)
68 67 71 69 275
B. Crenshaw (USA)
70 70 68 69 277
J. Nicklaus (USA)
73 67 71 69 280
C. Mason (unattached)
72 69 70 69 280

1987
N. Faldo (England)
68 69 71 71 279
P. Azinger (USA)
68 68 71 73 280
R. Davis (Australia)
64 73 74 69 280
B. Crenshaw (USA)
73 68 72 68 281
P. Stewart (USA)
71 66 72 72 281

1992
N. Faldo (England)
66 64 69 73 272
J. Cook (USA)
66 67 70 70 273
J.M. Olazabal (Spain)
70 67 69 68 274
S. Pate (USA)
64 70 69 73 276
D. Hammond (USA)
70 65 70 74 279
A. Magee (USA)
67 72 70 70 279
E. Els (South Africa)
66 69 70 74 279
I. Woosnam (Wales)
65 73 70 71 279
G. Brand (Scotland)
65 68 72 74 279
M. Mackenzie (England)
71 67 70 71 279

back of the green. 'But,' he emphasised, 'I was aiming at the hole.'

His faithful caddie, Willie Aitchison, insists that he had never thought it would go anywhere else: 'I looked down at Lee's ball, saw the lie and the line and, knowing what he had done already, I expected him to chip in. What followed,' said Aitchison, 'was the only bit of gamesmanship you could ever level at Lee. He pulled me to a halt and said, "Willie, stand here for a minute. Let Tony go on the tee first. He'll be thinking about the bogey he's just made." '

'God is a Mexican!' exulted Trevino. Bearing in mind that when he sank that chip at the seventeenth on the Sunday, he had already holed two wedges from off the green in his third-round 66, it could be that the combined eloquence of the Archbishop of Canterbury, the Moderator of the Church of Scotland and the Pope himself might have been pushed to persuade the galleries otherwise. Not when they thought about how fast that meteorite from the Merry Mex had been travelling from sand at the sixteenth on the Saturday when it hit the flagstick and subsided, judiciously stunned, into the hole. Some said it would be a hundred years before anyone enjoyed such bolts from on high again but Trevino did not like people to think that it was all down to luck: 'Besides which, what a lot of people don't realise is that Tony didn't finish second to me at Muirfield. He finished third and I beat Nicklaus.'

Muirfield has always rewarded the player who can place his tee shots and Trevino, whose staple shape of shot was left to right – 'You can talk to a fade but a hook won't listen' – was one of the most accurate drivers the game has seen. With his strong grip, open stance and late release, he was relentlessly repetitive in his action but yet a consummate shotmaker who could manufacture shots which lesser mortals could not even see.

He loved the bump and run of links golf and, at least when out on the course, the sun which that week beat down mercilessly. They had billeted Trevino and his entourage in the Border country seat of Yester House and, out of deference to the Americans, had turned up the central heating full blast. 'It's so hot,' said Trevino – and Shakespeare could not have coined a more felicitous image – 'the oil is dripping off the ancestral portraits!'

Tom Watson (1980)

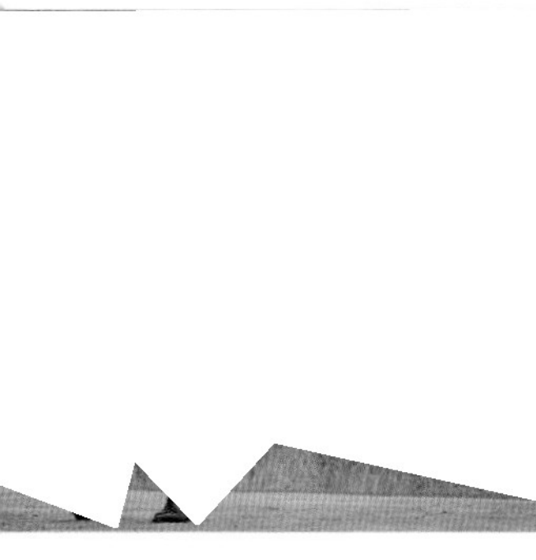

'WINNING in Scotland,' mused Tom Watson, after triumphing in the Open championship for a third time, 'is a different feeling to my wins elsewhere. I am a sentimentalist and something of a traditionalist and this, after all, is the birthplace of the game. You cannot but think of the champions in whose footsteps you are following on a course like Muirfield.' His quintet of Open championship victories – only one of which, at Royal Birkdale in 1983, has been accomplished in England – has included a quiver of iron shots destined, in the words of Rupert Brooke, to remain 'golden for ever'. At Muirfield, his shot of the week, as he himself described it, was a five-iron at the eleventh which, in the ancient phrase, 'bored a hole in the wind' to settle four feet behind the flag.

With Watson and Muirfield, it had been a case of love at first sight: 'Not a weak hole on the course.' Which, in itself, must have rung ominously in the ears of his fellow contenders for, on the eve of the championship, Watson had spoken of how, to win the Open, you had to marry the course. 'Court her, wed her,' as the *Scotsman*'s correspondent interpreted the approach of the engagingly fresh-faced golfer they used to call Huckleberry Finn, 'and trust that, come Sunday night, the old trophy will be winking knowingly at you as proof that the union has been blessed.'

The championship had opened in wind and rain, the worst day in an Open in terms of weather, declared Jack Nicklaus, since Tony Lema's Open of 1964. Trevino and Watson staggered in from the storm, clutching a 68 apiece, joint leaders who each had his own explanation as to why he could handle the inclement conditions. Watson, whose renown as a bad-weather golfer obviously owes not a little to the amount of practising he does in the winter in Missouri, had concentrated above all 'on catching the ball square on the clubface'. A precept in line with the injunction of John Jacobs, when playing into a wind, to focus on hitting the ball 'not harder but better'. Trevino's recipe was also one of which the old-timers would have approved: 'Save for that one-iron to the last green – I really laid into that shot – I was always swinging well within myself, taking a club or two more than I needed.'

In the eyes of a visiting American scribe, the second day's leaderboard had looked like 'the golfing counterpart of Burke's Peerage'. Trevino led, having added a 67 to his opening 68, with Watson, Jerry Pate and Ken Brown sharing second place and Seve Ballesteros and Jack Nicklaus among those lurking five strokes off the pace. But the round of the day had belonged to the Argentine Horatio Carbonneti who, like so many of the members, was the offspring of a family of lawyers. His hair was prematurely grey, less it was alleged (and again more than one of the Honourable Company may have identified with him a little guiltily) from reading legal briefs than difficult greens. After a seven over par first-round 78, he had packed his bags before setting off for Muirfield to do what no man had done before to the revered links – hole it in 64.

By Saturday night, Watson was four ahead, his third-round 64 eclipsed only by Isao Aoki's searing 63. In Hitler's War, James Logan, BEM, the Honourable Company's head greenkeeper, had fallen into Japanese hands. Had he known in his years as a PoW that the course record of his beloved Muirfield would one day suffer a similar fate, he might have been sorely tempted to take a leaf out of the enemy's book and commit hara-kiri. It was only the second 63 in the history of a championship dating back to 1860. The man Neil Coles had christened the Wizard of Oz, on the strength of his sorcery on and around the green, had had only 24 putts.

The evolution of Aoki's bizarre putting style stretched back to a round he had played some ten years before his Muirfield *tour de force* at a now defunct US services' base in Japan. Without his own comparatively short-shafted putter, he had obtained the loan of a model which was a great deal longer. Right through the bag, from driver to wedge, he naturally

Plus ça change, plus c'est la même chose

Harold Hilton, who was playing J.E. Laidlay in the second match, on the behaviour of the crowds which followed the head-of-the-order clash between John Ball and Robert Maxwell in the inaugural Scotland–England international at Hoylake in 1902

'The spectators who followed Messrs Ball and Maxwell were quite a disorganised rabble and the men in charge of the rope were quite unable to keep them in check. Everyone seemed so anxious to obtain the best situations that they run and scramble. They do not seem to understand that the bigger the circle made the better can everyone see. Another little matter which might be pointed out is the fact that it is not quite considered etiquette to break into unseemly mirth when a player misses a short putt. It may appeal to the spectators as ludicrous but is rather a painful matter to the player who is surely worthy of a little consideration.

Another disturbing element is the camera fiend. I had a little experience of one on Saturday last. Going to the first hole in the second round I had actually addressed my ball and was considering the advisability of changing my club, when I felt someone touch me on the arm and on looking round gazed upon an apparition with a camera. I cannot repeat my reply to his

request that I should stand still on swinging so that he could take a snap-shot. But I know I promptly hit my ball off the socket of the iron and put it into the field.'

The Honourable Company have had their staff troubles like everybody else and, wholly true or partly apocryphal, many have been much troubled by the tale of the steward who was sacked but left behind one very grateful member. The latter was on his way home from Muirfield when he was stopped by the police. Only too well aware of how much he had had to drink, he abandoned all hope when the breathalyser was produced. In fact, he passed with flying colours, so diligently had that rapscally steward watered down the gin.

carries his hands low and, rather than arch his wrists artificially, he had simply putted with the ball a long way from him and the toe of the implement in question rearing skywards. From the first putt, he had loved the feel it gave him.

Watson woke at eight o'clock on the last morning – and slept fitfully for another three hours, dreaming always of golf. 'I was playing up a narrow corridor,' he recalled – which would seem an allusion to playing up the slender tightrope that is Muirfield's first fairway. In fact, he began with a par, retrieving his four with an exquisite running chip executed with a four-iron – a stroke calculated in these days of the multi-purpose wedge to please the more elderly cognoscenti. To many, he had the championship won from the eleventh but he himself did not feel that the title was surely his until he stepped on to the penultimate tee. He had lost a shot at the par 3 thirteenth, his favourite hole on the course, but he hit the green of the short sixteenth safely. He got his par to remain at 13 under the card with Trevino – at nine under his nearest challenger – already in the clubhouse. With a last round of 69 and a 13 under par aggregate of 271, he won by four strokes with – horses for courses – the 1972 champion, Lee Trevino, second and, in third place, Jack Nicklaus. Henry Cotton, thrice himself the Open champion, doubted if he had ever seen a better swing than Watson's and, as he said, he could go back to the days of the Great Triumvirate of Vardon, Braid and Taylor.

The first Open with a Sunday finish had again, in terms of organisation, reflected well on both the R & A and the Honourable Company, though there will always be critics. As Watson made his birdie at the long ninth on the first day, the holing of the final putt was delayed by a scurrying mouse. 'I told you,' exclaimed an onlooker, triumphantly, 'the stewarding was patchy!'

Nick Faldo (1987 and 1992)

GEORGE POTTINGER has told of how a member of the Honourable Company had complained testily one uncharacteristically windless morning that he had nothing to lean against. On his arrival for the 1987 Open championship, Tom Watson's comment was different if a little risqué, likening a Muirfield without wind to a woman with no clothes: 'No challenge!' Before the Open was over, they were to see such wind and weather that when Nick Faldo, on the third day and his thirtieth birthday, received a large, unidentified wooden object from his wife, Gill, by way of a present, he suggested it was probably 'an ark'. But, before that, there had already been no lack of both colour and drama.

Eighty-seven players were exempt, leaving 66 to come through the qualifiers. Among those who did not make it was Jack Nicklaus Mark II whose caddie had won the 1966 Open at Muirfield. 'I had no yardages, nothing,' said father Nicklaus. 'If I had been working for me, I'd have been fired!'

At the close of the first day, Australia's Rodger Davis led with a course record of 64 by three strokes from Bob Tway, Lee Trevino and Ken

Green, with Paul Azinger and Nick Faldo but a stroke further behind. 'The guy who's going to win this thing,' declaimed Davis, prophetically, 'will not be the guy who stays out of the rough but the guy who stays out of the fairway bunkers.' The wind on the second day was from the west where, in the opening round, it had been more from the east. Seventy-eight players survived the halfway cut which came at 146, four over par – with, among the guillotined, Arnold Palmer who had taken five in a greenside bunker in compiling a 10 at the fourteenth. 'God could have got it out,' agreed Palmer, magnanimously, 'but he would have had to throw it.'

As for Nicklaus, he had had a first round 74 but was improbably saved by a total stranger, Doug Keddie, a 52-year-old golfer from North Berwick with a handicap of 23.4. Knowing that he was swinging badly, Nicklaus had repaired to the practice ground. 'I was hitting practice shots, some good, some bad,' recounted Nicklaus, 'when I heard this voice from the gallery: "You're crossing the line on your backswing." The amazing thing,' explained Nicklaus, 'was that that was exactly the fault I had been working on with my teacher, Jack Grout, shortly before I flew over from America.' A par 71 followed.

Nick Faldo speaking after receiving the coveted Open jug in 1992. Centre is Prince Andrew, with R & A officials on the left. At the right of the picture is Douglas Foulis, captain of the HCEG

Azinger, who had won thrice on the US tour, was in the lead at six under, a stroke ahead of Faldo, Gerard Taylor, Rodger Davis and Payne Stewart. Azinger's golfing pedigree struck a chord with the Scottish galleries. He was a pupil of John Redman who was himself a disciple of Scotland's Tommy Armour. Like the Silver Scot, Redman never discouraged a 'strong' grip if it were natural, his theory being that as the left hand naturally hangs down at one's side so should it be placed on the club.

So hard did the wind blow on the third day that a merciful R & A shortened four holes 'to give the players the chance to reach the fairways'. The fifth was reduced from 599 yards to 506, the tenth from 475 to 430, the eleventh from 385 to 350 and the seventeenth from 550 to 501. The links was thus reduced from 6,963 yards to 6,781 but such was the weather that, for instance, the US Open champion, Scott Simpson, had an 82 and even as powerful a golfer as the defending champion, Greg Norman, required a driver, a two-iron and a five-iron to get home at the fifth – and that though it had been chopped by over 50 yards. Nick Faldo, paired with Azinger in the afternoon, had a 71, as did the American who now led by a stroke from Faldo and David Frost. 'No matter what happens tomorrow,' remarked Azinger, philosophically, 'I'm going to be a better player when it's over. You cannot get this experience anywhere else and I'm enjoying it.'

Davis, four strokes off the pace with a round to go, set the target with a 69 for an aggregate of 280. For Faldo, the shot of the front nine was from sand at the eighth – it being perhaps no coincidence that, on a course where the bunkers play so large a part, the two men who were ultimately to fight out the championship, Faldo and Azinger, had led the tour statistics in sand saves on their respective circuits in 1986.

Faldo's second shot to the long fifth in the last round of the 1992 Open plugged in the face of a bunker. He could only play out sideways but managed to get his par

With two holes to play, Azinger, at six under, was once again leading by only a single stroke when those words of the Australian soothsayer, Rodger Davis, came to pass. At a time when accuracy and not length was what mattered, Azinger hit his driver at the long seventeenth. 'It was a ridiculous club to hit there,' he was to concede later. 'It cost me the champi-

onship. I should have hit my one-iron. I just don't know what I was thinking.' His tee shot had finished in a fairway bunker in the corner of the left-hand dog-leg – a six and, now but five under par, he was tied with Faldo.

For 17 holes, Faldo had marched with par and now, at the eighteenth, he followed a three-wood with a five-iron second of around 200 yards to within 40 feet of the flag. His first putt was too strong, finishing five feet beyond the hole but he sank a grisly sidehill-downhill putt for yet another par. Safely on the fairway, Azinger, clearly worrying about his choice of club, tossed grass to test the wind and tested it again. He knew as soon as the ball had left the club that his five-iron was headed for the left-hand greenside bunker. What he was not to know was that it would bequeath him such a satanic combination of sand and lie that even he could not rescue his four.

By the time of the 1992 Open, Muirfield had come so far from the early reservations of such as Andra Kirkaldy, J.H. Taylor and Bernard Darwin that almost the only criticism was the lack of a long shot into a par 3 green. Nevertheless, it had seemed almost defenceless on the first day under the lightest of winds, two Americans, Raymond Floyd and Steve Pate, ending their first day atop the leaderboard with Ian Woosnam and Scotland's Gordon Brand on the next rung after 65s, and Nick Faldo, Lee Janzen, Ernie Els and John Cook all returning 66s.

The next day, Faldo made his move, a superb 64 giving him a 36-hole total of 130 which broke the record of 132 first set by Henry Cotton in 1934 at Royal St George's and matched by Greg Norman and Faldo himself at St Andrews in 1990. 'I just felt so good inside,' observed Faldo. 'No matter what club I had in my hand, it always felt just right. Never before have I had such a feeling over a whole round. When you consider where we are and that, in a way, every shot is marked in history, it really is a unique sensation.'

The cut descended on 143, a mere stroke over par. Among the victims were Seve Ballesteros and three of Muirfield's former Open champions, Nicklaus, Watson and Gary Player. After 54 holes, Nick Faldo led by four strokes from Steve Pate and John Cook. 'I don't know anyone,' admitted Pate, 'to whom I would less want to give a four-stroke lead.' But that same summer Faldo had led by four strokes in the Irish Open and eventually won only on a play-off. Less than a month later, he had been five strokes clear with a round to go in the French Open but finished in third place. All that must have been in his mind when, on the last afternoon, the crisis came.

At the long ninth, Cook had hooked out of bounds to take seven and, falling back to nine under the card, was as many as four strokes behind Faldo with only nine to play. In the first three rounds, Faldo had played the back nine in 33, 31 and 34 but now, at the eleventh, he tugged a pitch into a greenside bunker. He took three from the front of the green at the short thirteenth and then, at the fourteenth, pushed his drive into a steep-faced bunker, dropping yet another shot. As Faldo stumbled, Cook counter-attacked to such effect that, by the time he stepped on to the penultimate tee, he was actually two ahead, a swing of six strokes in seven holes. But from that unlikely scenario, Faldo was to enjoy his finest hour. 'You had better play the best four holes of your life,' he told himself. His five-iron to the par 4 fifteenth dropped short of the green but ran on and on to finish within three feet of the flag. Not just the shot of the championship but possibly one which will be seen in retrospect as the shot of a lifetime.

He holed and up ahead Cook, who had previously had an eagle and two birdies at the seventeenth, was spilling a two-footer after his first putt for the eagle had grazed the hole. Faldo was a little strong with his tee shot to the sixteenth but got his three before, at the seventeenth, he held the green with a four-iron and secured his birdie four. Hard ahead, Cook, like Azinger before him, was puzzled by the wind, finally reaching for his two-iron a little uneasily. It finished through the fencing on the starboard side and, though he was allowed to drop his ball greenside of the fence, he could not save his par, his 70 for 273 giving Faldo his opening.

Faldo, in the classic situation of a four for the Open, hit a magnificent drive and a three-iron which covered the flag all the way but expired just through the green. His first putt lowered itself gingerly down the green, hand over hand, and he holed the short but missable putt it left him. In the most emotive moment of his career, Faldo broke down as he was to do again later in the press tent, gratefully accepting the loan of a handkerchief from David Begg, the press officer. In the event, what had saved him was not just his refusal to succumb but his unshaken belief in his own painstakingly rebuilt technique; a faith the very lack of which in his original swing had spawned the uncertainties which had given rise to those woundingly erroneous suggestions that he would always fold in the great championships . . .

Aside from the other alterations giving him a flatter plane and a lower trajectory, the takeaway and leg action were drastically different. Very obviously, the touch of drag had gone from the former while the dip of the legs into impact, which Henry Cotton had been inclined to deem essential in so tall a man, had given way to a considerable firming up downstairs. Not that his height, six feet three inches, has not remained a factor. 'I always have to watch,' he explained, the day after the 1992 Open, 'that my right hip does not get behind me too early in the backswing because, being so tall, if it does, I'm in real trouble.'

From the day in 1985 that he put himself under the tutelage of the English-born Floridian golfing guru, David Leadbetter, he had been steadfastly prepared to get worse in order to get better. And that in the face of much adverse criticism from those who believed that there had been nothing wrong with his old action which, with its elegant and athletic flow, had certainly been easy on the eye – unless that is, you happened to be David Leadbetter or one of his disciples, in which case it presumably caused you to emit a sharp cry of pain.

Faldo's detractors argue that, in four of his five majors (the exception being his five-stoke margin at St Andrews in 1990) he was eventually let in by a gruesome lapse by his immediate rival – Scott Hoch missing a very short putt at the first extra hole of the play-off for the 1989 US Masters and Ray Floyd dumping his second in the water in the 1990 Masters at the second extra hole. But, even aside from the fact that many more championships are won on the back of such opponents' errors than by spec-

'We couldn't let Payne Stewart play here — look at the silly way he dresses!'

THE PAYNE STEWART AFFAIR

It was on the eve of the 1991 Open championship at Royal Birkdale that Payne Stewart revealed that, on his pre-championship visit to Scotland and Scottish links, he had been unable to get on to Muirfield. Not get on? The newly crowned US Open champion? The flak flew. What almost no one bothered to find out was the Honourable Company's side of the story. Visitors to Muirfield are confined to Tuesdays and Thursdays and these days are booked up a long way in advance. In this instance, as Group Captain Prideaux tells it, a third party made the call – 'apparently a very polite, well-mannered gentleman' – and it simply did not register with the girl on the desk that the inquiry involved Payne Stewart, US Open champion. She looked at her list, said she was very sorry but there were no times available – and that was that.

When Stewart arrived for the 1992 Open at Muirfield and set about signing in, Prideaux was already in the hut and came up to

him: 'What the devil do you think you are doing. I'm the secretary and you don't think *you* are going to play here, do you?' Stewart cottoned on at once. 'Hell, man,' he cried, plaintively, 'I thought you would at least let me play this week.'
They parted on the best of terms and a tabloid journalist, hellbent on rekindling old flames, got very short shrift from Stewart when he brought up the happening of the previous year. 'Come off it, buster,' said Stewart, 'that was a misunderstanding . . .'
'If the American Open champion wants to play Muirfield and we knew it,' Prideaux emphasises, 'we would, of course, find a way of making room for him. As for the members, they would be queuing up to play with him.'

Payne Stewart putting in the 1992 Open at Muirfield

tacular outright winners at the denouncement, it should be remembered that each time Faldo himself, in the time-honoured but valid cliché, did what he had to do when it mattered most.

Long before he was being hailed as the best player in the world, Faldo had laid claim to the tag of golf's best pupil. He was both a ball-player and an athlete. Not only had he obsessive desire and ambition but, no mere dreamer of dreams, he was also a compulsive worker, an inveter-practiser. A player who, turning his back on a lucrative golf scholarship at the University of Houston, had come back to England because, without a car, he could not match the daily six hours of practice he had been used to getting at home. He was interested in technique, never bored by it, least of all as it applied to his own game. Above all, he had guts. Faldo's playing of those last four holes at Muirfield in 1992 ranked with the last day at Augusta in the 1989 US Masters, the year he defeated Hoch in the sudden death play-off. When play was finally suspended on the evening of that Georgian April Saturday, Faldo, with his pitch to the thirteenth green still to negotiate, was joint second, level par to the four under of Ben Crenshaw who had himself five holes of the third round still to play.

On the morning of the Sabbath, Faldo dropped shots to be home in 39 for a 77 which left him five strokes adrift of Crenshaw. Still more ominously, his putting was apparently in such disarray that he was to be seen at the break on the practice putting-green with an assortment of putters spread about him. In almost any other man, that would have indicated a fatal indecision. Indeed, that quintuple Open champion, Australia's Peter Thompson, used to go so far as to warn would-be wagerers to steer clear of the man who arrived at a tournament with even two putters protruding from his bag. Nor was that all. An English golf writer, who had approached Faldo during that midday crisis, had been brusquely told – to fall back on the expurgated version favoured by Ronnie Barker's Fletcher – to 'naff-off!'. Scarcely was the scribe back in the press-room before his phone was ringing with Faldo on the other end apologising – but again the incident hardly suggested the tranquillity of mind which Harry Vardon was wont to recommend as a prerequisite of great golf. But, in all this, as in so many other respects, Faldo showed himself something of a man apart. Exhibiting a rare strength of purpose, he mostly putted beautifully to be round in a seven under par 65, one of the immortal finishing rounds of the Masters.

At the prize-giving at Muirfield in 1992, he allowed himself a dig at the expense of the press which came out the wrong way, a little like a pitch where he had misread the lie. What was more, he who had been in tears the moment the last putt dropped to give him the most nerve-wracking of victories, also sang a line from *My Way*. It recalled nothing so much as the Welsh rugby team in New Zealand wistfully singing the songs of home until an old man in the corner of the tavern began showing obvious signs of distress. 'You from Wales?' asked the BBC's Alun Williams, sympathetically. 'No,' said the old man, 'I'm a musician!'

No matter. The way Faldo had risen in his agony to cover those last four holes in two under the card when nothing worse would have won had been a demonstration of golfing fibre never excelled in the 250 years of the Honourable Company's history.

PEN GOLF
MPIONSHIP

Caddies

THERE is more than one theory as to the origin of the word 'caddie' but Edinburgh in the days of Leith Links and the Company of Gentlemen Golfers has a claim. In 1774, a stranger in the city wrote of 'a society of men who constantly attend the cross in the High Street, and whose office is to do anything that anybody can want. Whether you stand in need of a *valet de place*, a pimp, a thief-catcher or a bully, your best resource is to the fraternity of cadies.'

There seems little doubt that they went regularly to Leith but, for all that caddies have been a motley crew across the years, many of today's have come a very long way from those – mostly – not notably pious opportunists who gathered round that Edinburgh cross. Fanny Sunesson, the 5 handicap, powerful but very feminine Swedish golfer who hefts Nick Faldo's bag and who was with him when, in 1992, he won the Open at Muirfield, is reputed to make over £100,000 a year. Indeed, she is a client of Mark McCormack's International Management Group in her own right.

And what, in some caddie shed in heaven or hell, would those High Street worthies of yesteryear make of Ian Woosnam's caddie, Wobbly, who, even allowing for some three hundred years' inflation, gets paid rather more than the two Scots shillings (or tuppence in English money) which Sir John Foulis recorded as the fee, on 17 December 1692, for 'the lad who carried my clubs'. After finishing joint second in the 1989 US Open at Oak Hill, Woosnam was anxious to return to the bosom of his family and was intent on hiring a jet to whip him by air from Rochester to New York – only to find that his credit card would not cover it. 'Never mind,' said Wobbly, casually. 'Use mine . . .'

Above: an old-time caddie, 'Caddie Willie', from a painting at Muirfield based on a photograph - it was some time before golf bags were introduced

Left: Fanny Sunesson and Nick Faldo in consultation during the 1992 Open at Muirfield

---

CLUBS AND SOCIETIES

At a rate of no more than two a week, from April to September, Muirfield will be played in the light evenings by some 48 clubs and societies, around 50 per cent of whom will be artisans clubs. Through the day, the Open championship links over the year will be visited by maybe a further 50 clubs and societies, mostly limited to a party of no more than 12. Special permission can be sought and obtained for a gathering of as many as 50.

The fees for such clubs and societies are worked out on an individual basis. If there are Honourable Company members within such a visiting body, the price is adjusted according to a fixed formula.

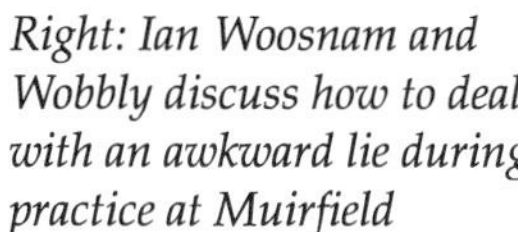

Right: Ian Woosnam and Wobbly discuss how to deal with an awkward lie during practice at Muirfield

Captains

Dalrymple

1744–1747	John Rattray
1748	Hon. James Leslie
1749	David Dalrymple
1750	Hon. Francis Charteris
1751	John Rattray
1752	Lord Drummore
1753	Sir Henry Seton, Bt.
1754, 1755	W. Cross
1756	Sir Henry Seton, Bt.
1757	Robert Clerk
1758	Thomas Boswall
1759	Andrew Hamilton
1760	William Hog
1761	William St. Clair of Roslin
1762	Sir R. Henderson, Bt.
1763	Col. Horn Elphinstone
1764	Colin Campbell
1765	Col. Horn Elphinstone
1766	William St. Clair of Roslin
1767	William Hog
1768	Alexander Keith
1769	Thomas Stoddart
1770, 1771	William St. Clair of Roslin
1772	James Rannie
1773	Duncan McMillan
1774	James Cheape
1775	Alexander Elphinstone
1776	James Cheape
1777, 1778	John Trotter
1779	Sir Alexander Don, Bt.
1780	Alexander Keith
1781	Alexander Duncan
1782–1784	W. Inglis
1785	Major George Hay
1786	Robert Allan

Inglis

1787, 1788	Lord Elcho
1789	Thomas Mure
1790	William Simpson
1791	James Dalrymple
1792	John Trotter
1793	George Cheape
1794, 1795	Robert Allan
1796	John Gray
1797	Sir James Stirling, Bt.
1798	Thomas Hay
1799	John Gray
1800	John Clerk
1801	A.M. Guthrie

Gray

1802	Thomas Mure
1803, 1804	John Gray
1805	A.M. Guthrie
1806	James Scott
1807, 1808	John Taylor
1809, 1810	George Mitchell
1811	Birnie Brown
1812	Burnet Bruce
1813	A.M. Guthrie
1814, 1815	John Taylor
1816	Col. R. Anstruther
1817, 1818	Walter Cook
1819, 1820	John Mansfield
1821, 1822	George Ramsay
1823–1825	John Taylor
1826, 1827	Henry M. Low
1828	John Taylor
1829–1835	Robert Menzies
1836	William Wood
1837, 1838	John Mansfield
1839–1842	Thomas Paton
1843, 1844	W.A. Cunningham
1845–1848	George Maclachlan

Keith

Anderson

Captains

Asher

1849–1851 Sir David Baird, Bt.
1852 W.M. Goddard
1853, 1854 Ord Graham Campbell
1855–1858 Alexander Mackenzie
1859 Robert Cowan
1860, 1861 D.B. Wauchope
1862, 1863 John Blackwood
1864 Gilbert Mitchell Innes
1865, 1866 The Earl of Stair
1867 Sir Alexander Kinloch Bt.
1868 Andrew Gillon
1869, 1870 Capt. Alexander Lindsay
1871 Sir Hew Hume Campbell, Bt.
1872, 1873 George Maclachlan
1874, 1875 J.L. Mansfield
1876, 1877 John Wharton Tod
1878, 1879 W.J. Mure
1880, 1881 B. Hall Blyth
1882, 1883 Arthur Makgill
1884, 1885 D.D. Whigham
1886, 1887 Sir Walter G. Simpson. Bt
1888, 1889 James Syme
1890, 1891 Col. J.W.H. Anderson

Laidlay

1892, 1893 Alexander Stuart
1894, 1895 A. Graham Murray
1896, 1897 William Hope
1898, 1899 G.F. Melville
1900, 1901 Henry Cook
1902, 1903 L.M. Balfour-Melville
1904, 1905 J.E. Laidlay
1906, 1907 A.R. Paterson
1908, 1909 Patrick Murray
1910, 1911 A.R.C. Pitman
1912, 1913 Robert Maxwell
1914–1918 C.J.G. Paterson
1919, 1920 A.G.G. Asher

Smythe

1921, 1922 David Lyell
1923, 1924 The Lord Kinross
1925, 1926 Stair A. Gillon
1927, 1928 R.K. Blair
1929, 1930 A.W. Robertson Durham
1931, 1932 John Cook
1933, 1934 Sir John C. Couper
1935, 1936 B. Hall Blyth
1937, 1938 Hon. R.B. Watson
1939- 1941 R.H. Maconochie
1942- 1945 R.Y. Weir
1946, 1947 J.A. Robertson Durham
1948, 1949 R.M. McLaren
1950, 1951 P.C. Smythe

Dallmeyer

1952, 1953 C.J.Y. Dallmeyer
1954, 1955 G.L.A. Jamieson
1956, 1957 A.L. McClure
1958, 1959 R.M. Carnegie
1960, 1961 J.R. Watherston
1962, 1963 G.T. Chiene
1964, 1965 Hon. W.D. Watson
1965–1968 Colonel T.R. Broughton
1968–1970 T.R. Macgregor
1970–1972 Hon. Lord Robertson
1972–1974 G. Robertson Durham
1974–1976 M.H. Cullen
1976–1978 D.H. Thorburn
1978–1980 T.S. Lewis
1980–1982 W.M. Miller
1982–1984 J.C.R. Inglis
1984–1986 G.R. Cockburn
1986–1988 G.F. Burn
1988–1990 H.M. Inglis
1990–1992 W.M.C. Kennedy
1992– A.D. Foulis

McClure

John Taylor, captain 1807-08, 1814-15, 1823-25, 1828, recorder 1816-23. From the painting by Sir John Watson Gordon on loan to Scottish National Portrait Gallery

Recorders

1783-1796	John Gray
1796-1798	John Edgar and Thomas Duncan
1799	Thomas Duncan and D. Murray
1800	Archibald Gibson
1801-1803	James Laidlaw and Alexander Lumsden
1803-1806	Alexander Lumsden
1806-1809	Joseph Gordon
1809-1811	Walter Cook
1811-1816	Adam Longmore
1816-1823	John Taylor
1823-1826	Walter Cook
1826-1828	William Wood
1828-1850	James Hay
1850-1865	James Blackwood
1865-1869	H.J. Wylie
1869-1876	J. Wharton Tod
1876-1882	Henry Cook
1882-1888	James L. Mansfield
1888-1896	B. Hall Blyth
1896-1910	R.H. Johnston
1910-1919	T.M. Hunter
1919-1924	H.D. Lawrie
1924-1932	William Robertson
1932-1946	R.M. McLaren
1947-1955	I.H. Bowhill
1955-1963	G. Robertson Durham
1963-1972	W.M. Miller
1972-1983	J.B.B. Stewart
1983-1992	D.M. Greenhough
1992-	M.J.P. Healy

Winners of the Gold Medal

competed for at Leith Links (2 rounds of 5 holes each)

Year	Winner	Score
1790	Robert Allan	
1792 Jan.	(after postponement from December 1791) Robert Allan	
1792 Dec.	Richard Stoddart	
1794 Feb.	Thomas Stoddart, Junior	
1795 Jan.	Robert Allan	
1795 May	Robert Allan	
1800	John Taylor	
1801	Wm. Oliphant	
1802	John Taylor	
1803	Wm. Oliphant	
1804	A.M. Guthrie	
1805	John Taylor	
1806	John Taylor	
1807	Walter Cook	
1808	Wm. Oliphant	
1809	Wm. Oliphant	
1810	Wm. Oliphant	
1811	Wm. Oliphant	
1812	Wm. Oliphant	
1813	Wm. Mitchell	
1814	Walter Cook	
1815	Walter Cook	
1816	Wm. Mitchell	
1817	Walter Cook	
1818	Walter Cook	
1819	Wm. Mitchell	
1820	Adam Longmore	
1821	Alexander Mitchell	
1822	Alexander Mitchell	
1823	Alexander Mitchell	
1824	Charles Shaw	
1825	Charles Shaw	65
1826	H.M. Low	60
1827	McGrieux (Samuel Messieux)	66
1828	John Taylor	63
1829	John H. Wood	(Competed for at
1830	John H. Wood	Musselburgh)

competed for at Musselburgh (2 rounds of 9 holes each)

Year	Winner	Score
1836	William Wood	93
1837	William Wood	87
1838	W.M. Goddard	85
1839	Thomas Patton	85
1840	James Skelton	88
1841	William Wood	85
1842	J.H. Dundas	85
1843	W.M. Goddard	85
1844	W.W. Goddard	87
1845	J.T. Gordon	99
1846	W.M. Goddard	87
1847	O.G. Campbell	94
1848	Charles Cundell	88
1849	H.J. Wylie	86
1850	Capt. Maitland, R.N.	81
1851	H.J. Wylie	83
1852	Capt. Maitland Dougall. R.N.	88
1853	John Bruce	90
1854	Capt. Campbell	84
1855	Robert Hay	81
1856	W.M. Goddard	76
1857	Robert Hay	84
1858	O.G. Campbell	86
1859	H.J. Wylie	90
1860	O.G. Campbell	88
1861	Gilbert M. Innes	80
1862	T.D. McWhannell	82
1863	O.G. Campbell	80
1864	H.J. Wylie	82
1865	Gilbert M. Innes	83
1866	W.J. Mure	86
1867	Gilbert M. Innes	80
1868	Robert Clark	81
1869	Gilbert M. Innes	75
1870	Dr. Argyll Robertson	83
1871	E.L.I Blyth	87
1872	John Dun	84
1873	E.L.I. Blyth	90
1874	Dr. Argyll Robertson	84
1875	Robert Clark	85
1876	Dr. Argyll Robertson	83
1877	James L. Mansfield	84
1878	Capt. A.M. Brown, R.N.	82
1879	W.J. Mure	82
1880	W.J. Mure	86
1881	W.J. Mure	87
1882	L.M. Balfour	81
1883	J.E. Laidlay	85
1884	L.M. Balfour	83
1885	James L. Mansfield	84
1886	L.M. Balfour	83
1887	J.E. Laidlay	79
1888	J.E. Laidlay	83
1889	L.M. Balfour	82
1890	J.E. Laidlay	85
1891	J.E. Laidlay	82

competed for at Muirfield – Spring meeting

Year	Winner	Score
1892	L.M. Balfour	79
1893	J.E. Laidlay	78
1894	R.H. Johnston	79
1895	G. Gordon Robertson	83
1896	Major D.A. Kinloch	85
1897	C.L. Dalziel	88
1898	J.E. Laidlay	82
1899	J.E. Laidlay	85
1900	T.M. Hunter	79
1901	Robert Maxwell	80
1902	N.F. Hunter	79
1903	Robert Maxwell	80
1904	Robert Maxwell	78
1905	G.F. Dalziel	85
1906	C.L. Dalziel	80
1907	J.E. Laidlay	82
1908	Capt. C.K. Hutchison	83
1909	Robert Maxwell	80
1910	Capt. C.K. Hutchison	76
1911	J.E. Laidlay	78
1912	Robert Maxwell	91
1913	R.T. Boothby	79
1914	Robert Maxwell	73
1915–1919	The Great War	
1920	A. Burn-Murdoch	86
1921	L.M. Balfour-Melville	83
1922	Robert Maxwell	80
1923	G.B. Crole	79
1924	F.W. Paulin	80
1925	Douglas Currie	79
1926	Douglas Currie	73
1927	P.C. Smythe	77
1928	W. Willis Mackenzie	79
1929	W. Willis Mackenzie	79
1930	F.W. Paulin	79
1931	G.T. Chiene	76
1932	Abandoned	
1933	W.A. Cochrane	80
1934	J.R. Pelham-Burn	78
1935	F.W. Paulin	79
1936	I.H. Bowhill	76
1937	Capt. W.L. Steele	77
1938	W.I.E. Thorburn	77
1939	I.A.D. Lawrie	77
1939–1945	World War	
1946	P.M. Smythe	80
1947	C.D. Lawrie	88
1948	Sqdn. Leader P.L. Arnott	76
1949	I.D.M. Considine	74
1950	T.R. Macgregor	79
1951	J.D. Tweedie	82
1952	G.W. Mackie	76
1953	I.D.M. Considine	77
1954	I.D.M. Considine	76
1955	G.R. Robertson Durham	75
1956	J.W. Draper	75
1957	J.W. Draper	77
1958	A.L. McClure	78
1959	P.R. Bryce	78
1960	A.L. McClure	76
1961	Major D.A. Blair	69
1962	Major D.A. Blair	70
1963	J.L. Mitchell	76
1964	A.C.N. Ferguson	79
1965	G. Robertson Durham	77
1966	R.H.J. Mackie	74
1967	R.H.J. Mackie	72
1968	C.D. Lawrie	73
1969	R.H.J. Mackie	76
1970	A.R. McInroy	76
1971	J.G. Salvesen	75
1972	R.P. White	75
1973	J.G. Salvesen	74
1974	R.P. White	72
1975	W.B.M. Laird	73
1976	G. Robertson Durham	75
1977	D.M. Greenhough	75
1978	R.M. Sinclair	77
1979	D.M. Greenhough	76
1980	Brooks Carey	73
1981	A.R. McInroy	74
1982	D.M. Greenhough	78
1983	W.B.M. Laird	76
1984	R.P. White	77
1985	J.R. Fraser	73
1986	P.A.K. Arthur	74
1987	W.B.M. Laird	78
1988	J.H. Bryce	75
1989	R.D. Inglis	75
1990	D.E.D. Neave	71
1991	J.H. Bryce	75
1992	J.E. Cook	76
1993	P.A. Burt	69

Winners of the Autumn Medal (Gold)

competed for at Musselburgh (2 rounds of 9 holes each)

1871	G. Mitchell Innes	85	1878	John Wharton Tod	83	1885	J.E. Laidlay	83
1872	G. Mitchell Innes	90	1879	E.L.I Blyth	83	1886	J.E. Laidlay	82
1873	Dr. Argyll Robertson	84	1880	John Wharton Tod	86	1887	J.E. Laidlay	80
1874	E.L.I. Blyth	84	1881	Alexander Stuart	83	1888	J.E. Laidlay	80
1875	W.J. Mure	80	1882	L.M. Balfour	84	1889	L.M. Balfour	87
1876	Robert Clark	83	1883	W.J. Mure	84	1890	J.E. Laidlay	83
1877	Robert Clark	86	1884	L.M. Balfour	82	1891	Alexander Stuart	80

competed for at Muirfield

1892	L.M. Balfour	81	1927	W. Willis Mackenzie	75	1964	J.M. Dykes	76
1893	L.M. Balfour-Melville	86	1928	S.G. Rome	77	1965	A.C.N. Ferguson	76
1894	W.M. De Zoete	82	1929	W. Willis Mackenzie	79	1966	G. Robertson Durham	79
1895	J.E. Laidlay	80	1930	P.C. Smythe	78	1967	J.G. Salvesen	78
1896	Major D.A. Kinloch	80	1931	I.H. Bowhill	77	1968	I.S. Dougal	76
1897	A.R. Paterson	81	1932	S.G. Rome	77	1969	J.B. Cochran	73
1898	L.M. Balfour-Melville	82	1933	I.H. Bowhill	76	1970	J.G. Salvesen	74
1899	J.E. Laidlay	86	1934	I.A.D. Lawrie	75	1971	R.P. White	75
1900	J.E. Laidlay	84	1935	J.N. Shaw	79	1972	P.G.H. Younie	75
1901	Robert Maxwell	77	1936	S.G. Rome	78	1973	P.G.H. Younie	72
1902	Robert Maxwell	79	1937	Capt. W.L. Steele	75	1974	Sir I.M. Stewart	79
1903	J.E. Laidlay	76	1938	J.T. Campbell	78	1975	W.B.M. Laird	75
1904	Robert Maxwell	76	1939–1945	World War		1976	D.E.D. Neave	71
1905	J.E. Laidlay	75	1946	I.H. Bowhill	79	1977	R.H.J. Mackie	76
1906	Robert Maxwell	78	1947	C.J.Y. Dallmeyer	77	1978	P.A. Burt	72
1907	Capt. C.K. Hutchison	74	1948	R.M. Carnegie	78	1979	R.P. White	77
1908	T.M. Hunter	77	1949	G. Robertson Durham	76	1980	W.G. Morrison	75
1909	Robert Maxwell	82	1950	A.L. McClure	77	1981	W.B.M. Laird	74
1910	L.M. Balfour-Melville	81	1951	G. Robertson Durham	76	1982	V.N.U. Wood	76
1911	Robert Maxwell	79	1952	R.M. Carnegie	73	1983	D.E.D. Neave	74
1912	Capt. C.K. Hutchison	79	1953	G. Robertson Durham	72	1984	D.E.D. Neave	73
1913	Capt. J.A. Orr	77	1954	G.W. Mackie	76	1985	A.J. Low	77
1914–1918	The Great War		1955	J.W. Draper	79	1986	D.M. Greenhough	79
1919	Robert Maxwell	82	1956	C.D. Lawrie	74	1987	D.E.D. Neave	77
1920	Robert Maxwell	79	1957	J.W. Draper	74	1988	J.A.R. Wood	75
1921	Robert Maxwell	82	1958	J.W. St. C. Scott	75	1989	D.E.D. Neave	75
1922	Major C.K. Hutchison	80	1959	G.W. Mackie	72	1990	J.A.R. Wood	81
1923	Douglas Currie	82	1960	J.M. Dykes	77	1991	Dr. J.H. Bryce	75
1924	G.B. Crole	80	1961	Major D.A. Blair	74	1992	D.E.D. Neave	74
1925	S.G. Rome	83	1962	R.H.J. Mackie	77	1993	P.A.K. Arthur	77
1926	F.W. Paulin	82	1963	J.T. Williamson	81			

1855 1870

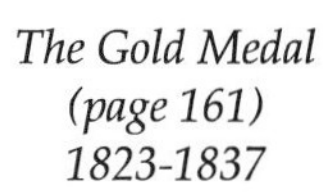

The Gold Medal (page 161) 1823-1837

1870 1899

Winners of the Silver Medal

Spring Meeting – presented by the Captain in 1887

competed for at Musselburgh (2 rounds of 9 holes each)

Year	Winner	Score
1887	L.M. Balfour	83
1888	L.M. Balfour	85
1889	J.E. Laidlay	86
1890	Robert Craig	86
1891	C.E.S. Chambers	84

competed for at Muirfield

Year	Winner	Score
1892	J.E. Laidlay	80
1893	R.H. Johnston	85
1894	J.E. Laidlay	81
1895	Major D.A. Kinloch	85
1896	H.F. Caldwell	85
1897	A. Stuart	88
1898	C.L. Dalziel	86
1899	A.D. Blyth	86
1900	C.L. Dalziel	82
1901	P. Balfour	80
1902	W.H. Fowler	81
1903	J.E. Laidlay	86
1904	J.E. Laidlay	78
1905	J. Younger, Junior	87
1906	J.E. Laidlay	83
1907	Robert Maxwell	83
1908	Robert Maxwell	84
1909	Capt. C.K. Hutchison	84
1910	L.M. Balfour-Melville	76
1911	Mark Tennant	78
1912	J.R. Gairdner	93
1913	Robert Maxwell	80
1914	J.R. Gairdner	79
1915–1919	The Great War	
1920	D.M. Wood	87
1921	Robert Maxwell	84
1922	Douglas Currie	83
1923	Douglas Currie	80
1924	R.K. Blair	80
1925	F.W. Paulin	80
1926	S.G. Rome	79
1927	W. Willis Mackenzie	78
1928	I.H. Bowhill	82
1929	F.W. Paulin	81
1930	I.H. Bowhill	81
1931	Major T.J. Mitchell	78
1932	Abandoned	
1933	James Haldane	80
1934	F.W. Paulin	78
1935	R.M. Carnegie	79
1936	S.G. Rome	78
1937	Major W.H. Callander	79
1938	R.M. Carnegie	80
1939	G.T. Chiene	78
1939–1945	World War	
1946	C.D. Lawrie	81
1947	G. Robertson Durham	90
1948	D.S. Middleton	79
1949	A.L. McClure	77
1950	I.D.M. Considine	79
1951	M.M. Thorburn	82
1952	D.S. Middleton	78
1953	G. Robertson Durham	77
1954	J.H. Campbell	76
1955	J.M. Dykes	77
1956	I.M. Stewart	77
1957	J.M. Sturrock	78
1958	G. Robertson Durham	79
1959	Lt.Col. A.M.M. Bucher	79
1960	J.D. Tweedie	76
1961	G. Robertson Durham	75
1962	G. Robertson Durham	76
1963	A.R. McInroy	79
1964	I.M. Robertson	80
1965	C.N. Hastings	78
1966	J.G. Salvesen	76
1967	W.B.M. Laird	75
1968	R.P. White	78
1969	I.W.H. Leslie	78
1970	D.R.J. Stewart	77
1971	G. Robertson Durham	76
1972	G.A. Hill	76
1973	D.E.D. Neave	78
1974	J.G. Salvesen	73
1975	G. Robertson Durham	75
1976	D.E.D. Neave	76
1977	J.G. Salvesen	78
1978	A.C.N. Ferguson	78
1979	R.H.J. Mackie	77
1980	R.D. Inglis	78
1981	W.B.M. Laird	77
1982	W.B.M. Laird	81
1983	Major D.A. Blair	77
1984	J.R. Fraser	77
1985	D.E.D. Neave	74
1986	P.A. Burt	77
1987	V.N.U. Wood	79
1988	B. Carey	77
1989	J.H. Bryce	78
1990	I.Q. Jones	77
1991	D.E.D. Neave	76
1992	J.R. Fraser	77
1993	G.D. Wuollet	75

The Silver Medal

Winners of the Musselburgh Medal (silver)

Autumn Meeting – competed for at Muirfield

Year	Winner	Score
1908	J.E. Laidlay	77
1909	Capt. C.K. Hutchison	85
1910	Capt. C.K. Hutchison	83
1911	J.E. Laidlay	80
1912	J.E. Laidlay	81
1913	Robert Maxwell	77
1914–1918	The Great War	
1919	J.E. Laidlay	84
1920	Capt. C.K. Hutchison	81
1921	W.F.C. McClure	83
1922	M.M. Thorburn	80
1923	A. Burn-Murdoch	84
1924	C.L. Dalziel	81
1925	D.M. Wood	86
1926	H.C. Stuart	85
1927	A.W. Robertson Durham	79
1928	C.J.Y. Dallmeyer	80
1929	R.A. Gallie	80
1930	R.M. Carnegie	80
1931	R.M. Carnegie	77
1932	J.R. Pelham-Burn	78
1933	R.M. Carnegie	76
1934	R.M. McLaren	76
1935	F.W. Paulin	79
1936	J.D.H. McIntosh	78
1937	G.T. Chiene	77
1938	P.J. Oliphant	79
1939–1945	World War	
1946	J.D.H. McIntosh	81
1947	G. Robertson Durham	78
1948	I.D.M. Considine	79
1949	R.M. Carneige	77
1950	G. Robertson Durham	79
1951	J.M. Cowan	76
1952	G. Robertson Durham	77
1953	I.D.M. Considine	79
1954	J.M. Dykes	78
1955	Alastair Walker	80
1956	P.R. Bryce	78
1957	A.R. McInroy	76
1958	P.R. Bryce	76
1959	J.W. Draper	76
1960	Lt.-Col. A.M.M. Bucher	79
1961	J.M. Dykes	74
1962	J.G. Salvesen	80
1963	R.J. Normand	81
1964	R.H.J. Mackie	76
1965	R.H.J. Mackie	77
1966	J.G. Salvesen	80
1967	G. Robertson Durham	78
1968	R.P. White	77
1969	C.N. Hastings	76
1970	W.B.M. Laird	76
1971	A.C.N. Ferguson	75
1972	C.N. Hastings	76
1973	D.M. Greenhough	75
1974	J.G. Salvesen	80
1975	R.P. White	79
1976	J.G. Salvesen	75
1977	J.G. Salvesen	78
1978	R.P. White	73
1979	R.M. Sinclair	77
1980	W.B.M. Laird	75
1981	J.E. Cook	74
1982	R.H.J. Mackie	77
1983	Major D.A. Blair	76
1984	R.P. White	75
1985	J.C. Briggs	78
1986	R.J. Normand	79
1987	S.L. Briggs	78
1988	I.Q. Jones	77
1989	Col. F.F. Gibb	77
1990	A.J. Low	83
1991	I.Q. Jones	78
1992	Dr. J.H. Bryce	76
1993	R.P. White	79

Winners of the Grant Cup (best aggregate score of Spring and Autumn Medal Competitions)

Year	Winner	Score
1954	I.D.M. Considine	159
1955	G. Robertson Durham	157
1956	P.M. Smythe	158
1957	J.W. Draper	151
1958	J.W. St.C. Scott	157
1959	G.W. Mackie	151
1960	Lt.-Col. A.M.M. Bucher	157
1961	Major D.A. Blair	143
1962	G. Robertson Durham	157
1963	J.G. Salvesen	162
1964	A.C.N. Ferguson	155
1965	G. Robertson Durham	158
1966	J.G. Salvesen	156
1967	R.H.J. Mackie	151
1968	R.P. White	155
1969	R.H.J. Mackie	154
1970	J.B. Cochran	155
1971	R.P. White	152
1972	R.P. White	155
	D.M. Greenhough	155
1973	P.G.H. Younie	150
1974	J.G. Salvesen	153
1975	W.B.M. Laird	148
1976	D.E.D. Neave	147
1977	R.H.J. Mackie	154
1978	R.P. White	152
1979	R.H.J. Mackie	155
1980	Brooks Carey	153
1981	W.B.M. Laird	151
1982	W.B.M. Laird	160
	R.H.J. Mackie	160
1983	Major D.A. Blair	153
1984	R.P. White	152
1985	A.J. Low	153
1986	P.A.K. Arthur	157
1987	D.E.D. Neave	158
1988	J.H. Bryce	156
	J.A.R. Wood	156
1989	R.D. Inglis	153
1990	D.E.D. Neave	155
1991	Dr. J.H. Bryce	150
1992	Dr. J.H. Bryce	155
1993	P.A. Burt	152

Winners of the Robert Allan Trophy

(Knockout Foursomes)

Year	Winners
1975	A.K.E. Finch Noyes and D.M. Greenhough
1976	J. Macpherson and R.M. Sinclair
1977	W.R. Alexander and D.M. Greenhough
1978	J.C.R. Inglis and R.M. Sinclair
1979	A.L. McClure and P.W. Millard
1980	G.C. Summers and A.S. Russell
1981	Major J.G. Vanreenen and G. Manca
1982	Lt. Cdr. A.L. Brown and K.W. Paterson Brown
1983	J.L. Trainer and J.A. Wolfe Murray
1984	Colonel G.S.K. Maydon and A.D. Hay
1985	P. Turnbull and R.J. Normand
1986	I.S. Boyd and M.J.P. Healy
1987	R. Gardner and I.D. Mackenzie
1988	J.B. Cochran and R.E. Henderson
1989	J.A. Crabbie and S.D. Wilson
1990	Col.F.F. Gibb and G.R. Russell
1991	W.M.C. Kennedy and P.S. Ballantine
1992	C.H. Ross and J.G. Salvesen
1993	V.N.U. Wood and D.K. Stuckey

Winners of the Graeme Warrack Quaich

Year	Winner	Score
1985	H.D. Jamieson	92–16=76
1986	Dr. H.N. Macphail	84–16=68
1987	R. Brereton-Smith	90–18=72
1988	I.M.D.N. Farquharson	100–24=76
1989	R. Brereton-Smith	86–16=70
1990	Dr. J.L. Trainer	93–18=75
1991	Lt. Gen. Sir Chandos Blair	83–12=71
1992	J.D. Lumsden	85–15=70
1993	T.F. Creamer	86–16=70

Winners of the A. Logan McClure Quaich

Year	Winners
1989	Mr and Mrs J.H. Marshall
1990	R.H. Bell and Miss M. Bell
1991	R.M. Sinclair and Mrs C.S. Sinclair
1992	Dr. and Mrs J.H. Grant
1993	D.M. Simpson and Mrs E.C. Simpson

Index

Note: Names appearing only in the Foreword or Lists of Captains, Prizewinners etc, and references to Muirfield and the Honourable Company are not indexed. Page-numbers in italic refer to illustrations.

Photographic acknowledgments

All the paintings, prints, historic photographs and precious objects reproduced in this book are either part of the Honourable Company's archives or from private collections, unless otherwise stated. We apologise if, by being unable to trace photographic sources, we have unknowingly failed to acknowledge copyright material.

p.41 Drawing of Leslie Balfour-Melville from *The Badminton Library* by Horace G. Hutchinson; pp.50-57 Photograph of County Cup team by the *East Lothian Courier*; p.89 Photograph of Henry Cotton from *Thanks for the Game* by Henry Cotton; pp.138-139 Photographs from *Golf* by Henry Longhurst; pp.142-143 Photographs of Henry Cotton and Gary Player from the *Glasgow Herald* and *Evening Times*; p.154 Cartoon from the *Daily Mail*.